# Path to Biculturalism

# Path to Biculturalism

**MARLENE KRAMER, R.N., Ph.D.**

*Professor, School of Nursing,*
*University of California,*
*San Francisco Medical Center,*
*San Francisco, California*

**CLAUDIA SCHMALENBERG, R.N., M.S.**

*Research Assistant and Project Director*
*Reality Shock and Conflict Resolution*
*   in Neophyte Nurses Research Grant*
*University of California*
*San Francisco, California*

Contemporary Publishing, Inc.
Wakefield, Massachusetts

**Library of Congress Cataloging in Publication Data**
Kramer, Marlene, 1931–
    Path to biculturalism.

    Includes bibliographies and index.
    1.  Nursing—Psychological aspects—Problems,
exercises, etc.  2.  Nursing—Social aspects—
Problems, exercises, etc.  I.  Schmalenberg,
Claudia, joint author.  II.  Title.
RT86.K68   610.73'01'9     77-7202
ISBN 0-913654-30-2

*In Memoriam to Ricky Lawrence*

*a friend and a bicultural nurse who
served as a model for the authors*

# Contents

# Preface

Reality shock is a universal phenomenon. It occurs any time an individual moves out of a subculture in which he is competent and feels comfortable and into a new subculture wherein he must function and is probably less competent and less comfortable. The term *reality shock* is used primarily in reference to newcomers into an occupational field, to describe the specific shock-like reactions of new workers when they find themselves in a work situation for which they have spent several years preparing and for which they thought they were going to be prepared, and then suddenly find that they are not. The shock-like reactions occur when the aspirant professional perceives that many professional ideals and values are not operational and go unrewarded in the work setting. When an individual encounters this disparity in values, he can resolve the conflict in a number of ways—by adapting fully to the new subculture, by fleeing the work scene, or by job hopping, to mention a few. However, one of the most productive ways of resolving the conflict is to become bicultural. Biculturalism means being as competent and effective in the new subculture as in the old. The result: one can work equally well in either subculture.

Becoming bicultural is what this book is all about. It maps out the knowledges and competencies needed to achieve biculturalism—to achieve competence in the new work subculture while retaining values from the old nursing school subculture. It was written expressly for student nurses and for new graduate nurses about to enter their first work experience. However, the content is valuable and useful for all nurses—and, in fact, for members of other occupational groups—who are contemplating a change in position or place of employment. The reality shock experienced by a staff nurse moving into a head nurse position, by a supervisor becoming a Director of Nursing Service, or by a staff nurse joining the faculty of a School of Nursing differs from that experienced by the senior student moving into a staff nurse position in degree rather than in kind.

The *Path to Biculturalism* consists of five instructional programs, each containing two or more modules. Incorporated into each of the instructional programs are learning activities designed to help the reader grasp and make use of the material. The learning activities are meant to encourage and guide thinking. Analytical thought processes are more important for the reader than formulating her thoughts into specific words. For this reason, examples of completed learning activities have been omitted. We want to avoid patterning the thinking of the users of the activities. The reader may choose to do all or part of the learning activities; or she may choose to do none of them. People learn in different ways. Some readers may wish to write out their responses to the questions and activities, while others may learn best by thinking about and/or discussing the questions. The content of these programs represents what we believe new graduates need to know in order to become bicultural, to effect a smooth and productive transformation from the role of student to staff nurse. The first program, "Reality Shock," consists of two modules. "Make It Work For You" describes the phases of reality shock, its signs and symptoms, and most important, it suggests ways in which an individual might handle herself while experiencing the various phases of reality shock. "Letters from Lynn," the second module in the program, is the diary of a new graduate on her first job. It is hoped that it will provide the reader with insight into the dynamics of reality shock.

"A Look At You" is the title of the second program; it consists of two modules, "The Me Module" and "The Proving Ground." Becoming bicultural means becoming both an effective, competent person and an effective, competent nurse. "The Me Module" is especially concerned with the personal dimension. It focuses on the nurse as an individual, guiding her in an assessment and development of those behaviors that are needed to meet the goals she establishes for herself. Although all the programs in the *Path to Biculturalism* are aimed at helping the individual become interpersonally competent in the new work subculture (it is assumed that the individual was at least minimally competent in the school subculture), it is quite possible that some of the material will also help a person become more interpersonally competent in any subculture.

The other module in the "A Look At You" program is called "The Proving Ground." It is designed to help the nurse ferret out the Content, Criteria, Circumstances, and Appraisal of the informal tests that she constructs for herself as well as those that others in the work setting construct for her. If she can identify the content of tests and the criteria for passing them, the newcomer is free to decide whether she wishes to pass such tests.

Often, the work setting provides sparse feedback. And this at a time when the new nurse needs it most and is most vulnerable to its absence. "The Elusive Quest," the third program in the *Path to Biculturalism*, talks about getting feedback, or an answer to the question, "How Am I Doing?" This program consists of three modules. "Why is the Quest Elusive?" explains differences in feedback between school and work; "Disguises of the Quest" acquaints the reader with the various forms that feedback can take; and "Eliciting the Elusive" discusses ways of eliciting and providing feedback.

To become as interpersonally competent in the new work subculture as in the former school subculture, one must be able to interpret accurately a given situation from the point of view of someone well adapted to the work subculture. To do this, one must understand what values and attitudes are all about, how values are organized, and how they can be changed. This content is presented in the first module of the "Walk A Mile in My Shoes" program, and is entitled "A Look at Shoes in General." The second module, "Work Shoes and School Shoes," discusses the similarities and differences between the values taught in school and those emphasized in the work scene. What do values sound like when they are cloaked in everyday speech? The module "The Work Shoes Speak" is based on a series of tape-recorded interviews with nurse aides, orderlies, LVNs, and staff and head nurses. It acquaints the reader with the variety of work values expressed by these people—in their own words. The last module, and perhaps the most important one in this program, is entitled "Putting Your School Shoes to Work." A common and frequently heard complaint of new graduate nurses is, "I can't practice nursing as I've been taught," or put another way, "I can't put my school values into practice." The goal of this module is to offer the newcomer practical, useful ways of operationalizing her school ideals. There are no magic secrets, but having learned how values can be changed, and where differences between one's own values and those of others are likely to occur, the reader should now be in a position to utilize the suggestions offered in this module.

"Conflict Resolution: The Mating of Dreams and Reality" is the last program in the *Path to Biculturalism*. Productive conflict resolution is the goal of the journey that began with the realization that "the way I was prepared to nurse isn't the way nursing is practiced in the real world." If an individual wants to change the status quo, to improve nursing practice, to establish her own identity as a nurse, to put her school ideals into practice, then she must set goals for herself and develop the abilities needed to reach those goals. Obtaining needed feedback is one skill that must be developed to enable an individual to realize her ideals. Anytime a newcomer enters an established work group and tries to do things a little bit differently, tries to put school ideals into practice, tries to influence others in the performance of their duties to the end of better patient care, some conflict will occur. Conflict, if handled productively, is healthy and growth-producing. If avoided, submerged, and mishandled, it leads to stagnation, dissatisfaction, and maintenance of the status quo. Productive conflict resolution makes the difference. The three modules in this program are designed to help the reader become a productive handler of conflict. "Conflict: The Cutting Edge of Growth" focuses on the positive value of conflict, while the second module, "Reality," describes the usual kinds of conflicts encountered by new graduate nurses. In the third module, "The Mating Process," the reader is introduced to six principles which, if effectively implemented, will result in productive conflict resolution.

The five programs in the *Path to Biculturalism* were developed as the second component of a three-part Role Transformation Program. The first component was a series of six seminars in which new graduate nurses discussed the feelings and events they were experiencing. It was hoped that in this way they would develop and use a valuable reference group—other new graduates—to begin productive resolution of any difficulties they were experiencing in the new environment. The third component of the Role Transformation Program was several all-day Conflict Resolution Workshops for new graduates and for their head nurses. The purpose of these workshops was to permit new graduates to utilize the knowledges and skills gained from the instructional programs in the resolution of typical work conflicts. A systematic study of the results of the three-part Role Transformation Program indicated that it was effective in producing biculturalism, empathy, and effective change agent activity in new graduates during their first year of employment. Use of the program was also related to maintenance of a professional role concept and longer length of employment in the initial job.

The cognitive material presented in the five instructional programs was developed through a synthesis of material in the literature and the personal experiences of the authors. References and bibliography are cited at the end of each instructional program so that the user may refer to these sources if additional material is desired, and also to give credit to some of the sources used in the construction of the programs.

Ricky Lawrence and Patricia Benner, each of whom made contributions to some of the modules in this work, deserve recognition. We acknowledge the help and insight given by Ricky Lawrence in the original development of The Me Module. Ms. Benner contributed to the development of the Reality Shock Program, and played a key role in the development of the material incorporated into The Proving Ground and The Work Shoes Speak Modules. We also thank Linda Lewandowski for her critical reading of the manuscript, and Gerry Miller for her long hours of typing. Grateful acknowledgment is also made of the support received from Grant NU00505 from the Division of Nursing, Bureau of Health Manpower, USPHS, Washington, D.C.

Many other nurses in the United States and Canada donated their time to listen, read, and offer ideas and suggestions. Their critique of the material was invaluable. To these nurses, as well as to the more than three hundred new graduate nurses who used the Role Transformation Program, we extend our heartfelt thanks and gratitude. We have incorporated your ideas and suggestions and we feel that the programs are improved because of you.

Acknowledgment for permission to quote their material is given to: Lynn Maloney Pittier; Susan Caghan; Patricia Benner; The Sparta Florida Music Group, Limited; Music City Music, Inc.; ATV Music Group (Maclen Music); Lowery Music Company, Inc.; Holt, Rinehart and Winston, Publishers; The C. V. Mosby Company; The American Journal of Nursing Company; America Press, Inc.; Pantheon Books, a Division of Random House, Inc.; Fearon Publishers, Inc.; and University of California Institute of Industrial Relations. Special thanks to *The Journal of Nursing Administration* which has presented many of our ideas in the articles "Dreams and Reality: Where Do They Meet?," "Conflict: The Cutting Edge of Growth," and "The First Job—A Proving Ground: Basis for Empathy Development."

# REALITY SHOCK

# Module 1

# Make It Work For You*

**INTRODUCTION**

Do any of the following statements about work sound familiar to you?

It's fantastic being out of school — I learn at least ten new things a day!

I can't believe how incompetent the RNs are, how lazy the aides and orderlies are, and how unconcerned *everyone* is about the patient!

It's incredible! *No one cares — no one!*

I love working in Pediatrics! I'm learning so much. I love working with the families as well as the children.

I see no way that people can be true to themselves, true to the patients, and work in this place!

But it shouldn't be that way! The aides and orderlies take advantage of the RNs. The RNs are afraid to ask for competent help so they go around defeated trying to do everything themselves or else they just throw up their hands and do the bare necessities and get by as light as they can!

I had no idea it would be this way. You can't believe the merry-go-round of IVs, medications, admissions, treatments. My whole day consists of interruptions. Surely this is not the whole story!

---

*The contribution of Patricia Benner to the development of this module is gratefully acknowledged.

If these statements strike a familiar chord, if you have found yourself or your friends making similar statements, you or your friends might be going through the process of reality shock. This learning module will describe the four phases in the process—honeymoon, shock, recovery, and resolution—and is designed to help the reader recognize:

1.  The perceptual distortions that may occur with reality shock.
2.  Ways to make reality shock work for you.
3.  Constructive outcomes for reality shock.

The concept of reality shock is borrowed from the literature and experiences of culture shock. Culture shock is the surprise and disequilibrium experienced when a person moves from an understood, familiar culture to a new culture that has new demands and new, unfamiliar meanings for familiar events. While the initial response to the new environment is often one of enchantment and interest in the novelty, over time the novelty, if too strange and demanding, brings on shock, disbelief, and rejection of the new environment. The same kind of shock occurs when a new graduate, coming from the understood, familiar subculture of nursing school, encounters the novel, strange, often unpredictable and seemingly illogical subculture of work. Moving out of school into the work world can be compared to moving into a new cultural system—a place where values, rewards, and sanctions are different from those experienced in school. When you move into a new subculture, you can count on experiencing at least some of the phases of culture or reality shock. This module will identify the phases of reality shock so that you can recognize them in yourself and others and make reality shock work for you.

**Honeymoon Phase**

Immediately after taking your first job as an RN you may experience the honeymoon phase. This is a kind of exhilaration, an excitement about arriving at a long-awaited goal.

EVERYTHING IS WONDERFUL

Redrawn from Kramer, Marlene. *Reality Shock: Why Nurses Leave Nursing.* St. Louis: C.V. Mosby, 1974.

During the honeymoon phase, the new graduate looks at the world through rose-colored glasses: the world is all good; everything is wonderful. The new nurse receives a regular paycheck; she can pay her bills and buy new clothes. Because she spends a lot of time on the work scene, the new nurse will probably get lots of positive feedback and recognition from her patients. And that feels good! You hear new graduates saying things like:

My head nurse is just fantastic, really fantastic. I can talk to her about anything. She always has really great ideas.

The exhilaration is heightened if the first job is a highly prized one — as opposed to a job taken because it was the only one available or because it was close to home.

The thrill of arriving, of being in a place where you can try out your wings, where you can at last really nurse, carries with it some perceptual distortions that you need to be aware of. See if you can detect the perceptual distortions in the following quotes from recent graduates describing their first job.

> Oh, it's just super. I love it; I really do. It's all so perfect. Everything. Better than I ever thought it would be!

> The nurses are really super, and the physicians on the unit constantly seem to be explaining what they are doing and why. All one has to do to get an EKG explanation is to look ponderingly at a strip. Also the chief cardiologist expects the nurses to follow him on rounds of the four patient wards and listen in and possibly participate in patient discussions. I can't really help but enjoy every day here.

> There is nothing but praise and respect for the physicians and no competition raging and the patient care is really the issue. It's really exciting, and when the nurses go home, it isn't with a sigh of relief that the day is over.

And here is the response of a recent graduate nurse when asked to describe a dissatisfying experience:

> I can't think of any really. I guess it seems like I'm trying to be difficult, but I'm not. I can't think of anything that's been frustrating . . .

Did you notice that the evaluations have a superficial quality and that there is some distortion in the perceptions of these recent graduates? Things are described as all good; everything is wonderful. This is most characteristic of the honeymoon phase. It can be compared to travelling through a country and seeing only the novel, the romantic, the enchanting aspects. For example, when travelling through Switzerland, you might see farmers raking hay and putting it in haystacks and view it as something enchanting and refreshing. But if you were to move into the Swiss countryside and actually rake hay for a while, your perception of the experience would change. Your new perception might be less pleasant and would certainly be more reality based. The same is true in the first nursing job. Getting through to the irascible, demanding patient may at first seem stimulating and challenging, but after a while, both the patient and his demands become much less pleasant.

During the honeymoon phase, the new nurse's appraisal of her job is characterized by almost unbounded enthusiasm. Problems are not recognized, they're not even perceived as yet. This is indeed an enjoyable time for the newcomer.

How can you take advantage of the honeymoon phase? It's not too difficult, actually. Just sit back and enjoy the enthusiasm, the novelty, the enchantment. However, avoid wiping out anyone else by your enthusiasm and energy. Consider how the high energy and enthusiasm of an individual in the honeymoon phase might affect others at work. How would a person with unbounded enthusiasm affect a person who is quite discouraged and disenchanted with his job? Or, how would it affect an individual who was very much into the game of "ain't it awful around here?" Enthusiasm in this kind of situation is not "catching"; in fact, it's usually the opposite: the "ain't it awful" syndrome is much more catching. If you come on strong and enthusiastic, your energy tends to make others more tired and more cynical. Often, their reaction is "Just you wait, you haven't hit it yet." If you alienate people like this, they will "turn-off" to you, and later, when you really need it, both information and support will be denied you. To make your honeymoon phase work for you, try to share your enthusiasm and high interest with others who are enthusiastic and interested. Gaining awareness of how your actions and attitudes affect others in the work situation is the first step toward gaining interpersonal competence. Interpersonal competence is the ability to work effectively with others, the ability to interpret accurately and predict their interpretations and responses to events and to your own behaviors. Achieving interpersonal competence in the work world is necessary if you are to make your work world a liveable, enjoyable, and productive place.

Because you are usually preoccupied with the novel aspects of your work world during the honeymoon phase, you cannot see the overall picture, and you are not apt to be very effective at processing information. An example of this can be seen in the new graduate who just "has to" make rounds with the physicians because it's new and exciting and she can learn so much. While doing this, she completely misses the verbal and nonverbal messages being sent by the head nurse and other staff nurses regarding some of the total unit work that must be done. This is not to say that you should not attend ward rounds, or that one behavior is right and the other wrong. No, it is just to remind you that when you are excitedly focused in on a patient, or on some activity that is challenging and/or novel, it is highly probable that you will not be accurately processing information related to the larger unit picture. Due to this information processing problem, you might be supercritical of your own performance—thinking that if something goes wrong, it's all your fault—rather than noticing aspects of the environment that might be causing problems or impinging upon your performance.

If you view the honeymoon phase as a respite, a calm before the storm, then you can make good use of this untroubled, high energy time. Evaluating your own skill needs, assessing your proficiencies, and noting what skills you want to improve is a good activity for this time. A note of warning though: trying to learn everything at once, or expecting all your co-workers to have a sound rationale behind all their performances can catapult you into disappointment and disillusionment. It's best to focus on the skills

that your particular work group or hospital are best prepared to teach you while everything is so new and things are going so well. During the excitement of learning new skills and procedures, you may notice that these things are occupying such a large portion of your time and energy that you sometimes forget the patient. Try to remember that skills are means to an end, not ends in themselves. There is more to nursing than just skills and procedures.

It's a good idea to be as helpful to your co-workers as you possibly can during the honeymoon phase. It may be somewhat difficult to find the time to help others when you are learning the system that you have just entered, but this is a high energy time for you and you may be able to provide assistance in the area of patient care. Make it a point to offer help to one co-worker each day if possible. In this way you will begin to build up a support system that you will almost certainly need during some future venture.

The honeymoon period, when all is going well, is a good time to get to know your co-workers. As a newcomer, you can ask questions now that you may not be able to, or may not want to, later on. Find out what your co-workers think and believe about nursing care. What are their goals? What do the aides and LVNs see as the duties of a team leader? What do others on the unit view as a reasonable patient assignment? Obtaining information about and from your co-workers will enable you to begin to develop the interpersonal competence mentioned earlier. In order to predict and interpret responses accurately, you must know something about the other person, his values, his ideas. You may find that you do not see eye-to-eye with your co-workers in some areas. But please note, this is not the time to attempt to change the views of your co-workers—it is only a time to learn about their values and beliefs. If you attempt to introduce new ideas, to persuade others to change their behavior now, before you have earned the right of membership into the group, before you have built a reputation for competence, before you have been around long enough to learn some of the history, you are doomed to failure. It's not only the failure but the negative reactions you will provoke that will make it more difficult for you to change the views of your co-workers later on.

### Shock Phase

Sooner or later, the bliss, high interest, and energy of the honeymoon phase will pass. You might wonder why. Must it pass? Why does it have to pass? There are no simple, obvious answers. But the answers have something to do with *infusing your own identity and values into a new system whose values and identity are different from yours and which inherently resist disruption.* Some comments from new graduates illustrate what happens.

> Initially I was so busy mastering all these skills that I was too busy even to look around. I was learning a lot and I had all this stimulation—very much like the university atmosphere. But then one day, I slowed down and looked at the work I was doing and what the others were doing and I realized that nursing had become just a job, and that was a big disappointment.

> I thought, my God, where has all this stuff gone? You know, like the care plans, and goals and objectives, and all this stuff. That really shocked me! I looked at the notes I had been taking and they were terrible, just terrible. It was a bloody mess. It really was!

> And another thing, when you're in school, you study a lot. And you're always doing something, studying personally. But once you get out at work, you're too tired, and no one else is doing it, and it just goes.

> You have to deal with your own feelings. I'm really not the kind of nurse I was led to believe I was. I went out to work. I went there to learn and I didn't see myself as having, well I felt I had a little bit to contribute, but I wasn't there as a change agent. And then I stopped to think, oh my gosh, what would my instructors think of me if they knew what it was like here, and I'm not even trying to change anything.

> I finally decided I had to get settled into something that would raise my estimation of myself as a nurse. I was so worried about all the skill type things that I found I was disregarding the skills and knowledges that I *did have* and felt comfortable with—teaching, history taking, and communication.

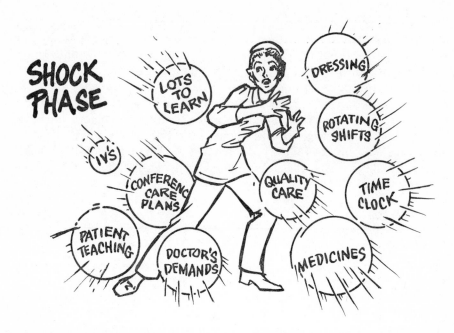

This sudden realization that nursing isn't what you thought it would be, or that you aren't satisfied with what you have become as a nurse might be called the pre-shock or introductory shock phase. It may be the beginning of the realization that you are "in a rut." Some new graduates go through it, while others move directly into the real shock phase, which occurs when you try to change the way you do nursing, or you try to introduce new ideas and ways of doing things to co-workers and you meet resistance. Any established system inherently resists disruption. When you try to achieve some personal objectives, when you try to get things done the way you think they should be done, when you try to infuse your identity and values into the system, it is likely that reality shock will develop. This is particularly true when you offer values, beliefs, or ways of doing things different from those of the work group. "I found I wasn't surrounded by people who supported my point of view, who believed and understood my background."

What are some of the sounds of reality shock? See if you can identify the perceptual distortions characteristic of the shock phase in the following quotations from new graduates:

Like, wow, it's awful! I can't believe it. I never thought it would be like this. I knew it wouldn't be a picnic, but this is ridiculous! The stupid way they do things. Sometimes I wonder if any of these gals have ever been to nursing school. They know nothing at all about care plans, or histories, or discharge summaries. And the aides are so mean to the patients. Boy, I hope I never get like that!

I'm somewhat disappointed because they don't care as much about patients as I had been led to believe. And nurses don't make the decisions my instructors always said they would. (Also, there's) no feedback, positive or negative. It's hard to know what's expected of you.

I had just started but immediately I thought that the care was so bad, that I didn't want to be a part of it. I was not able to effectively change the work in that environment to the degree that I had any pride in what I was doing.

Besides the disappointment and disbelief, can you hear some perceptual distortions?

First, you might notice that the criticism is just as superficial as was the blanket praise during the honeymoon phase. In other words, we've switched from one extreme to the other. The criticism is all pervasive; all things are bad. The new graduate is very extreme in the way she perceives co-workers. They are either good nurses or bad nurses. There is no in-between.

Why do you suppose a person perceives things as either all good or all bad? One reason is that a person is taken by surprise by many things in the

new work environment—things that exposure to clinical settings during school had not prepared her for. In school, students are exposed to the "front stage" reality of events on the nursing unit. Front stage reality is the performance that the unit staff puts on for particular audiences (like students and faculty, nursing supervisors, physicians, etc.). For these audiences, a certain picture of the ward situation is presented—and students are given the impression that all nurses know the actions of all drugs they give, for example. Some time after beginning employment, the new graduate discovers or uncovers the "backstage" reality, the things that go on everyday when everyone's guard is down and they are not putting their best foot forward. This can really be a shock and a surprise; it causes a great deal of anger because these graduates had not been prepared for the "backstage" reality. A frequent sound of reality shock is:

> It's not fair. I've been robbed. No one told me it would be like this.

> My instructors should have known what I needed to know to be a nurse and seen that I learned it. I've put in four years and I don't know anything! I've been robbed!

Another characteristic of the shock phase is a tendency to reject the way things are done at work. People become polarized on certain issues and practices and you hear a lot of "we" and "they." "We" are the good guys who do things the right way—the way we learned in school. "They" are the bad guys who give routinized, sloppy nursing care. Listen to the language of reality shock in this excerpt from a new graduate:

> It has really been hard to motivate people to do anything because they've just been there so long. And I know that new graduates, well it's not hard to motivate them to do things. In the past, when you would tell the night nurse about something that should be done you'd just get this long line of defenses. You would just feel like you were talking to a brick wall. But somehow, I don't feel that way when I talk to a recent graduate. At least she will listen to me. They don't have those hard shells built up yet.

Whenever you hear talk about two camps—"we" and "they"—it is quite likely that those talking are experiencing reality shock and expressing rejection.

Moral outrage is another characteristic of the shock phase. It can be recognized by the overuse of the word "should." "That's not the way it *should* be." Nurses *should* care about the patients, but they don't." "Patients really *should* get better care; they have the right to better care; it *shouldn't* be this way."

> Just because she wears a white uniform and dirty shoes, does that make her a nurse? No! If she's going to prove to me that she's a nurse, I think she has to offer realistic suggestions and be able to actually do nursing the way it *should* be done on the unit.

"Shoulds" are prescriptions for behavior; they are statements of how things ought to be. Moral outrage is the anger experienced at finding out that things are not as they ought to be.

The consequences of shock and moral outrage are also felt physically. In fact, physical signs may be the first clue to identifying the shock phase. The following excerpts point up some of the physical signs and symptoms of reality shock:

> I would go home every night really upset and cry and cry and be so exhausted I'd have to go to bed.

> I talked with Jean the other day. I told her that I was in a slump. I felt my first slump. I had never been in such a slump before in my life. You know, apathy. I didn't care about any of this junk; one hour I'd be excessively a go-getter and the next hour ugh! I'd just be down. I've never been this way in my life. It's so weird. I don't understand it.

> And then there's the sleep syndrome, when you go home and all you want to do is sleep, so you can get up and go to work the next day. Pretty soon all you're doing is sleeping and working.

The excessive fatigue and need for sleep are sure signs of conflict and anger.

Although the phases of reality shock are being presented as though they are separate and distinct, this is not quite so. You will not wake up one morning and say to yourself, "Well, I think I'm going into shock today." No, it's much more subtle. What you will begin to notice is that you're having more bad days than good, and that you seem to be tired all the time, even though you're getting the same amount of sleep as you used to. That's how you'll recognize the beginning of the shock phase.

Okay, now that you can recognize the signs and symptoms of reality shock, how can you make the experience work for you? You must deal with the *anger* experienced during reality shock before you can map out possible solutions or behavior changes. Describing your anger, your frustrations, your feelings of surprise and injustice won't make the experience any less painful, but it will help you deal constructively with it.

One way to deal with the anger of reality shock is to find someone to discuss your anger with. Learning to accept the feelings of surprise, disappointment, and anger is a first step in resolving the conflict. Find someone who can understand your position, someone who doesn't become defensive or tell you that you "shouldn't have such high expectations" or be so "idealistic." That you don't need to hear. You need someone who will be able to listen to your anger and help you determine why you are so angry but who will not be judgmental. And you need to do this with someone who won't

hold it against you or use it against you later. A good person to talk with is another new graduate who started working about the same time you did—she will understand. It doesn't have to be someone who is a friend. And it's probably better to express your anger to someone who is not working on the same unit as yourself. Trying to explain things to someone outside your unit will force you to concentrate first on expressing your feelings and then to take a more objective view of the situation as you try to sort it out. And finally, you need to let the person know that you are seeking only a listening ear and support—not interventions or solutions. These you must work out for yourself. You also need a safe place to deal with your anger, so try to do this over coffee or at lunch, rather than on the unit.

One way to make reality shock work for you is to make use of your view of the unit as a newcomer. During reality shock, your ability to view the unit as an outsider is coupled with a tendency to be hyper-critical and almost hyper-alert to various aspects of the unit's functioning. With your ability to see things differently than anyone else, you might generate sweeping suggestions for wholesale change on the unit. Take advantage of your unique perspective: write down all the things that you see wrong and all your recommendations for change. Notice, I said write them down, rather than share them with other personnel at this point. There is good reason for this reserve.

> You know my biggest mistake when I first started was immediately introducing all these great ideas. I figured the rest of the place should know about these great ideas and now I'm stuck with them because nobody thinks they're great.
>
> I was so busy telling everybody about something new and they didn't want to know. All the time they're saying to me, "Who are you? You can't even do all these other things that we can do, so why are your ideas so much better?"

During reality shock you probably have little or no social power on the unit, so it will be very difficult for you to sell your ideas or get others to accept your view of things. And introducing an idea before you can ensure its acceptance often creates resistance toward it. Furthermore, the hyper-critical appraisal done during reality shock may be the product of some blind spots. There may be aspects of the problem that you are not yet aware of. You can begin to determine this by describing (and writing down) how things are now and how they came to be that way—sort of a little sleuthing into the history. You may find that your suggestions and your criticisms will change as you learn more about the unit, or that you can use the "history" to help make the desired change. The important thing is to make use of the unique perspective you have during this time by capturing your ideas on paper. You won't pass this way again, and you might end up with two or three really good ideas that could make a difference and have an impact on the nursing care on the unit after you've moved out of the state of reality shock and have gained some social power to make changes.

Sooner or later, you will pass through the shock phase of reality shock. The shock phase is too enervating, too exhausting for you to remain in it very long. Anger, frustration, and disappointment take a lot out of you. Sooner or later, you will pass into the recovery phase.

### Recovery Phase

Recovery is marked by a new sense of balance, by the ability to see more than one perspective, and by a return of one's sense of humor. Instead of seeing things all rosy and wonderful as you did in the honeymoon phase, or all black and despairing as you did during the shock, you begin to see things as shades of gray. There's more balance to your perceptions. Let's listen to some sounds of recovery as expressed by recent graduates.

> I think you really do have to get rid of the emotional thing. You can't go around horrified all the time. As a nurse, there are so many horrifying things that you have to deal with, it would interfere with your job if you reacted to everything.
>
> It's not good to work with all new graduates because there are problems with that too. We have a lot of energy but we also lack a lot of experience.
>
> Remember how outraged I was about these cockroaches before? Well, I have adjusted to my horror of cockroaches. I can laugh about them now. One night I was assisting a doctor with a Pap smear, and a cockroach crawled right across the slide. Later the doctor wanted to know how to get this specimen down to

# Return of Humor !!

the lab real fast, and asked, "What's the fastest mode of transportation?" I answered, "Well, you could strap it on the back of a cockroach."

What you notice in the above excerpts is a somewhat more relaxed and multidimensional view of the situation. Because of her newly acquired (or restored) perspective, the new graduate is free to sit back and listen to incoming messages. She can begin to hear other people's sides of the story. The anger and tension are reduced, and energy that was used to express anger is now available to work out a constructive resolution to the conflict.

The recovery period is crucial to constructive conflict resolution, because in this phase the newcomer realizes that her previous perspectives and strategies probably will not work and that new ones are called for. Thus it becomes a time of growth, a time of creative problem solving in which new strategies and new perspectives are developed, and these can lead to a growth-producing resolution of the conflict produced when a newcomer attempts to establish her own identity and values in an established system.

### Resolution Phase

During reality shock you will probably wish you were elsewhere; you may daydream about the ideal or perfect job; and you might be tempted to switch rather than fight, to look for greener pastures, to find the "perfect" job in order to resolve the conflict and turmoil you feel. While some may

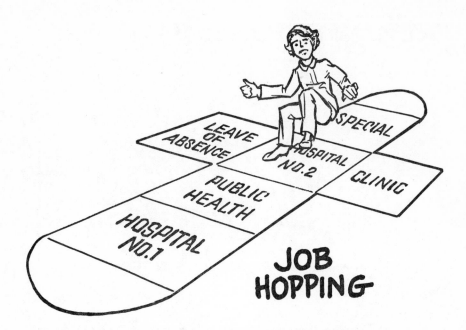

find jobs closer to their ideal, jobs that fit their expectations and values, most people will find that job hopping only delays the needed conflict resolution. The perfect job simply does not exist! Decide whether you want to go on a hunting expedition for another job. What are the pros and cons? Well, if you change jobs often enough, you can remain perpetually in inservice orientation. Being a new employee can be a very nice, comfortable role. You can perpetually play the game, "I'm new around here, teach me, show me." By always "being new," you can generally avoid responsibility and involvement. A doubtful way of resolving conflict for the individual, job hopping is extremely costly for the system (Directors of Nursing Service report that it costs between $1,000 and $3,000 to orient one new nurse), and a person cannot make a contribution if she is not in the system long enough to earn informal power.

In most cases, your energy would be better spent *by investing a little extra time on that first job,* resolving some of the conflict and anger experienced there—instead of job hopping. Granted, you may eventually come to the realistic decision that your present work setting is not for you. But to leave it when you're in the state of conflict, anger, and confusion is less than growth-producing. You cannot make a real contribution to a job if you do not remain in the system long enough to earn informal power. Before moving to another job, try to constructively resolve some of the conflict that you are experiencing.

A person can stand the tension and the feelings of reality shock only so long, and then ways must be found to reduce the tension. Unfortunately, many people choose ways that avoid *constructive* conflict resolution. They may resolve the conflict, but not constructively. For example, the new-comer may drop all the professional values learned in school that are caus-ing discomfort and conflict and wholeheartedly adopt all the dominant work group values. Such an individual has "gone native" in much the same way that an American living in India "goes native" when he relinquishes his own cultural values and adopts India's culture, values, practices, and mores. By adopting the work values wholeheartedly, the individual be-comes a highly competent, organized, efficient nurse, the epitome of the Organization Woman. Such a nurse becomes determined to keep the bureaucratic system functioning in a highly efficient manner. For the indi-vidual this can be an effective way of resolving conflict, but for the organi-zation it has the drawback of maintaining the status quo rather than empha-sizing growth, improvement, and progress in patient care.

Another way of resolving the school-work value conflict is to flee the work scene, capitulate and reject the values dominant there, and return to school, where the more idealistic components of care are highly valued and rewarded. Performing a "lateral arabesque"[1] the newcomer, disliking and feeling uncomfortable in the work setting (in a sense, incompetent in this setting), pirouettes away from the patient's bedside back to the ivory tower of academia, a setting where she feels comfortable and competent because her values are upheld there. Often, the goal of nurses who return to school for the above reasons is to become faculty some day, so they can teach others to "nurse the way I couldn't." This does not mean that all faculty in

## LATERAL ARABESQUERS

Redrawn from Kramer, Marlene. *Reality Shock: Why Nurses Leave Nursing.* St. Louis: C V   Mosby, 1974

all schools of nursing have necessarily done "lateral arabesques," but a goodly percentage have. This is especially true of those who have followed this kind of pattern:

> Graduate with a B.S. degree in June. Work for three summer months, during which you "love taking care of patients" but "can't stand to practice nursing the way we're forced to." Return to graduate school in September, receive an M.S. degree, and then go directly into teaching, probably without any additional experience of nursing practice.

Nurses who follow this pattern have in all probability adopted the lateral arabesque mode of resolving conflict, as have other nurse faculty who have a limited, unsuccessful, and unenjoyable nursing practice work experience. This does not mean that they aren't good nurses according to school subcultural values. It means that in the work system they were not perceived by themselves or by others as successful. To teach others to nurse the way you would like to, but found you couldn't, is not a constructive mode of conflict resolution either for the individual or for the health care system. It does little more than add another generation of frustrated nurses to a system already overburdened with them.

Still another option for the newcomer who is experiencing the pull and tug of the conflict between work and school values is to subjugate both value systems to outside interests and become a "Rutter." A Rutter is a nurse who says, "I know it's a cop-out, but too bad. Nursing is just a job. I'm in a rut and I know it. I'll put in my eight hours and do what I have to do, but then I'll go home and forget about it." The Rutter resolves the school-work value conflict by limiting her involvement in the job and her commitment to the profession. This will probably help the nurse handle her value conflict if her initial investment in nursing wasn't too strong. However, in no way can this mode of conflict resolution help improve the kind of care patients receive.

THE RUTTERS

Redrawn from Kramer, Marlene. *Reality Shock: Why Nurses Leave Nursing.* St. Louis: C.V. Mosby, 1974.

Other, potentially more destructive modes are available. A person can turn the conflict inward and become a "burned-out." Although she may appear calm (at least sometimes), inwardly she is churning, frustrated, and very unhappy. Not infrequently, "burned-outs" become chronic gripers and complainers, offering suggestions in a negative tone of voice that says, "I know you won't listen to me or accept this change, but I'll tell you anyway." The "burned-outs" are the nurses who often are nursed by the patients themselves: "Oh, nurse, you look like you feel so bad today. Would you like to tell me about it?" Obviously the "burned-outs" never really resolve the conflict. By turning the conflict inward, they make themselves unhealthy, which doesn't help either the individual or the quality of patient care.

A final unconstructive way of resolving the conflict between school and work values is complete withdrawal. Those who choose this option

"throw in the hat and tear up the license," and leave nursing practice altogether. They can be found in graduate schools, studying other disciplines, preparing to be art teachers, elementary school teachers, or accountants. Or they are already pursuing other occupations not requiring RN licensure—working as travel agents, librarians, clerks, etc. In a nationwide study done to look at the career pattern of 220 nurses over a two-year period, it was found that almost one-third of the sample (N=72 or 29.33 percent) were "Quitters"—leaving nursing practice altogether. Upon interview, all stated that their major reason for leaving the profession was frustration and disillusionment with it. Abandoning nursing practice may be a constructive and healthy resolution for some, but the loss of their creative ideas and input certainly slows the growth of nursing and the improvement of patient care practice.

None of the above conflict resolutions can be considered constructive in terms of both the individual and the health care system. The conflict is

# THE QUITTERS

not really resolved but rather suppressed; or the individual becomes fused into the system at the expense of her own values and identity. Instead of maintaining her identity by incorporating new values and integrating old values with the new circumstances, she permits *the new circumstances and environment to dictate her identity* to herself and to others.

The most useful and healthy conflict resolution is a bicultural adaptation. In this type of resolution, the recent graduate re-evaluates school-bred values, keeping the ones she thinks are worthwhile, and translating those worthwhile values into the terms and the realities of the work setting. A bicultural adaptation permits the new graduate to be the kind of person she

wants to be and the kind of nurse she wants to be. It is a process in which one works out one's own unique nursing role by infusing the role with school-bred values and by accepting some work-world values. Neither value system is all right, all wrong, all good, or all bad. It is a question of what is most useful. What is most valuable in terms of delivering the best patient care possible? What action is most likely to take care of immediate problems as well as working to effect system changes to take care of long range problems?

A bicultural adaptation permits the new graduate to assess the real situation without feeling moral outrage, without crying internally, "But it shouldn't be that way!" Now don't misunderstand, a bicultural adaptation does not mean freedom from conflict nor absence of anger. It means only that one can *perceive and interpret accurately* the values in the work situation and the values from the school experience that are the sources of conflict, so that realistic strategies for resolving the conflict can be developed. Biculturalism means integrating the two conflicting value systems. Some examples of bicultural adaptation are given in these interview excerpts:

> Yeah, it's not all good to work with all your friends. I mean, it's really groovy to come on and see your friends, but it's not so great to have to say, "Why didn't you take those orders off in the daytime." That's really hard to say. Plus, it's both good and bad to have new grads, too. I don't know how to say it, but the unit is really crazy and the new grads are not sure of themselves. You need some with some experience too. It's just not all that good to have all new grads.

> The duties of the RN, the LVN, and orderlies are really defined. The orderlies take care of the urine. It is almost to the point of being ridiculous. When I started doing these things, Mrs. Smith, (the LVN,) really got offended because she thought I was doing these things because I thought that she wasn't doing her job. The other night she got angry because I was out changing the patient. She doesn't say anything when she is angry, she gets very silent when she gets angry, but I knew that she was angry. When she came back to the nurses' station I said, "Mrs. Smith, I wasn't doing that because I thought you wouldn't do it, but I just happened to be out there and it seemed stupid for me to come in and call you when I was there and I could do it in the time it would take me to walk to the desk and ask you to do it." And you know, she responded quite favorably to my understanding.

What do you notice about these examples of bicultural adaptation? You may have noticed that these new graduates can see several sides of the issue. Not only that, they are more relaxed and are able to interpret and predict accurately the effect of their behavior on co-workers. In the second excerpt, notice that the recent graduate is able to achieve her goals without alienating Mrs. Smith, the LVN, because she understands Mrs. Smith's expectations and her interpretations of the event. Doing this requires the newcomer to interpret accurately the values prevalent in the work setting. Without the "know-how" gained from recognizing the predominant values in the work setting, the newcomer is handicapped and cannot introduce her own ideas and goals.

In order to introduce your own ideas and goals in the work setting effectively, you must approach others in the right way. Furthermore, you should ask yourself several questions before you try to operationalize your goals in the work setting. Some of these questions are:

1. What are my values and goals?
2. What are the values of the others on the unit?
3. How do I know if (and to what extent) I am reaching my goals?
4. What effect will the accomplishment of my goals have on others?
5. How do I resolve conflict constructively?

If you can answer these questions, you know how to approach others. Biculturalism permits you to answer these questions accurately, because biculturalism means understanding social situations so that you can (1) accurately predict the effect of your behavior on others, (2) accurately interpret the behavior of others in terms of *their* frame of reference, and (3) choose the appropriate approach for operationalizing your goals in the work setting. Biculturalism does not mean losing your identity or being co-opted into the system. It means freedom to choose your responses.

The following quote from *I Never Promised You a Rose Garden* captures the essence of the kind of challenge offered by the first job experience. The wise therapist is saying

> Look here, Furii, I never promised you a rose garden, I never promised you perfect justice, and I never promised you peace or happiness. My help is so that you can be free to fight for all these things. The only reality I offer you is challenge, and being well is being free to accept it or not at whatever you are capable. I never promised lies, and the rose garden world of perfection is a lie and a bore too.*

While you may long for a more boring and perfect work situation, the challenge and opportunity provided by conflict, by disagreement are a means to growth. By viewing your first job in this framework, you will be able to recognize the perceptual distortions you're prone to and you should be able to make reality shock work for you. Hopefully, you will choose a bicultural type of conflict resolution, one that gives you the freedom to choose your *actions* instead of limiting you to a set of *reactions*. It is the purpose of the remaining four programs in this book to help you develop your abilities to know yourself, to obtain needed feedback, to develop empathy, and to resolve conflict constructively—abilities that will help you to operationalize your goals on the journey along the path to biculturalism.

At this time, complete the learning activity entitled "Coping with Reality Shock." This will give you some notion of how well you have absorbed and can use the material presented in this program.

---

*From *I Never Promised You A Rose Garden* by Hannah Green (Joanne Creenberg). Copyright © 1964 by Hannah Green. Reprinted by permission of Holt, Rinehart and Winston, Publishers.

**COPING WITH REALITY SHOCK**

*Directions:*    Based on the characteristics described for each of the four phases of reality shock, determine where you are in the reality shock process. To do this, answer each of the following questions.

1. Reflect on the signs and symptoms of reality shock as described in this module. Which of them are you currently experiencing; which have you experienced in the past?

2. What are some comments you have made that illustrate the signs and symptoms of reality shock? You may want to casually ask some of your co-workers, "What are the things you hear me saying most often about my job?"

3. List some reactions of others on the unit to your actions and comments.

4. Develop a plan for dealing with the signs and symptoms of reality shock that you are now experiencing. You may want to write this out, or you may just want to develop it mentally.

This completes the "Make It Work For You" module. The next module, entitled "Letters From Lynn," lets you watch the reality shock process unfold and see how one new graduate copes with it.

### REFERENCE

1.    Peter, L.J. and Hull, R. *The Peter Principle*. New York: Bantam Books, 1969.

# Module 2

# Letters From Lynn*

## INTRODUCTION

The following "letters" are one new graduate's account of her experiences in her first job, actual excerpts from her diary describing her trials, successes, feelings, hopes, and aspirations as she entered the work world. Included in the account is a dialogue between Marlene Kramer and Pat Benner—nurses who have been studying the work adjustment of new graduates. The dialogue is included to help the reader zero in on the main points of the "Make It Work For You" module. However, reading the dialogue is optional, and can be omitted without loss of Lynn's message.

The "Make it Work For You" module will help you identify the signs and symptoms of reality shock. After reading these "letters," you should have more insight into the signs and symptoms of your own reality shock, and you may discover new ways of dealing with it.

In this module, Lynn refers several times to the proving ground, and to testing herself out on her first job. This material will be covered in more detail in the second module of the program, "A Look at You." You may wish to re-read some part of the "Letters from Lynn" after you read "The Proving Ground" module.

The material regarding value differences between school and work is covered in detail in "Walk a Mile in My Shoes."

---

*Reprinted with permission from Kramer, Marlene. *Reality Shock: Why Nurses Leave Nursing.* St. Louis: C.V. Mosby, 1974.

*Late September, 1970*

*After I started my job, it became obvious that I could never get any of the nurses in the orthopedic surgical ward excited about nursing, or even cooperative about some of the things I wanted to initiate, like nursing histories. I started them, but they remained on the Kardex unused, except for extra space to write other things . . . Also this orthopedic ward would not have provided me with the technical skills that my classmates and I craved. The patients were mostly post-amputees awaiting a prosthesis fitting. The two weeks that I served on the floor involved the care of fifteen to twenty patients. I was floored! The care was minimal, granted, but with so many I felt like a guard pacing up and down the halls. So many of these young Vietnam amputees needed someone to sit down with them and just talk. Some had histories of battle neurosis and poor adjustment to their disability. But you just couldn't spend any time on these problems—even to scratch any surface. It made me think of when I was in school, and all the time I spent on some wards, and in visiting families, trying to think up patient problems to satisfy the instructor. Here there were all these problems staring me in the face, but I had neither the time nor energy to do anything about them . . . All in all I requested a transfer to the Coronary Care Unit. I was refused for two weeks because of my inexperience. But they finally put me in; I really had to talk them into it.*

*This area really fascinates me. I've been coming home every night and studying the EKG's and reading almost more than when I was in school. The nurses are really super and the physicians in the unit constantly seem to be explaining what they are doing and why. All one has to do to get an EKG explanation is to look ponderingly at a strip. Also, the Chief Cardiologist expects the nurses to follow him on rounds of the four patient wards and listen in and possibly participate in patient discussions. I can't help but really enjoy each day here; it is an area that we sort of trained for all along with its one-to-one patient-nurse relationships, observational responsibilities, and the heavy psychosocial aspects of the disease. As far as technical skills go, the patients have constant IV's running, which the nurses initiate and re-start. We give IV meds, draw all our own blood, and defibrillate those in ventricular fibrillation if there are no doctors handy. Yesterday I was drawing my first blood from a jugular intercath and managed to squirt blood all over my uniform and the patient. He was really concerned that he would have to pay for the embellishments on the polka dot sheets, and he laughed and laughed about it.*

*The most valued skill in the CCU is observational in nature. This is quite a contrast to the orthopedic station, where I reported some swollen lymph nodes and an earache and sore throat to the resident physician (surgeon), who sharply informed me that he was a surgeon, not a medical man. Think of the problems I might have encountered if I had taken it to the medical man myself! . . .*

*My impressions with my first job really convince me that all that psych emphasis wasn't so useless. On the other ward I really felt like a middle man who had to understand and then deal appropriately with every staff member. The surgical residents were uptight and defensive, and the nurses were really aggravating the situation by trying to gain some satisfaction for themselves. Then the LPNs, two males, had to maintain their position both as men and nurses. By the time the IPR with staff members are waded through, it's no wonder lots of people have no energy left for that poor patient, labelled difficult. With a 40-bed ward and five-staff ratio, it's understandable that one tends to become involved in interpersonal struggles with staff members, including the doctors. Anyway, it seemed that the difficult doctor often received more attention than the difficult patient. The CCU is as different as night and day. There is nothing but praise and respect for the physicians, with no competition raging. And patient care is really the issue. It really excites me! And when the nurses go home it isn't with a sigh of relief that the day is over.*

*Actually, the switch to this ward is a blessing for me. I was never very satisfied in nursing school and seemed to look for each clinical as perhaps a little more satisfying, which it wasn't really. By the end of basic training I felt I couldn't leave the academic setting until something caught my interest about nursing on a long term basis. Going to the university with physiology type electives made me even more uneasy about nursing as a lifelong career. The upshot of all this is the crucial importance of this first job. As it stands now, I'm neck deep in nursing. Yet I feared I might hate my compulsory one year of clinical experience. (One year seems to be the magic number. It was quoted to me ad nauseum as I applied for various jobs for which I was turned down.) See—I was trying to avoid the hospital setting before ever really encountering it. My supposed clinical expertise in Medical-Surgical Nursing requires a bit of experience if it is to mean anything to me or the nursing world. The dramatic end to this episode is that I really do like what I am doing in the hospital, and it looks as though this may last on a day-to-day basis.*

### COMMENTARY

KRAMER:  It looks as though Lynn didn't go through any kind of a honeymoon phase on that Orthopedic Unit, doesn't it?

BENNER:  No, I don't think she did—I think there might be several reasons for that, since she did experience a rather striking honeymoon period in the CCU. First, Lynn did not choose the Orthopedic Unit as a place where she would like to try out her new status, whereas she did have a decision commitment to the CCU. She had to fight to get into the CCU and I think this initial commitment, which stems from her own choice, gave her a positive view of the CCU even before she entered the unit. And secondly, I think that the CCU met the testing criteria that Lynn had set up for herself.

KRAMER: Let's look at some of the examples Lynn gives us of her honey-moon phase in the CCU.

BENNER: Lynn begins her work in the CCU with all the characteristic enthusiasm and fascination that can occur with a new environment.

> The nurses are really super and the physicians in the unit constantly seem to be explaining what they are doing and why. All one has to do to get an EKG explanation is to look ponderingly at a strip. Also the Chief Cardiologist expects the nurses to follow him on rounds of the four patient wards and listen in and possibly participate in patient discussions. I can't help but really enjoy each day here.

Lynn exhibits the wholesale praise and acceptance that is characteristic of the honeymoon phase.

> The CCU is so different. There is nothing but praise and respect for the physicians, with no competition raging. And patient care is really the issue. It really excites me! And when the nurses go home it isn't with a sigh of relief that the day is over. Actually, the switch to this ward is a blessing for me.

This wholesale acceptance and praise is almost like a "cook's tour" mentality. There is not enough reality testing to provide a critical, balanced view of the new environment. Expectations soar. And these high expectations are fertile ground for the impending crash of reality shock. It is at the point of serious navigation and goal seeking that the honeymoon phase wanes. Because the initial euphoria of the honeymoon phase does not allow for cue sensitivity, and accurate perception of social reality of the new social system, the entrant gathers very little objective information. The excitement and "high" over the new environment's assets effectively block energy for receiving and accurately processing information about the prevalent cultural values and norms in the new social system. The resulting absence of information makes goal accomplishment in the new social system next to impossible. The entrant bumps up against reality in the form of blocked goal achievement. At this point, both Lynn and her perception of the CCU staff seem to be almost completely focused on the patient.

*Early November, 1970*

*My request for transfer to the CCU was based on: (1) their initial decision to turn me down because of my lack of experience. I usually aim for that which is just out of my reach. (2) It was really painfully evident that any* concentrated nurse-patient relationships would be impossible for any nurse as overloaded with technical tasks and patients as I was on the orthopedic unit. (3) Our CCU has a maximum patient load of four, so there is ample time to really learn the technical and emergency skills and to enjoy the one-to-one relationships I became so accustomed to during nursing school. (4) The night duty was my own choice even though my family situation demanded it. I really enjoy an isolated independence.

On days, there are a million secretarial and task-oriented duties which consume so much time. At night it is more patient-observation oriented. And very important for me now are the free hours in which I read and study the progress notes. I am really frustrated if my work day is not constructive for me in some way. At night one can sit at the bedside and listen for the gallop of rales reported in the physician's notes. My goal is to gain enough clinical competence to observe subtle changes in the patient as they occur. For example, if I begin to hear that gallop for the first time or if an existing one becomes louder I may be picking up the first signs of congestive heart failure. It will eventually be a function of the nurse to report the CHF anyway when the clinical signs are more overt, so why let the patient progress that far if one can avoid it.

I try also to read at least one article a night or go over EKGs. On days one just doesn't sit down to read, there is always someone coming through — and we must look productive. Even before I ever worked, I felt that hospital nursing was a form of stagnation, a job with a ceiling on it. I still feel this can easily happen as a person settles into the rut of the work-a-day world. You may hear this from lots of students who approach their first job. I fear lapsing into mediocrity. Making progress means more to me than performing well on the job, and with respect to the number of patients and the shift, the CCU is ideally suited to give me the satisfaction I need to keep out of that "rut." I can't help feeling that this is one more transitional stage in my education, but I'm not sure just what I'll eventually go after. So much for rationale in job selection.

Since I've begun working in the unit with a relatively limited and close-knit group of girls, the Blau article you sent me has become increasingly relevant[1]. It's funny that I can currently and in retrospect analyze the social interactions. However, I seem to fall into every pitfall that Blau mentioned as inhibitive to social attractiveness. As I see it, security in the nursing role demands the acquisition of clinical competence. In my zeal to learn EKGs, for example, I approached the understanding of them by the 12 lead interpretation. People on all sides of me were pushing the literature, but didn't anticipate that I would immediately be so thorough. I didn't realize at the time that I was a threat. The head nurse would occasionally ask me a question which I would really answer as completely as I could. Blau states that the social processes generated by excessive concern with making a good impression actually set up an impasse to integration within a group. That's me! Further, I complicated the scene with what Blau terms self-deprecation.

*(Incidentally, that's a great article and its relevance increases as my socializa-
tion in the unit progresses.) I feel as though I've really blown it with the head
nurse, who is obviously uneasy around me. The socialization or social integration into this group really deserves about ten pages. An interestingly large
part of one's on-the-job energies are focused on the maintenance of interrelationships with colleagues.*

*Late November, 1970*

*I feel quite guilty about this delay, but I've just reached the point of
exhaustion. One could see it coming when I averaged about two or three
hours sleep a day. When given an hour, I'm the type who will plan two hours'
worth of projects. There were so many things I planned to do after graduation
which I have been compulsively fitting in during sleeping hours. Now I have
to face the reality of limiting myself. I am finding this to be true in nursing,
too. Throughout my education I migrated toward the sciences, but I found it
hard to become attached to any specific area. So here I find myself in one of
the most specialized areas of hospital nursing. I think about this a
lot . . . . . . at some point in time—preferably the near future—I should direct
my energies toward whatever I want to pursue in depth over a long period.*

*This brings me to the unit where I work. When I first entered the CCU my
attention was focused mainly on the oscilloscope. I was reading like mad to
catch up with the other nurses, and was, I'll have to admit, awed and curious
about the expertise that supposedly sets this group apart from the rest of the
staff at this hospital. (I imagine this may hold true at many establishments.)
During my orientation the emphasis was on the arrhythmias. The nurses still
seem to concentrate on this as opposed to the clinical aspects of cardiac
pathology. They seem to rise to the challenge of the electrocardiographic
diagnosis but they don't try to acquire any clinical type of diagnostic skill.
Perhaps one reason for this is delegated responsibility. The physician will inquire about a patient's current rhythm, and the nurse is expected to have
interpreted both the type and relative significance of the rhythm. The physician would never inquire about the patient's progressive rales or heart gallop.
So, in this circumstance, the physician is the major determiner of the type of
interest and responsibility the nurses assume. After the first two to three
weeks on nights, I got tired of looking at the oscilloscope and began to spend
a lot more time with the patients. My clinical expertise was low as I had really
seen very little. So my husband proceeded to teach me about how to
approach a patient. His method is logical, concise, and of course oriented
toward the diagnosis of the patient's physical problem. So, for a short time, I
was very systematic, examining the patient from head to foot and then comparing my results with the progress notes. This wasn't what I was looking for
at the time, so I began to approach the patient as a person-patient.*

*At this point I was beginning to get tremendously tired and I lapsed into
that which came naturally (considering my U.C. nurturing). There is a pro-*

cess . . . I am becoming more cognizant of it all the time. I can see my interests and needs changing weekly. It's not something I can control.

I have found that the process of becoming the type of professional I want to be is very much related to my need to compensate for inadequacies, real or perceived. I have found that I am quite aggressive yet unsure of myself. My confidence is usually proportional to my competence in a given area. In areas where I feel quite insecure I become quite intense. This holds true for skiing or any other activity as well as nursing. Once the threat has passed and I have conquered my fear I typically migrate to another area that is threatening. One would be amazed at the number of challenges I have attacked. The staff in the CCU did not see me as defensive; in fact they thought I was quite sure of myself. Both the RN who oriented with me and the head nurse made this clear to me a couple of times when I expressed feelings of inadequacy. Apparently, part of my way of handling an uptight situation is to appear somewhat confident. This was a shock to me as I always perceived myself as one who was entirely too passive and apologetic for my actions.

In retrospect, my functional rapport with the staff is rather poor. Apparently I made myself a threat to them when I attempted to integrate myself at their level of competence too quickly. The head nurse is a shy girl who finds leadership difficult, I think. I was an instant threat to her, and increased the initial gap between us by trying to impress her with my progress in learning my assigned task (interpreting EKGs). When we attempted to establish some sort of social rapport, I again distanced myself by exposing too many of my interests. Perhaps this was another attempt to prove myself. It was almost immediately evident that she was very uneasy around me. This has a tendency to snowball when one begins to respond with a similar uneasiness and confusion, and the tension escalates. She made several comments to me that were inconsistent with her good nature, including: "I hope you won't get bored with this unit." "The books you bring are very impressive." "I don't know why I'm explaining these (EKGs) to you, you probably know more about them than I do." The tone of her voice smacked with as much sarcasm as she could muster. I was shattered and sat down at home to have a good cry. She is just not given to sarcasm and is friendly with the whole crew. So I guessed that the major problem was my own and I cooled it completely. Sue, the other new RN, immediately hit it off with the head nurse.

One day, I attended a Cardiology Convention where I had to sit in the only seat left, which was next to Sue and the head nurse. That was quite a coincidence, and a bit embarrassing for them. Everyone is typically told about education opportunities. They told me they had tried to contact me. They hadn't. Since that time I have eliminated any real attempt at social rapport. Instead I have focused on giving reports and have avoided a defensive attitude. We are like friendly business partners but we avoid personal involvement. Her uneasiness seems to be subsiding and I know mine is. I hide my book in my purse before she arrives in the morning . . . and I try to use her *as a resource, which I think she needs. I'm so conscious of the situation that I take care to be subtle.*

*I am still a threat to her; if I avoided all activities that posed a threat to her I wouldn't be satisfying my own needs in this role. My report, for instance, is well prepared and includes the psychosocial status of the patient. I really enjoy giving a comprehensive account of the night's events, writing pertinent progress notes, etc., in hopes of increasing the continuity of care, with special emphasis on the patient's feelings about his progress or prognosis. Sound textbooky? This is the area where most of our current contact is made.*

*According to Blau, I've passed through the phase of caring so much about acceptance that I would act defensively in ways that interfere with it.*

1. *I avoid self-deprecating modesty. I no longer apologize for what I don't know. And I don't give defensive rationalizations for each action. I am increasingly quiet about the little decisions I make and I simply present what I have done at report time.*

2. *I've gradually reduced the social aspects of interaction with co-workers for a more business-like congeniality. I'm less uptight and less concerned about their good will toward me.*

3. *I've reduced the amount of energy I expend in social interactions with the staff, and I've re-directed it toward my patients.*

4. *I still try to impress my co-workers, perhaps, but now by hiding my persistent weaknesses. For instance, if something is bothering me about a procedure or medication I keep it to myself until I get home where I look it up or ask my husband about it. The point where I am now has allowed the tenseness with the head nurse to recede a bit.*

*Now to my LPN. I wrote you a couple of pages about her one day that I couldn't possibly have sent at the time. They represent complete abandonment of objectivity. I simply hated her for about two weeks. And about that time the tensions with the head nurse were brewing.*

*In the beginning, I attempted to make myself acceptable to her by using her as a resource. She took right over by carefully explaining "how we do things here." Well, considering my defenses and my desire to move in my own way, I instantly resented her authoritarian attitude. So I cut her questions with such comments as, "I think Mr. X needs a repeat of his Seconal, don't you?" She used any opening I gave her, and I began to wonder who was making the decisions. And every morning at five she insists upon waking the patients for TPR and weights. It's not so bad that she wakes them up . . . . but she makes them get out of bed and onto those darn scales, which wakes them up for sure. A couple of times I've requested that she not start until six, which would give her plenty of time to finish. My emotional agitation made me so tense that I was fearful of my tone of voice, so I decided to cool it until I could get my bearings. Obviously there was more to it than the five o'clock arousal.*

*These diaries have been a tremendous help in seeing what is happening. I think about situations by saying "Dear Miss K." And I analyze the situation as a person who is looking in at what is really taking place. By doing this I finally figured out that this LPN has no idea in the world what I am upset about, if she is even aware that I'm upset. Her Filipino background makes her very old country in the way she approaches things. I began to understand her nursing actions when she related her life-style to me. Her marriage was arranged; her children are ruled with an iron hand; and she wouldn't let her daughter be Prom Queen at a Catholic girls' school because she didn't want her (a high school senior) to meet any boys until after college. There are set ways to do things.*

*I really did give her too much credit for thinking, and would secretly get angry when she didn't. That statement isn't sarcastic; I expected her to problem solve each little problem. But I guess some people find their security in performing tasks on an assigned schedule without questions or any deviation in style. When I realized this, my anger cooled down a lot.*

*Initially, I really tried to establish a social rapport with my LPN. It was very energy consuming, as it required that I try to make conversation with an older woman with whom I had nothing in common. As I began to feel comfortable with the silent periods, my tension subsided a lot. Now we often have four-hour stretches when I may be reading and getting the hourly B/P and she goes about her tasks. She is also a quiet woman and she enjoys the silences, I think. Our relationship is much improved now. And I think it is curious that she was probably unaware of the turmoil that I had been experiencing.*

*I haven't even talked about the poor man in the bed yet—the patient—but in writing this I can see that patients are only about 25 percent of my concerns now. I sound pretty bad to myself as I write along—but I try so hard on a constant basis.*

*I have approached patients in a number of different ways since I started. I was at first fearful of "breaking" the man with the vulnerable heart and hidden vessels. Now it seems like all the veins are pipelines ready to be tapped. Patients aren't breakable, and, for a while, I found them interesting specimens for learning on. I even began to try for veins I couldn't see. But when I wasn't too successful I decided to stop. Then I was hot for hearing rales, cardiac auscultations, etc. And finally I settled back with the patient himself. I've run the gamut of nursing approaches all in two months' time.*

## One Week Later

*One thing I am beginning to miss on this job is any kind of good old nursing conversations. I mean, you can't really discuss what you see happening with anyone: the inadequacies, advances, or even patient progress. There is a loneliness about being unable to discuss one's interests. It is also a cause for frustration. As a novice, I am keenly interested in becoming proficient within my role. Fresh from school, I am still close to participant learning . . . hashing things out with my colleagues. To gain the type of proficiency I value, I need a close association with my co-workers. For example, this hospital's organization is complex in terms of administration. The nursing services department seems top heavy with administrators and deficient in concern for quality patient care. Ever since I began working, I have been interested in learning the function of each of these administrators. I have asked many different RNs what the DNS actually does on a day-to-day basis and what her overall function is. There is a general discontent with her, and the answer is typically a complaint about her. One nurse referred me to the formal write-up of job descriptions. The job description is ambiguous and tells me very little.*

*Lesson number 34 on the job has been to AVOID mentioning any reading you've done either recently or in the past. It is super threat number 1. This again makes me feel alone. The real excitement I feel about this job is supported by, and sort of proportional to, what I learn. I read an article the other day about the dangers of strokes caused by arrhythmias. These strokes are especially common in the elderly and occur when the perfusion to the brain is temporarily decreased. We can sit there watching the oscilloscope and because of the patterns, tell when perfusion is decreased somewhat. It is really exciting to know that in a susceptible person we can be alerted to this danger and act appropriately.*

*But the nurses don't want to hear about these things . . . they find them threatening. I may still be approaching things so awkwardly that I stifle interesting conversations that could go on. I'll have to keep this in mind.*

*I wonder if part of my disenchantment is due in part to the assignment of night duty. The autonomy of nights seems at first a reward in itself. After all the schooling, one gets a chance to try oneself out without displaying to the world a knack for making all those initial mistakes. And aside from getting the routine down in an efficient way, I wanted to try myself out — establishing and becoming comfortable with nurse-patient communications, going over my nursing notes and rewriting them when needed, taking time to organize and establish a regimen for giving report, spending extra time listening to hearts and seeing what edema really looks like all over the body.*

*Developing a good nurse-patient communication style really does take time. What I mean is, I have a particular way of expressing myself that hadn't been used to the fullest before. In school, I could always think about and prepare myself psychologically for patient contacts, but now I have to do it more quickly.*

**COMMENTARY**

BENNER:  Lynn's November diary entries have a different flavor from her October entries. It's as if she's begun her journey for real. She is very involved in finding out what kind of nurse she is and is becoming. I really get the feeling that Lynn is caught up in developing her proving ground.

KRAMER: Yes, Lynn seems unusual in that she had quite clear conceptions of what is important in *her* self-constructed test or proving ground. She says that she viewed this job as an opportunity:

> 1) to develop one-to-one relationships that she felt she was trained for in school
>
> 2) to make observations that are valued
>
> 3) to develop clinical diagnostic skills
>
> 4) to attend to the psychosocial aspects of illness
>
> 5) to practice and become expert in "important" high-level technical skills such as IVs, drawing blood, defibrillating patients
>
> 6) to learn    . and perceive progress in her accomplishments.

BENNER: Those are very clear, explicit objectives. In terms of technical skills, Lynn did differentiate between technical skills in the CCU, which she valued, and technical skills on the Orthopedic Unit, which she did not value.

KRAMER: Apparently the Orthopedic Unit was a totally unacceptable proving ground. Lynn points out that the Orthopedic Unit did not meet the conditions that were important to her on several counts. The number of "important" technical skills is one of the missing pieces, I think. If Lynn had had school socialization that taught her how to influence others to effect better patient care, rather than to value "one-to-one relationships" with patients, do you think she might have perceived the Orthopedic Unit as an ideal place to test herself?

BENNER: I think she might have. That's a thought provoking question. One of her objectives was to "attend to the psychosocial aspects of illness"; certainly she perceived more than enough psychosocial needs on the Orthopedic Unit.

KRAMER: But her perception only served to frustrate and overwhelm her. She could not meet patients' psychosocial needs in the *way* she was prepared to or expected to—that is, on a one-to-one basis. After her sensitive perceptions of psychosocial needs on the Orthopedic Unit she is left with the proverbial "empty bag." She lacked a repertoire of approaches to plan and execute interventions through others.

BENNER: So her sensitivity only served to frustrate her?

KRAMER: Exactly . . . . Let's get back to the testing idea.

BENNER: I am primarily aware of the test that Lynn is constructing for herself. Many new graduates seem more aware of the tests constructed by their work group. Do you see any evidence of the staff constructing tests for Lynn?

KRAMER: A little, but they seem quite subtle at this point. Rather than tests, they seem to be almost daring Lynn to be competent without making them feel threatened. The LVN that Lynn is working with is sending some strong socialization messages, however.

BENNER: Yes, she really tried to cut Lynn in on the back-stage reality, didn't she? She took right over by carefully explaining "How we do things here."

KRAMER: We don't know whether Lynn was aware of this possible entry into the back-region, but it is evident that Lynn knew what she wanted:

> Considering my defenses and my desire to move in my own way, I instantly resented her authoritarian attitude. So I cut her questions with such comments as. . . ."

And then there's Lynn's attempt to influence the aide, to effect change. Unfortunately, she was not yet powerful enough within the social system to succeed.

BENNER: I think that Lynn is beginning to be anxious to make contributions, to effect change, to make a difference in her work setting.

KRAMER: Yes, I think Lynn's quest for competency comes across in her desire to be clinically competent enough "to observe subtle changes."

BENNER: Lynn is aware that she has created distance between herself and other staff members. I think Lynn's quest for competency plus her reality shock distanced her from other staff members, and interfered with her reception of their socialization.

KRAMER: That could be. She saw herself as an almost instant threat to the head nurse. This produced uneasiness and distrust in both of them. The more Lynn tried, the more the tension increased, until finally it produced such comments from the head nurse as these:

> "I hope you won't get bored with this unit." "The books you bring are very impressive." "I don't know why I'm explaining these to *you*. You probably know more about them than I do."

These are very strong socialization messages, but because Lynn is not yet ready to accept the notion that she must deal with the human side of the organization, she has difficulty interpreting them correctly.

BENNER: Yes, and I think part of the reason for Lynn's difficulty in interpreting the messages correctly stems from her reality shock, which began to set in in late November:

> I've just reached the point of exhaustion. . . . Now I have to face the reality of limiting myself. I am finding this to be true in nursing, too.

Throughout my education I migrated toward the sciences, but I found it hard to become attached to any specific area. So here I find myself in one of the most specialized areas of hospital nursing. I think about this a lot......at some point in time—preferably the near future—I should direct my energies toward whatever I want to pursue in depth over a long period....

In retrospect, my functional rapport with the staff is rather poor. Apparently, I made myself a threat to them when I attempted to integrate myself at *their* level of competence too quickly.

Although this beginning rejection is not as strong as it will be within a week or two, it is in strong contrast to the initial euphoria and wholesale acceptance and praise Lynn felt upon entering the CCU. It is clear that she no longer sees the CCU through rose-colored glasses.

KRAMER:   What do you think triggered the shock phase for Lynn?

BENNER:   From Lynn's diary, it's not clear what the triggering events for the wholesale rejection and reality shock were. One can postulate that she had a series of value clashes and that her different values served to alienate her from her co-workers. As you noted, she did not accept the physician's socialization regarding the importance of oscilloscope observations and interpretation. This may well have been one difference that served to alienate her from her co-workers. I think that Lynn's description of her value clash with "her LPN" is also instructive:

> And every morning at five she insists upon waking the patients for TPR and weights.... A couple of times I've requested that she not start until six, which would give her plenty of time to finish. *My emotional agitation made me so tense that I was fearful of my tone of voice, so I decided to cool it until I could get my bearings. Obviously there was more to it than the five o'clock arousal* [italics added].

The LPN's task orientation clashed with Lynn's patient-centered orientation. Lynn was correct in concluding that there was more to it than the five o'clock arousal. The task orientation clashed with a whole set of school-bred values that put patients' needs ahead of task accomplishment. Lynn was not prepared for the set of responses that this activity of the LPN evoked. Lynn's wholesale rejection and criticism reflects the lack of objectivity that characterizes this phase of reality shock. Lynn was aware of this and was candid about it.

> Now to my LPN. I wrote you a couple of pages about her one day that I couldn't possibly have sent at the time. They're handwritten and represent complete abandonment of objectivity. I simply hated her for about two weeks.

KRAMER:  At least Lynn is aware of her predicament, her abandonment of objectivity. . . . I think Lynn is also experiencing some longing for or idealizing of the past.

> One thing I am beginning to miss on this job is *any kind of good old nursing conversations* [italics added]. I mean, you can't really discuss what you see: the inadequacies, advances, or even patient progress.

BENNER:  That's a good point, since one of the hallmarks of the rejection phase of reality shock is the longing for familiar symbols and idealization of the past. Here Lynn is longing for the collegial relationships experienced in nursing school.

KRAMER:  But side by side with this rejection stage of reality shock, I also see signs of recovery and increasing empathy, for example, in her analysis of her interaction with the LPN. She is aware that the LPN has "no idea in the world what I am upset about." Notice Lynn's increased empathy and role taking:

> I guess some people find their security in performing tasks on an assigned schedule without questions or deviation in style. When I realized this, my anger cooled down a lot.

BENNER:  There is evidence that writing the diary helped Lynn increase her objectivity and empathy. . . . I remember in the last commentary, you raised the question of whether Lynn would begin to get involved in interpersonal relationships with the staff—you know, to move from seeing everything as patient focus, to accepting the fact that some time and energy must also be devoted to dealing with the human side of the organization.

KRAMER:  Lynn does seem to be struggling with the necessity of dealing with the human side of organization. School teaches the student to rationalize away the human side of the organization. Students learn rational goal achievement but know nothing about all the familiar work group personality constraints. Some students never learn to accept the human side of the organization. Lynn was taught to value the worth of solving difficult interpersonal problems with patients in nursing school; however, she did not learn to equally value solving difficult interpersonal problems with staff members:

> By the time the IPR with staff members are waded through, it's no wonder lots of people have no energy left for that poor patient, labelled difficult. With a 40-bed ward and a five-staff ratio, it's understandable that one tends to become involved in interpersonal struggles with staff members, including the doctors. Anyway, it seemed that the difficult doctor often received more attention than the difficult patient.

BENNER: Lynn's initial reaction—or perhaps it was a planned action in view of how well she is in touch with herself and her strengths and weaknesses—to this perceived pull and tug between the task and maintenance goals of an organization, was to pull out. "I really enjoy the isolated independence on night duty in CCU." And initially she believed that the patient would be *the central issue in the CCU.*

KRAMER: This view was not to last long. Within two weeks after entering the CCU, she realized that she could devote about "ten pages to socialization and social integration into the work group." She states with some surprise: "And interestingly, a large part of one's on-the-job energies are focused on the maintenance of interrelationships with colleagues." The point here is that Lynn was not prepared for and found it difficult to accept the fact that she would have to devote energies to the human side of the organization—to interpersonal relationships and "gaining acceptance" with staff members.

BENNER: One senses some of the isolation Lynn feels when she talks about "the staff," "they saw me," "I made myself . . . when I attempted . . . their. . . ."

Later she notes:

I've gradually reduced the social aspects of interaction with co-workers for a more business-like congeniality. I'm less uptight and less concerned about their good will toward me.

KRAMER: Yes, she still believes that she can gain acceptance on a purely rational, professional basis and attempts to seek *respect* rather than *acceptance.* But this does not work for Lynn in this small unit. Still, in November she notes:

Being unable to discuss one's interests causes loneliness and frustration. As a novice, I am keenly interested in becoming proficient within my role. Fresh from school, I am still close to participation learning . . . hashing things out with my colleagues. To gain the type of proficiency I value, I need a close association with my co-workers . . . . Lesson number 34 on the job has been to AVOID mentioning any reading you've done either recently or in the past. It is threat number 1. This again makes one feel alone.

*Early December, 1970*

*I have just completed a seven-day run of nights. As I mentioned before, I live a full life during the day. I wonder how many of the girls who enjoy a fast pace on the job also continue the pace at home. I have this thing about energy spent—being spent constructively. If I spend an hour doing something and it is not something learned or constructive, I feel the time is wasted. Because of this, routine is frustrating, housework is boring, and so I undertake a lot of projects to keep me somewhat satisfied. You were right about the effect of home life on the quality of work done while on the job. On day seven a compulsion for good patient care is obscured by exhaustion. . . .*

*Hospital nursing is something I probably won't stay with for very long. There is a ceiling to it.*

*Two Days Later*

*I feel closed in on the job. I don't think I am practicing anywhere near my peak. I have been horribly depressed for the past week; most of it is due to my dissatisfaction with work. I often wonder why I ended up in nursing when I find interpersonal relations so unmanageable. Perhaps this characterizes the nurse who seeks satisfaction in the emergency care situation.*

*In addition to the limited setting I'm in, I am also on permanent nights. And I'm beginning to wonder just how pathological that decision was. I still find the interpersonal staff relations more energy-consuming than the patient care activities on a busy night.*

*Perhaps it's just my generation, but I absolutely abhor the clenches the establishment has on one's behavior. Right now, specifics matter very little. . . . It's a feeling of wanting to break out and throw one's arm all over the place just to prove that there is room and the energy can be spent any way it wants to!*

*I mentioned the ceiling inherent in hospital nursing. The ceiling is low and the four walls around it seem thick to me right now. There isn't any place in the system where one can advance to free expression. Higher positions seem to mean more money and more precisely defined roles.*

*Three Days Later*

*It is becoming interesting to me that every time I write about my job, my attitude toward it is completely different from the time before. The exhaustion finally did catch up with me and it seems to be affecting my performance at work to a greater degree than I would have expected. The first area of care that I've neglected or given lower priority is the patient's emotional status. Somehow, giving physical care requires less of one's energies than does standing for long intervals at the bedside allowing the patient to talk it out. Even more difficult is the attempt to help the patient express what he is shouting covertly. For the past week I've attended less to the patients' emotional needs; the problem with this is that job satisfaction has decreased even more. I go home feeling I've accomplished very little. . . .*

*Although our unit is set up strictly for coronary patients, the doctors like to send in other patients who require close observation. There is no ICU yet.*

*And out on the ward close observation is difficult due to lack of help. The doctors complain about the nursing care out on the wards. I spent several days out there and came back to my comfortable four-bed, carpeted unit feeling that those ward nurses are really superwomen who have been beaten down by the overwhelming number of patients and tasks. I was really slow out there in comparison to the aide I was helping. Inwardly, I criticized her for whizzing through those patients without saying anything to them or asking how they were. Then I got behind on all my duties. The concern for poor Mr. Jones quickly passed in the effort to get that next patient weighed or something.*

*The medical ward where I relieved is chronic in the sense that most of the men seem to be there for at least two to three weeks. And yet there is much less interpersonal interaction than in our "emergency" unit. So, for this hospital, the CCU is the place that provides much more opportunity for one-to-one nurse-patient contact.*

*Actually, nights are much less ideal for patient observation than I originally thought they would be. I hesitate to really wake my patients up with bright lights to look at their coloring, veins, etc., unless they are critical or already unable to sleep. This means that I can't really follow a progression throughout the night like I should. But once these apprehensive fellows finally do get to sleep on their second sleeper, it seems terrible to wake them up. Consequently, I find myself waiting until morning to really check them out. Sometimes this worries me; I'm caught between "good nursing care" and a little compassion for the patient. Originally, one real lure of the unit was the constant presence of doctors and medical students. They stand around six to ten at a time hashing out what is happening to the patient. It is also an area where the attendings pull out the chalk and give quasi-lectures that nurses can bend an ear to. Every day I see new diagrams on the little blackboard in the unit and feel sort of bad about missing the session that went with it. I do have more time to read the progress notes, which isn't quite the same.*

*There are many more small, everyday realizations that are beginning to add up to dissatisfaction. I don't feel that I am doing a very good job. I'm carrying out all the activities that the job description requires . . . I really try to be conscientious. But I feel as though I am helping the unit to hold its own without advancing.*

*Late December, 1970*

*This portion should really have a different sound from what I wrote during the last few days. I've had some sleep. . .*

*My purpose in this first job in the CCU is to gain experience so that I may comfortably move into some other area of nursing. As I said previously, I am still a bit unsure just where I am heading. The important point, though, is that this is less a "job" than another learning experience for me. It is like an extension of my student clinicals, except that it is my first effort to show myself* what I am made of and to learn what I can expect in my future career. . . . I am consciously critical of my failings as a leader, innovator, and in inter-personal staff relations.

Within the clinical situation, I have felt closed in for many reasons. One of these is the authoritarian structure I must function in. I mentioned the cooling process I went through when I felt that I was threatening the head nurse. She was not a person to be alienated from—especially while she was orienting me. And she probably has some influence in my socialization with the staff. Lately my fears of alienation have been overshadowed by the frustrations I feel about not progressing.

The head nurse is talking about some good innovations in the charting for-mat. In the new format there will be a space allocated to nurse-patient teach-ing. Hopefully, it will be specific enough to be really effective. Our charting is extensive—it covers both sides of one page. The change will be a positive step toward one-to-one involvement. Also I bet it will open up a lot more awareness of the patient's emotional status. I had two strong personal feel-ings about her change: (1) I felt a sting . . . that she had thought of it first, and (2) I felt relieved to know that I might be able to add something without social penalty. What's this bit with my preoccupation about being accepted??????

I feel I have so much to offer, so many things I'd like to suggest, things that would help the patient. But . . . but what? I don't want to threaten the others. I want so much to be accepted. For instance, there is a constant awareness of the EKG and significant changes in the rhythm. This is as it should be. However, another very important aspect of nursing care is the pa-tient's hydration. We usually seem to follow the physician's orders blindly about fluid restrictions, flow rate of the intravenous fluids, etc. And if we don't, we sort of sneak our opinion in without charting what we've done. At least I've found myself doing it. Twice now since I've begun in the unit, we have overloaded a patient with IV fluids by following the doctor's orders. And in one case, I recall saying at report "this man will be overloaded if we keep up the fluids at this rate." The day nurse agreed with me, but both of us continued the fluids. We slowed them down so that we were behind, but in our notes or comments to the doctors we should have said that we were doing it intentionally and given our rationale. The last fellow I had was total-ly miserable 24 hours a day because he was allowed 75cc/shift. His tongue was dry and furrowed despite almost constant applications of swabs to his mouth. He groaned continually. Gradually I just began cheating. The doctor increased the IVs to a good rate, but not the oral intake. I poured out some of the fast running D5/W and gave him an equivalent amount of $H_2O$ with some jello for osmotic purposes. Bad, bad, bad. There is a neat article in a recent AJN about the clinical application of fluids and electrolytes. In it Voda suggests that nurses be somewhat responsible for the consequences of the intravenous fluids that they monitor, just as they are responsible for the medications given with respect to dosage, allergic responses, etc. I would like to introduce the article to the girls at work; perhaps we could prevent *these unnecessary fluid disasters. Every person in our unit is constantly on IVs so that medications can be administered through the veins. Hydration is our business. . . . But I'm afraid to introduce it — the social penalty.*

*Since the last letter my relations with the staff have again completely changed. I'm just more relaxed. Things seem to fall into place better and when I request the aide to do something or get something, it is not quite so stiff. Also my permanent LPN is on vacation so I have a breather from the continual problem about having patients wakened every four hours so that they can never sleep after five.*

## COMMENTARY

KRAMER: Lynn begins her December diary entries by commenting on the demands of her home role versus the demands of her work role. Like most professionals, she finds routine boring in either setting.

BENNER: Lynn's feelings of rejection for the hospital seem to have increased too:

> Hospital nursing is something I probably won't stay with for very long. There is a ceiling to it.

and then, two days later she writes,

> I feel closed in on the job. I don't think I am practicing anywhere near my peak. I have been horribly depressed for the past week; most of it due to my dissatisfaction with work.

KRAMER: Sounds like a combination of moral outrage and despair, doesn't it? This is also the first hint that Lynn sees flight as an acceptable alternative in coping with the high level of frustration she is experiencing.

BENNER: It's not hard to empathize with her frustration, especially when you take into consideration the high degree of investment Lynn has made in her job.

KRAMER: Yes . . . Lynn is also aware that she brought with her some bias against the organization, which may be above and beyond the discomfort she is experiencing with its method of organizing work. Lynn says it better than I can:

> Perhaps it's just my generation, but I absolutely abhor the clenches the establishment has on one's behavior. Right now, specifics matter very little. . . . It's a feeling of wanting to break out and throw one's arm all over the place just to prove that there is room and the energy can be spent any way it wants to!

> I mentioned the ceiling inherent in hospital nursing. The ceiling is low and the four walls around it seem to be thick right now. There isn't any place in the system where one can advance to free expression

Higher positions seem to mean more money and more precisely defined roles.

BENNER: Given Lynn's level of activity plus this amount of frustration, it is little wonder that fatigue is a persistent problem.

KRAMER: I think Lynn's lack of interpersonal power in her social system is beginning to take its toll too. Perhaps she is experiencing frustration from a lack of interpersonal competence in this social system. By interpersonal competence, I mean the ability to bring about desired effects by predicting how one's actions will affect and be interpreted by others. At this point Lynn feels powerless to bring about desired effects in her new social system, and understandably so.

BENNER: Feeling powerless is probably one of the most trying things about being new in a social system. And for Lynn, the feeling of being unable to make a difference or effect change made her work world unbearable. If she could not make a difference in the social system she did not want to stay:

> There are many more small, everyday realizations that are beginning to add up to dissatisfaction. . . . I really try to be conscientious. But I feel as though I am helping the unit to hold its own without advancing.

KRAMER: Lynn's desire to "make a difference" really puts the onus on the organization to create an environment that will enable her to contribute. Lynn noted earlier that her commitment to this organization was temporary, probably around one year. She reiterates her conditional, temporary commitment here, and I think this helps her. By refusing a commitment to stay for a long period, she decreases the stress and pressure to conform in a situation that she finds frustrating. Unfortunately though, interpersonal competence is never mastered through flight behavior.

BENNER: Yes, Lynn notes that she is still unsure where she is heading, but that her present job is less a "job" than another learning experience.

KRAMER: For Lynn, this first job is truly an extension of professional school socialization.

BENNER: That makes sense. And yet Lynn can't quite talk herself into viewing her first job as just another clinical since the first job had special meaning to her as a proving ground. Notice she says:

> It is like an extension of my student clinicals, except that it is my first effort to show myself what I am made of and to learn what I can expect in my future career.

KRAMER: Yes, like many other new graduates, she does give considerable weight and importance to her first job.

BENNER:    One is struck by the high level of motivation that persists in spite of frustration and fatigue. Lynn shows continued interest in learning and indicates that she misses the teaching aspect of the physicians' socialization.

*January, 1971*

*I received a note of suggestions from the night nurse concerning things I have neglected throughout my shift. After the initial resentment over what I felt was admonishment, I looked up the job description for my shift and found how wrong I had been. I had read it in the beginning — even took notes so that I wouldn't forget every detail. But as the fog of orientation cleared, so apparently did the memory of what I read. Little things, like renewal of narcotics, are really important and shouldn't be done by the busier shifts. I talked with her about it briefly — I think she felt uneasy at the time — but I thanked her for it and haven't missed the extras lately. I'm not very routine-oriented — it's something I always have to remind myself to do.*

*After four months I'm still not completely "settled" in the job as "one of the girls." As time passes, I find it much easier to converse with and socialize with the RNs and less so with the LPNs. This is in contrast to the rapport that I established with the staff when I first began working. I also find that if I have a suggestion or if criticism is passed my way I am much more able to handle it with the RNs. My leadership qualities with the aides are almost nil. I really become irate with myself for being unable to give even the most minor directions. As I see it, the reason for this right now is my defensiveness. The aides are older and more set in their ways and thoughts. My rapport with them is slipping, I think. I have worked with more of them lately, so my subjectivity is lessened. The energy consumed in worrying about staff rapport tells me I shouldn't look for any sort of administrative position in the near future.*

*Although I'm tired and absolutely everything seems to be getting worse in the way I handle life and the job, I am beginning to realize that I do like nursing. Now to figure where I fit in. I mentioned previously my frustration with nursing as a "nowhere profession." But it sure allows for flexibility — to excel in an area of one's choice. Hospital staff nursing is not a fertile place for me to find job satisfaction. The proportional frustrations outweigh the satisfactions.*

*Frustrations*

*1. Lack of medical knowledge*

*2. Lack of responsibility*

*3. Lack of time to accomplish patient care meeting personal standards*

*4. Lousy hours (worked Xmas, New Years, Thanksgiving)*

*5. Employee of an institution (completely expendable)*

*Satisfactions*

1. *Patient satisfaction*
2. *Satisfaction with care given and rapport established with patients*

*I hate to keep belaboring my fatigue, but it really does play a top role in this girl's career goals. I expect to become pregnant again within the next couple of years, and the teacher at my daughter's school tells me that my daughter is becoming increasingly anxious, less able to concentrate, and louder than usual. So, mama better tend to a bit of motherhood also. My next job will have to involve either better hours or fewer hours. I am seriously looking around for another job—one in which I hope I can get more satisfaction. I have applied to some of the local nursing schools for teaching positions. Maybe if I can't find satisfaction in nursing, I'll find it in teaching.*

*One Week Later*

*I haven't actually initiated any teaching session with the patients about their cardiac pathology, which was one of my goals. I usually explain the importance of deep breathing, etc. Also it took me quite a while to say "heart attack" around the patients. The "injury to heart muscle" skirted the issue a bit. The men didn't collapse with the mention of an attack and did show interest when I began to explain a little about the nature of an attack (in the heart itself). I haven't spent as much time as I'd like to yet, but I think patient teaching may be a good way to establish a rapport with mutual exchange—patient responds with questions, asks for clarification, and gives more voluntary information about past medical history (clues one in on extent of understanding about his health and its maintenance). Anyway, I'll try it—it would be great for the patients and would provide me more nursing satisfaction.*

*I am gradually learning how to follow a routine. I don't "think routine," and therefore I forget the details. My reports are less organized than previously because I'm less apprehensive about giving report, and I don't have time to rewrite my stuff completely as I hastened to do before. Again, I forget. To be organized, I've run off a bunch of itemized report sheets that I can fill in as I go and integrate into my routine. As I finish charting I can jot down information in the appropriate spot.*

*Job satisfaction has been at a low ebb. Perhaps because of two or three months without much sleep. I don't feel like I'm a very good nurse—as far as nurses go. Efficiency is energy consuming, and to complete a day's work well, I don't have the energy to read. I haven't done any reading for a while and this really bugs me—not only am I not particularly confident with my nursing abilities, but my theoretical base isn't building. Drugs—I'm behind on those. I know what's wrong: I'm not contributing to the betterment of the unit as I'd like to—or something.*

*Now that I've had some rest, my attitude is changing—I'm not quite as fatalistic, I give more time to what satisfies me in the job. It's the con-*

centrated personal contact. I really like to build a rapport with the men — in particular, their trust in me as their nurse.

## Several Days Later

*I've been fussing around long enough trying to establish a social rapport with the staff members on my ward. As you must realize, it has already thwarted what I might be doing for my own self-improvement on the ward and, un-naturalness comes through as stilted for me. I have guarded myself against competing with anyone and can you imagine, the upshot of this fiasco has been a show of lack of confidence in me as clinically competent and socially as a flop. Yesterday, the head nurse asked to talk to me "in the back room." Have you ever gotten that feeling in the pit of your stomach when you know someone is going to tell you that you just don't add up? The first part of the admonishment session was devoted to the fact that I had come into work one night with liquor on my breath. Granted, this is serious if someone has had too much to drink. Well, I was completely sober after some beers at a big Italian dinner at the Spaghetti Factory. My whole family had been up from San Francisco and I had had four days off. The liquor may have been on my breath from dinner, but the complaint was unfounded. Also, one of the aides I'd never worked with started complaining about the milk I drink while on duty. She reported the fact to the head nurse, who told me that the kitchen was complaining. It hadn't.*

*The head nurse continued to say that the staff members thought something was the matter with me; that I was too nervous for them and that she wanted me to come onto days. I know that if I were to come on days I'd be daily transferred out on to the ward. I can't make the shift anyway because of my home situation. Throughout the conversation I felt that I was a chronic irritant to the girls and that the head nurse goes in spurts in being friendly and uneasy around me. It can't always be me on that score. The whole thing really hurt. I tried so hard to do things just right. In addition, I'm always the first to be nice to people, ask them how they are and compliment them. If I didn't give a damn it would be a different matter, but I feel that I try harder than some of these girls. I guess I've come across as an agitant. The girl who works evenings hasn't talked to me since the night I had "liquor on my breath."*

*At the conference with the head nurse, I defended myself only slightly by showing complete surprise at being put down for drinking. Then, like a complete idiot, I began to help her tear myself apart. I solicited from her what she was really concerned about. Was it my inability to socialize with the girls or something? I continued to say that I realized it might be hard to like a person who is very intense and talks fast, etc. She wouldn't say, just that most liked me, and then she hesitated. . . . So, I've screwed my first job. After the initial depression I felt like the nurses had opened up for me whatever had been preventing me from being myself. I had failed on their terms as I saw them set, but perhaps me as me won't be any the worse for it. I am not going to compete with the staff but with myself.*

*I've revised the little report form to include activity and weight and diagnosis. . . . I think this form really will be a help. . . . I haven't shown the printed-up form to the nurses yet, so I'm not sure if they'll like the idea. I've done it by hand and I revised it as I went. Hopefully it will help me at least, and will not be rejected for its originator but for the idea itself, if it's not valuable to the others.*

*This is my day off, so when I go back and feel a bit cooler about this whole thing, I'll talk to the head nurse. Another thing, I think the idea about the patient teaching is really great as I indicated to you before. It was the head nurse's idea, and she said she would include it in her next run-off of nursing notes. She didn't; perhaps she'll dump the plan. I'd like to help get something specific down and thought I'd find something written on it and do a work-up on paper: a preliminary form that all of us could work on as we go. I could get started teaching and pass on, by way of this form, specific things that are important and should be included. Teaching is so important in this area. The men often fear procedures that they shouldn't fear . . . like the frequency of blood pressures, EKGs, and so forth. Also, the doctors come in in packs and leave the patient to huddle outside his door. This would scare anyone, and a little forewarning would help.*

*Funny, just before the head nurse approached me I was beginning to feel more comfortable with everything. My LPN and I have worked together long enough that she and I know what to expect and things move along smoothly. I understand her more now and appreciate her for her clinical competence. You may remember the upsets I used to experience when she woke everyone up at five. Now she doesn't do it quite so much. She takes their temps when they are awake or turns out the lights after she is done so they can go to sleep again. And also, I was writing down all the different things from the job description and extras like the number of charts I want to make up in advance, certain things to stock, points I want to remember about the patients, getting their social histories, and so forth. I am not regimen-oriented, so I have to have reminders for all the red tape. And I chart extensively, which requires a lot of patient contact. So I was feeling better. Then this. Rise to it, Lynn, and show yourself you've got what it takes! Are any of the others having so much trouble or am I some kind of nut?*

*Having read what I just wrote, I can see that I am skirting the issue. I can't solve my current problems by innovating projects. But right now I can't see through it all. So until next time. . . .*

### COMMENTARY

BENNER:  Lynn seems to be beginning to pick up on work values in this series of entries.

KRAMER:  Yes, one of the things I particularly noticed was a beginning acknowledgement and perhaps a realization that there might be something to organizational values. This is very difficult for Lynn and other young graduates who find the organizational values — for example, the stress on routines or on replacement of supplies — very hard to tolerate.

> Little things, like renewal of narcotics, are really important. I am gradually learning to follow a routine. I don't think routine. Therefore, I forget the details. . . .

BENNER: Did you notice that Lynn found it necessary to translate the reminder about the things she had neglected doing into her own school-bred value system before acquiescing? She says "after the initial resentment over what I felt was admonishment, I looked up the job description . . . and found how much in error I had been." Lynn isn't accepting bureaucratic authority, rather she is handling this situation by "looking things up for myself." But I would agree with you that, on the whole, Lynn is becoming more open to some of the subcultural values of the work system. Where do you think Lynn is in the socialization cycle now, Marlene?

KRAMER: Well, she definitely moved out of the skill mastery state — I don't believe she's mentioned any of that for quite a while. She's still consciously trying to master routines though, but it seems to be on an acceptance, rather than a rejection level. There is still definitely shock and moral outrage. Perhaps this is best expressed in Lynn's description of her feelings about the conference with the head nurse. She was "completely surprised." She thought she had been doing well. She was beginning to feel more comfortable, and felt her IPR with the staff was going along more smoothly. And then this! It's quite possible that Lynn was so busy trying to get across the things she believed in that she was literally unable to hear or perceive messages that others were sending her. On the other hand, the staff did not appear to be very aware of this new graduate's plight. It probably never occurred to them that a young woman of today would not consider it nonprofessional to have a light alcoholic beverage with dinner and go on duty at 11:00 P.M. There is also considerable data that Lynn is still experiencing fatigue as a result of her reality shock.

> I hate to keep belaboring my fatigue. . . . I'm tired and absolutely everything seems to be getting worse. . . .

Part of Lynn's fatigue, no doubt, is due to her night shift work and her high level of activity during the day. But in part it's due to the personal toll of making so many adjustments, and feeling discomfort and rejection in her new environment.

BENNER: It seems to me that one of the major symptoms of reality shock that Lynn is manifesting at this point is the sense of total defeat and failure.

I don't feel like I'm a very good nurse—as far as nurses go. Efficiency is energy consuming and to complete a day's work well, I don't have time to read. I haven't done any reading for a while and this really bugs me—not only am I not particularly confident with my nursing abilities, but my theoretical base isn't building.

So, I've screwed my first job. After the initial depression I felt like the nurses had opened up for me whatever had been preventing me from being myself I had failed on their terms as I saw them set, but perhaps me as me won't be any the worse for it.

There are many more, small, everyday realizations that are beginning to add up to dissatisfaction. I don't feel that I am doing a very good job. I'm carrying out all the activities that the job description requires . . . I really try to be conscientious. But I feel as though I am helping the unit to hold its own without advancing.

I am consciously critical of my failings as a leader, innovator, and in interpersonal staff relations. Within the clinical situation, I have felt closed in for many reasons. One of these is the authoritarian structure I must function in.

KRAMER:   That's interesting. I had thought that Lynn's sense of failure was more particularistic and goal related. But I would agree with you that her sense of failure does seem quite general and pervasive—she really verbalizes this quite often. As such, it is probably much more a manifestation of recognized interpersonal incompetency, rather than the pervasive, nebulous frustration and defeat associated with reality shock.

BENNER:   I see your point, and I agree that, just like the euphoria of the honeymoon phase, the feelings of failure associated with reality shock are pervasive and diffuse rather than particularistic. But don't you think her statement, "I am consciously critical of my failings as a leader, innovator, and in interpersonal staff relations" is quite general? There really isn't too much of a nurse role left, is there?

KRAMER:   I guess you're right. There's no doubt that Lynn is expressing a feeling of failure. And it is true that Lynn is subjecting herself to very "one-sided" criticism. Lynn could be making progress and contributions that she could value and appreciate if she were not caught up in rejecting her environment. And you're right; this one-sided derogatory criticism is characteristic of the rejection phase of reality shock.

BENNER:   Do you see any signs of recovery yet?

KRAMER:   Yes, I see two in fact. One is healthy, and I mentioned it a few minutes ago. Lynn is beginning to reach out. She is beginning to see some worth, logical meaning, and rationale to some of the work values and bureaucratic red tape. Did you notice what she said about getting better organized in giving reports? Now that's very much a work system value—the emphasis on organization. In beginning to comply with this value, Lynn says:

> So to be organized, I've run off a bunch of itemized report sheets that I can fill in as I go and integrate into my routine.

BENNER:  Complying with a work value, but doing it in her own individualistic style?

KRAMER:  Right. I've noticed many new graduates doing this sort of thing. They take some kind of organizational form or routine, and adhere to it in principle, but modify it so that it is somewhat closer to their value system. The other example of adaptation is, I'm afraid, less growth-producing than the above. I think you mentioned it in your previous commentary, and it also comes up again later on.

> I am seriously looking around for another job—one in which I hope I can get more satisfaction. I have applied to some of the local nursing schools for teaching positions. Maybe if I can't find satisfaction in nursing, I'll find it in teaching.

This "flight-into-teaching" pattern of conflict resolution is similar to that used by foreigners suffering from culture shock. By congregating into homogeneous groups having similar values, they form a "little America" or a "little Italy."

BENNER:  You think maybe schools of nursing are "islands of idealistic professional nursing?"

KRAMER:  Well, I would say that they are good candidates. . . . But I'm not ready to give up on Lynn yet. Judging by the insight she has displayed so far, I'd be willing to bet that she sees through this flight behavior, realizes it's a nongrowth-producing conflict resolution.

BENNER:  I think Lynn is showing some growth-oriented conflict resolution in her perceptive entries. They indicate that she is perceiving differences between her value system and that of the staff.

> I had failed on their terms as I saw them set, but perhaps me as me won't be any the worse for it. I am *not* going to compete with the staff, but with *myself*.

KRAMER:  In a sense, she is saying that she's going to try the "loner" strategy—going off to do her own thing. You'll remember, right in the beginning of the diary, Lynn said that this is one reason why she "chose" CCU and nights. But all along, she seems to be in conflict between wanting to compete with and win respect from the staff as part of her quest for proving herself, and wanting to be able to "do her own thing all by herself."

BENNER:  It seems that within a few short weeks we are seeing a variety of resolution strategies, and some signs of recovery as well. There is evidence that she's thinking of flight into teaching; she also says she's going to "go it alone." But then at the same time, there is some evidence of constructive resolution. She is beginning to identify different value systems; she's acknowledging the worth of some work-related values; and particularly in her description of her interactions with the LPN she was having difficulty with, there are signs that she's developing empathy and ability to predict the behavior and reactions of others.

> My LPN and I have worked together long enough that she and I know what to expect and things move along smoothly. I understand her more now and I appreciate her clinical competence.

And then too, even earlier, we saw that keeping this diary helped Lynn get in touch with her lack of objectivity to the point where she developed considerably more empathy for the LPN.

> These diaries have been a tremendous help in seeing what is happening. . . . I finally figured out that this LPN had no idea in the world what I am upset about, if she is even aware that I'm upset. . . . I guess some people find their security in performing tasks on an assigned schedule without questions or any deviation in style. When I realized this, my anger cooled down a lot. . . . And I think it is curious that she was probably unaware of the turmoil that I have been experiencing.

That's really quite considerable growth and insight into a conflict situation, and it certainly indicates that Lynn is making a positive adaptation. We'll just have to wait and see what happens in the next entries.

KRAMER:  Yes, but before moving on, there's one other point I'd like to make. In this section, we haven't commented on the extent to which Lynn is or is not making progress in the second phase of the socialization process—establishing workable IPR with staff. A couple of Lynn's sentences give us some insight into her attitudinal perspective regarding this goal.

> I've been fussing around long enough trying to establish a social rapport with the staff members on my ward. As you must realize, it has already thwarted what I might be doing for my own self-improvement on the ward.

It seems quite reasonable to deduce from this comment that Lynn still sees the human side of the organization, the need to work out staff relationships, as a "necessary evil" rather than an avenue to interpersonal competency and influence.

BENNER:   Yes, and she hasn't learned yet that in order to be influential, she must get into the "back-stage" reality. She doesn't seem to realize that in the conference with the head nurse, she was being judged and evaluated on "back-region" criteria.

KRAMER:   It's no wonder that the conference was a surprise to her. Do you remember that when the LPN tried to clue her in earlier, Lynn rejected it? The sense of failure that Lynn experienced in this conference is undoubtedly related to some missed perceptual cues from the "back-region" reality.

By the way, Lynn, rest assured that you aren't some kind of nut. Most of the other girls are having problems very similar to yours. You are not alone.

*Late February, 1971*

*It's been quite a while since I've written. . . . I've lost a lot of the hyper atti-tude about the job, also a lot of my enthusiasm, and sort of just sat back to let things cool down.*

*It would be so easy just to relax and let the job flow around me. Maybe I should stop fighting and join the others in the deep chasm that is the rut around here. Sometimes I get so discouraged. . . .*

*I think I'm extremely paranoid, and I really need to be as objective as possible. Also I'm pretty ambitious and impatient with the job, and my seemingly slow adaptation to it. A person can make just as big a mess of things by trying too hard as by not trying at all. So I have been trying to relax with it. Everything is going along fine. I'm gradually able to squeeze in some additions to the nursing care plans. The nurses are still negative to the nursing histories. Little additions are the only form of change accepted and even those not with any zest. I've been mostly adjusting things to suit my job needs. For instance, that report form has really been a help to me. I began using it and gradually offered it to the nurses who came on days. It was politely tolerated a few times and then they said it was confusing and quit us-ing it. Another little thing I've set up for myself and anyone who would like to use it is an IV kit. Whenever an IV needs to be re-started there are umteen things to jam together: tapes, bandages, intercaths, lidocaine, swabs, neo-sporin, etc., etc. I inevitably forget one thing in a rush—so I put together a little set in a square disposable emesis (cardboard) basin. It doubles as the receptacle for everything and will always be a sanitary carry-all. On nights I play around with these things, but this kit has been a real help for me, especially with admissions. There is always rushing and confusion at that time and I don't have to take the time or thought to assemble the IV equip-ment. It paid off the other night, and I was pleasantly surprised with myself. I've told the other girls about it and said that if they wanted to use it I would* keep one made up for them on the IV cart. Someone put it out of reach in the back of the cart, so I haven't said anything more about it. I like it though and will keep using it. I can see patterns forming in the way I do things; for instance, I've found myself writing a small summary on the patients at 12:00 when I first check them — gives me a feeling of thoroughness and keeps clear in my mind those things I should observe for. If they are stable I don't say much. My initial enthusiasm for cardiac auscultation, lung sounds, etc. is sort of settling into part of the routine. Nights are somewhat boring — and time is precious to me, so I've talked with the nurse on the ward just outside the unit about trading places for a week or two to get some additional clinical experience. I mean, I haven't irrigated a catheter (Foley) since I was a sophomore. I know the routine but can't do it with any ease. The other night I felt embarrassed in front of a doctor because I couldn't do it snap, snap. Still uptight about these things. The supervisor liked the idea that I get more practical experience. She feels that the practical nurses are worth much more than the university girls. She has had poor luck with their length of stay, ability to work hard, and the amount of time it takes her to train one to be a "nurse." She also feels that "total patient care" has been in use since nursing began — that we've not progressed one inch as a profession and that we are not professionals but technicians. Further, the night supervisor feels that care plans are a farce and that patient care doesn't require much more than physical management. When asked if she would like to reserve the "psychosocial," etc. to a clinical specialist who could tie the patient's needs together, her response was: "They cost too much and don't do anything." She returned to the university for her degree a few years back and felt it was a big waste of time — as she knew more nursing than the instructors did. After quite a talk, where I mostly listened and sought her opinions, she concluded that this hospital is backward: the care isn't up to today's standards. She is especially critical of the medical staff — interns, residents, etc. The time I've spent in giving her opinions in this diary is because they reflect my views and also what I feel is generalized opinion here, especially among the older staff. I won't work here beyond the point of learning for me. After a couple of months, I'd like to get some ward experience in concentration — perhaps switch to the postsurgical ward-recovery room area. And I'm definitely pursuing a teaching position. I don't want to be a teacher who is one step (clinically) ahead of the kids. By spreading out, hopefully I'll understand the workaday world of nursing before I go back to the ivory tower. I really do enjoy the fast pace of the hospital intensive care units. I enjoy medicine — the disease process, what's done about it, and the clinical return to equilibrium. Perhaps I really am heading for the Nurse Practitioner role? Clinical specialist? It all remains to be seen.

Interstaff relations have been better simply because I control myself. I am trying to relax, keep my private life behind the scenes, and maintain a pleasant "how's-the-weather?" rapport. This way I can't be too much of an irritant and cause for social discord. . . .

*Early April, 1971*

*In my earlier diaries, I was really wrapped up in my own niche in the CCU and wasn't paying much attention to the rest of the hospital and the system. Since then I've expanded a lot with my interests and I've discovered how really sick this place really is. The incentive to work is strictly money and fringe benefits. Any patient care incentive is frowned upon (at best). If you suggest a change in the size of the IV bottle used in the unit, it must go through several administrative channels. The night supervisor told me that in order to fit in with the system one must become passive or suffer brain damage from beating one's head. The system's inadequacies are all too clear. I'm glad I've been here, because I can approach any other job with hope. Also it is beginning to be a profitable learning experience about the hard cruel paths of administrative bureaucracy.*

*The ironic part of the conclusion of this job is that I am becoming more idealistic all the time. I refuse to lose my idealism — I'm learning where best to place it now. For instance, I had no orientation to the unit; the materials available for comprehensive instruction (especially drugs) were sparse. I've continued the drug data collection system I started and I've just started a pretty nice library of all the most current and classic articles on (1) arrhythmias, (2) clinical aspects of myocardial infarction, (3) pacemakers, (4) electrocardiography. I'm really enthusiastic about it and I've duplicated all the copies so that I have a separate library at home for myself. Then also, I have teamed up with my LPN, who is quite enthusiastic about learning how to read EKGs. We spend the nights together going over the strips taken the day before. I've written up in duplicate the principles behind the particular topic we discuss, which she has added to her home collection. . . .*

*I'm going on days next week. I am afraid that when seeking another job, night duty will be something of a handicap. I understand that I will become an instant aide. Neither the head nurse nor Sue will bathe a patient or empty a urinal. I will be interested to see how they pull that off. Joan, one of the other RNs, says that she often doesn't get to draw bloods, pass the meds, etc. when working with these two. Needless to say she is unhappy about the situation. But she won't say anything for fear of turning the friendly tides in this neat, tight, little group. I'm there to learn as much as work, so I have no idea yet what I'll do.*

*I'll be leaving here soon — running into teaching before I'm ready for it. But maybe I can teach others to succeed where I have failed.*

*I've sort of ruled out a job at the university for this year. . . . I plan to look for a clinically oriented job . . . inservice, specialized clinic area, or maybe something out of nursing. In a lab or something.*

*May, 1971*

*After nine months on the job, I'm ready to step out into an area where I will fit, function better, and be happier. These months have been spent learning* about my "bent" in this profession. Hopefully, the next job will satisfy it. I've been sitting in on the Medic I — on my own time, of course. For someone with no background in anatomy and physiology, these lectures are quite sophisticated. They spend quite a lot of time on the treatment and technical skills required in each anatomical site covered. This emphasis on treatment is somewhat new and fascinating. The lectures have provided quite a lot of new information, very useful to nursing observations. I can't help but love to get to the poor patient and evaluate what we learned the night before. The oscilloscope is not my bag unless it can be applied directly to what I see happening. Often their heart conduction system snaps along with some irritability while the other systems are really showing significant findings.

The heart is more interesting at the bedside. When in the unit, my responsibility is to "man the scopes." I often fail to keep as close a watch as the others, and drift into the patient rooms. If I catch some form of irritability on the scope it excites me less than if I catch rales, a gallop in the heart, or can feel the degree of liver enlargement, and I enjoy autonomy — being in a position where my opinions and suggestions have weight. Secretarial jobs in nursing really can pull one away from that distended neck vein one would like to re-check.

I wonder where I'm heading. Clinical specialist? Or out of nursing completely? I'm actively seeking employment elsewhere; I've begun calling other hospitals to inquire about opportunities that might be coming up — inservice, specialty area, etc. . . The job must include clinical experience that I still don't have. Perhaps a position in a combination CCU and surgical ICU would do it. I'd like to be assistant head nurse in this area to pick up some administrative experience.

The Medic I doctors are planning a new program where the fireman will be trained to perform treatment in several other needed emergency areas. The bill is in the state congress now. Its implications should be even more far-reaching than the heart team. I'm "antsy" to get involved in the movement. Emergency community medicine is wide open and new! It just may be what keeps me in nursing!

*June and July, 1971*

My attitude about this job has taken a complete about-face from what it has been for the last several months. I decided it was time for me to meet and talk with the DNS. I had an appointment with her last month. The session was quickly turned into a "counseling hour." Apparently I have been backing myself up into the corner. A lot of the backing up involved backing down from my beliefs about nursing and about what I should be doing in my job. I was really frustrated in not being able to do these things and most days went to work with a pit in my stomach. It's not as though I wasn't thinking about what was going on, but the focus was narrowed quite a bit and interpersonal relations with staff and doctors were magnified way too much. My feelings about usurping the head nurse's leadership function forced me into a passive-

*aggressive role that wasn't honest for myself, and probably wasn't pleasant for the rest of the girls. Also the approach didn't accomplish anything really worthwhile. My anxieties about the supposed diagnostic end of the nursing role in a CCU were terribly out of proportion when one considers what I was forfeiting—the humanistic side of nursing— to learn them. And that includes a campaign for increasing the continuity of care and the whole patient bit. The nursing care activities in the CCU are unique in that many of them close-ly approach a physician's duties: EKG interpretation, individual judgment in treating certain arrhythmias, quasi-responsibility for catching early signs of certain clinical complications, etc. An aggressive nurse (alias me) tends to compete somewhat, abandoning the care role for the diagnostic activities.*

*Having satisfied myself in this situational tragedy, I began to look back again to nursing. I felt safer coming back to it after having proven myself as a "CCU Nurse"—the concept of this as it is known and understood by the nurses on this unit. There has got to be much more to nursing than the CCU role as it is practiced here—I don't think I was facing up to what I had to do next. Quitting an institution like this would be passing up one of the most fertile areas for effecting change that I can think of. Also, when considering the autonomy that I enjoy, what better place to do one's own thing! The DNS very pointedly demonstrated to me (from what I told her) how I was backing down.*

*The upshot of the talk is that there are no utopias (which I realized, of course) and that this hospital is in particular need of leaders who will make their ideas viable to the staff. She felt that a leader should stick out like a sore thumb for her qualities, not necessarily assuming the head nurse's position, but giving functional leadership in terms of progress ( . . . right, right, right!). She also felt that this could be effected in whatever position the nurse held—staff nurse in particular, as this is where one must inevitably prove her-self anyway.*

*I went home feeling both elated and guilty that this had to be pointed out to me. Just think, after almost a year, I would (hopefully) begin to function as I should have all along. I had been developing a teaching plan for the cardiac patients but I left it home because I didn't want to upset things any more. I was really feeling the sense of destructive competition that I was very much helping to foster.*

*I've assembled two plans (an alternative if needed), and presented my idea about the need for planned teaching to those RNs that my shift permits contact with. Our hit-or-miss (mostly miss) explanation to the patients just doesn't approach teaching. A teaching plan is one step toward nursing con-ferences and regular care plans (very badly needed). The approval is there; but their saying yes to an idea or plan means nothing. So I began to talk about its implementation. The head nurse hasn't bought it with any enthusiasm; she simply wanted to go home while I talked to her about it. With my new courage in hand, I decided not to wait three months for her approval but to start at least presenting it to each nurse, and eliciting ideas and getting agree-*

ment about the need for nursing conferences. In the ward communication book I pasted a sample of the teaching form that another private hospital has found useful, and I left spaces for ideas about how we might adapt it to fit our particular needs. I left an explanation of what I hoped they would say or how they would like to help implement the teaching. Response: nothing—no one has contributed at all. So that's where I am—on the bandwagon with something that more appropriately fits my nursing role, something I can accomplish and which is much more satisfying, and I don't have to leave here or leave nursing!

I'm not sure what's happened, but my perspective about hospital nursing is changing—I no longer feel that it is a second-rate area where one obtains necessary experience and then leaves. There is a hell of a lot to do here and it can be a challenge for any of us, I guess. I had a particularly hard time adjusting to the staff role, I feel, basically because of my notions about interstaff relations, my role as a "staff nurse," my desire for more responsibility, and because of the changes I wanted to make. I really failed to understand how I might perform openly as an underdog to no one; that I didn't have to "stay in my place." There is certainly a lot of backtracking to do. I feel bad that you've been a witness to my behavior in this respect. My desire, of course, would have been to impress you, utilizing what my education had offered—in a creative way. Fear not; I feel as though I'm just getting started. The termination of this particular job won't be with the frustration that I've spoken of before. Take any area that one works in . . . the staff turnover may be complete in two to four years. However, if one effects some positive changes in the care of patients that persist through these turnovers, then the original resistance to the changes counts for zero. The totality is becoming clearer now.

It's also 4:30 A.M. — I'm on nights and may shortly loose coherency. This year, riddled with mistakes, was really a learning experience and hopefully I won't stumble into the same pitfalls again. The greatest feeling, though, is that I don't have to stop working here and get another job in order to start over or re-emphasize what I should have. I don't feel I am backing out or down in the least. As far as staff relations go—they really are quite fun to watch. They are all right now—the reverse of what they were originally. I get along well with the aides. They enjoy my efforts to include them in teaching about arrhythmias, etc. and I think they respect me for the effort and care I give to the patients. The RNs are hostile and somewhat tense around me. This I see as reversible. It will take time, but I intend to start.

1. My demeanor must be calmer and I must approach people with more personal conviction.

2. Any time I present an idea that challenges them I must elicit their involvement and their opinions. This should make the idea a joint effort, one that is not so readily dropped, I hope.

3. Others are beginning to add to the educational library—sort of following what I started. And would you believe they're listening to

*chest sounds and cardiac sounds! This brings them closer to the patient and away from the darn scopes. Also, I initiated IV daily care where the site is completely cleaned and redressed. The catheter is again secured and antibiotic re-applied. Others are beginning to do the same and the incidence of puffy infiltrated arms and red phlebitic lines all the way up the arm is dropping.*

So the personal business has to step aside somewhat if the idea is good enough.

### COMMENTARY

BENNER: Unlike other sections of the diary, this section covers a rather long period—about five months. In it, we see the culmination of some changes in Lynn, and the continuation and beginning of others.

I think one of the most interesting entries are her remarks relative to her view of the bureaucratic organization. Consistent with her earlier entries, she still sees the organization with limited commitment. "I won't work here beyond the point of learning for me." But there's also evidence of some change and growth in this area. It seems she can now relax enough to take off her blinders and see more of the organization than just the CCU.

I was really wrapped up in my own niche in the CCU and wasn't paying much attention to the rest of the hospital and the system. Since then I've expanded a lot with my interests and I've discovered how really sick this place really is.

KRAMER: Yes, I noticed that too, and I would agree that that is a sign of growth, but doesn't it sound like she might encounter "reality shock" again on a larger organizational level?

BENNER: I suppose that's possible. The above statement certainly does sound like the wholesale criticism and rejection characteristic of reality shock. For the time being though, I think the widening of perspective is healthy. And a statement she makes later on suggests that she's viewing the organization and her association with it in a more favorable light:

I'm glad I've been here, because I can approach any other job with hope. Also it is beginning to be a profitable learning experience about the hard cruel paths of administrative bureaucracy.

KRAMER: Lynn seems to be more aware of some of the socialization messages being sent to her. Whereas earlier they seemed to surprise her, she now seems to be cognizant of them—although she still doesn't buy them or the value system upon which they are based.

BENNER:  I can't say I blame her for that. I was struck with how common and consistent these kinds of socialization messages are. No matter where you work the same kind of priority system comes through. Direct caring for patients is lowest in status.

> I understand that I will become an instant aide. Neither the head nurse nor Sue will bathe a patient or empty a urinal.... I will be interested to see how they pull that off. Joan, one of the other RNs, says that she often doesn't get to draw the bloods, pass the meds, etc., when working with these two.

KRAMER:  Often, this kind of status ranking of tasks is explained by saying that more professional nursing skill is needed to draw bloods and observe monitors than to bathe patients. Lynn and many other new nurses have been taught just the opposite. Drawing bloods and monitoring vital signs are really quite routine tasks with predictable levels of resistance, but bathing patients in the CCU can be quite demanding. I suspect the real reason for this very common hierarchical arrangement of nursing tasks is something that Hughes commented on a long time ago[2]. "Ranking has something to do with the relative cleanliness of functions performed . . . no one is so lowly in the hospital as those who handle soiled linen."

BENNER:  It's been quite a year for Lynn. Where do you think she is now in her process of conflict resolution?

KRAMER:  Well, Lynn's opening remarks in this set of diary entries show that she realizes there is another path of conflict resolution open to her, different from the ones she's already cited ("flight into teaching"; "leaving nursing altogether"; "go it alone").

> I've lost a lot of the hyper attitude about the job, also a lot of my enthusiasm. . . . It would be so easy just to relax and let the job flow around me. Maybe I should stop fighting and join the others in the deep chasm that is the rut around here. Sometimes I get so discouraged. . . .

That's the only place I see mention of this attitude, and with the tremendous fight Lynn has been putting up all along, I think it's quite doubtful that she would seriously consider becoming a "Rutter."

BENNER:  I would agree. I see much more evidence of recovery and possible bicultural adaptation. One goal that Lynn has been working toward since she started her job is competence acquisition. Achieving this is very closely related to her view of herself as "becoming" a competent, self-confident individual with a sense of power and pay-off. A feeling that what she does is important and meaningful. One can sense some of this desire for power and efficacy in Lynn's patient care goals:

It is really exciting to me that in a susceptible person we can be alerted to this danger (stroke), and act appropriately when the situation arises.

I would like to introduce the article (on titration of IV fluids) to the girls at work; perhaps we could together prevent these unnecessary fluid disasters.

If I catch some form of irritability on the scope it excites me less than if I catch rales, a gallop in the heart, or can feel the degree of liver enlargement, and I enjoy being in a position where my opinions and suggestions have weight.

KRAMER: She doesn't seem to have experienced this same sense of power in her relationships with staff or in her ability to influence others. In fact, Lynn has vacillated between wanting to go it alone —having "isolated independence"—and wanting to influence her co-workers.

I think this (report) form will really be a help. . . . I haven't shown the printed up form to the nurses yet, so I'm not sure if they'll like the idea. . . . Hopefully it will help me at least, and will not be rejected for its originator but for the idea itself, if it's not valuable to the others.

I think I'm extremely paranoid, and I really need to be as objective as possible. Also I'm pretty ambitious and impatient with the job and my seemingly slow adaptation to it. A person can make just as big a mess of things by trying too hard as by not trying at all. So I have been trying to relax with it. Everything is going along fine. I'm gradually able to squeeze in some additions to the nursing care plans. The nurses are still negative to the nursing histories. Little additions are the only form of change accepted and even those not with any zest.

I began using it [report form she developed] and gradually offered it to the nurses who came on days. It was politely tolerated a few times and then they said it was confusing and quit using it.

I've told the other girls about it [the IV tray she designed and set up] and said that if they wanted to use it I would keep one made up for them on the IV cart. Someone put it out of reach in the back of the cart, so I haven't said anything more about it. I like it though and will keep using it.

The above incidents seem to substantiate her feelings that she was unable to change the unit to help it move forward. Her innovations were rejected and she was left feeling ineffective ("helping the unit hold its own without advancing").

BENNER: Lynn has been slow in developing interpersonal competency in respect to influencing staff; she seems to have been much more competent in influencing patients. Maybe this was because interpersonal competency with the staff was never one of Lynn's goals. From the very beginning, she saw her primary role as one of nursing patients and building her competence in this area. In fact, initially, she seemed unaware that she would have to get involved in staff relationships and the human side of the organization. It was because it was almost literally forced upon her that she began to become involved and motivated to develop interpersonal competence with staff.

KRAMER: Yes, I think you're right. In fact, I'd almost say that it wasn't until after the intervention provided by the Director of Nursing that Lynn really was strongly motivated to develop interpersonal competency in this area. And furthermore, only then did she have confidence in her ability to do so.

BENNER: In order to be willing to invest herself in interpersonal relationships with the staff, I think Lynn had to have some hope. I think she needed to feel that her investment in interpersonal relationships would be worthwhile and would help her achieve the patient care goals which were so important to her. It was not until after her counseling session with the Director of Nursing that Lynn had any hope that her investment would be worthwhile:

> Fear not; I feel as though I'm just getting started. . . . If one effects some positive changes in the care of patients that persist through these turnovers, then the original resistance to the changes counts for zero.

And appropriately, at the end of the diary Lynn notes *that she is making a difference.*

KRAMER: Yes, that was really quite a counseling session—a timely and effective intervention on the part of the Director of Nursing. Through this interaction Lynn developed both insight and hope that allowed her to take up her involvement with the staff again. Lynn leaves the question of work group acceptance and interpersonal competency on a hopeful note.

> I don't feel I am backing out or down in the least. As far as staff relations go—they really are quite fun to watch. They are all right now—the reverse of what they were originally. I get along well with the aides. They enjoy my efforts to include them in teaching about arrhythmias, etc., and I think that they respect me for the effort and care I give to the patients. The RNs are hostile and somewhat tense around me. This I see as reversible. It will take time, but I intend to start.

BENNER: Lynn's move toward biculturalism demonstrates one extremely important point. To get Lynn to move into a state of hope and comfort about her ability to adapt and innovate in the CCU, the support and counseling of someone in her social system was required. For Lynn, it was the Director of Nursing. (Remember, at the beginning, Lynn reported that other nurses said the DNS was unapproachable.) I wonder how many other young nurses feel they don't have anyone to turn to who can help them gain hope and perspective in respect to their value system, and insight into the potential conflicts between school and work value systems?

KRAMER: Lynn really expresses the recovery of hope and the beginning of biculturalism beautifully, doesn't she?

> I'm not sure what's happened, but my perspective about hospital nursing is changing—I no longer feel that it is the second rate area, where one obtains necessary experience and then leaves. There is a hell of a lot to do here and it can be a challenge for any of us, I guess. I had a particularly hard time adjusting to the staff role, I feel, basically because of my notions about interstaff relations, my role as a "staff nurse," my desire for more responsibility, and because of the changes I wanted to make. I really failed to understand how I might perform openly as an underdog to no one; that I didn't have to "stay in my place."

Lynn no longer expresses the glowing one-sided praise of the honeymoon phase, nor the derogatory one-sided criticism of the shock phase. Nor does she still feel "a bit above" hospital nursing as she did in her recovery phase. She can now understand the social system and can see her potential for making an impact there. This is no small accomplishment! It is at this point that any descriptive system is inadequate. Who can explain the hope and the energy, the commitment for making a difference, for making a creative contribution? We can only be grateful to Lynn for sharing with us what was at times a painfully honest description of her journey.

### REFERENCES

1. Blau, P. A theory of social integration. *Am. J. Sociol.,* Vol. 65, No. 6, 1960, pp. 545–556.
2. Hughes, H. *Men and Their Work.* New York: The Free Press, 1958, p. 72.

### BIBLIOGRAPHY

Green, H. *I Never Promised You a Rose Garden,* New York: Holt, Rinehart and Winston, Inc., Publishers, 1964.

Kramer, Marlene. *Reality Shock: Why Nurses Leave Nursing.* St. Louis, Mo.: C.V. Mosby Co., 1974.

Schmalenberg, Claudia E. and Marlene Kramer. Dreams and reality: Where do they meet? *J. Nurs. Admin.* Vol. 6, No. 5, June 1976, pg. 35–43.

Shaffer, David R. Clyde Hendrick, C. Robert Regula, and Joseph Freconna. Interactive effects of ambiguity tolerance and task effort on dissonance reduction. *J. Personality,* Vol. 41, No. 2, June, 1973, pp. 224–233.

# A LOOK AT YOU

# Module 3

# The Me Module

**INTRODUCTION**

The central theme of this module relates to you—to you in terms of how you see yourself and how you feel about yourself as a nurse. The module is designed to help you:

1. Understand the effects of entering the work world on your self-concept and self-esteem.

2. Examine your concept of yourself as a nurse.

3. Examine your employer's concept of a nurse as reflected in the role demands placed on you.

4. Determine the concept you would like to have for yourself as a nurse.

5. Determine your goals and the congruence between your goals and your present activities.

6. Identify the personal and situational barriers to your goal achievement, and decide which of these you might wish to change or alter.

7. Decide which behaviors and corresponding traits you wish to strengthen and/or eliminate.

In your day-to-day living, you seldom stop to really think about who you are, what you hope to accomplish, and how you might achieve your goals. Exploring these matters is important because an adequate self-concept can help make you a fully growing, self-fulfilling individual—one in whom all potentialities are in the process of being fully developed. What is the state of your self-concept? Before you can determine who you are and how you feel about yourself, we need to discuss self-concept.

## SELF-CONCEPT

Self-concept has numerous definitions. James said that a person's self is the sum total of everything that an individual can call his own[1]. Others have postulated the formation of the self in terms of a looking glass self, dynamic social interactions and interpersonal interactions[2, 3, 4]. One of the best definitions was offered by Kinch, who believes that an individual's self-concept emerges from social interaction and, in turn, guides or influences his behavior[5]. This definition indicates that the self-concept is an accumulation of all one's interpersonal and interactional experiences. It is a dynamic process. Your self-concept continues to develop and change as it encounters and responds to new influences. This experiential background forms an integrated framework from which you operate or behave. Although your self-concept is constantly developing and changing, the changes are very slow and gradual. It is your basic self-concept that provides you with a stable sense of who and what you are in the world.

In addition to this more or less *stable* self-concept formed as you grew and developed through childhood, you also possess many *constructed* social selves or self-concepts. The "constructed social self" makes it possible for you to fulfill your expectations of your various roles[6]. The constructed social self consists of assumptions about, perceptions of, and claims upon a given social situation in which your role expectations may be more or less well defined. In short, the constructed self deals with your image or concept of yourself in different occupational or social roles such as wife, mother, nurse, friend, and so on.

You attribute worth or value to both your enduring self-concept and to your constructed self-conceptions. You attribute "goodness" or "badness" to your self-conceptions; this value is referred to as self-esteem. When an individual has positive or high self-esteem, he feels good about himself. When a person has negative or low self-esteem, he feels bad about himself.

Our overall self-esteem is derived from three types of self-esteem: chronic self-esteem, task-specific self-esteem, and socially influenced self-esteem[7]. Chronic self-esteem refers to the relatively persistent level of esteem that is associated with your stable self-concept and is present in all situations. Task-specific self-esteem refers to your feelings of competence for specific task performances. Socially influenced self- esteem is related to others' expectations of you. Just as others affect the formation of the self-concept, so too, their communications of their feelings about your behavior affects how you will feel about your own behavior. The combination of the latter two are associated with your constructed self-concept — for example, the "goodness" or "badness" of your self-concept as a nurse is derived from both the tasks associated with that role (task-specific self-esteem) and from feedback from others as to how they feel about your behavior in the role (socially influenced self-esteem).

Each of you has a basic self-concept and a chronic level of self-esteem associated with that self-concept. During your developmental years, you have formed a concept of who and what you are and you have a fairly stable level of self-esteem. This is not to say that the self-concept and the self-esteem are static and unchanging. Changes occur as you grow and develop as a person, but there are few major fluctuations from day to day.

Each of you has a set of constructed social selves. The major concern of this module is with your constructed social self as a nurse. While you were going to school, you were taught the norms, values, attitudes, and behaviors necessary to fill the occupational role of a nurse. As a result of this socialization, you developed a constructed social self. You developed a concept of yourself as a nurse. Your concept is quite individual. However, you will share certain aspects of your nurse self-concept with others due to the more or less common nurse socialization process. Let's look at some items that are likely to be part of your concept of yourself as a nurse regardless of level of education and region of the country where you attended school. A nurse:

Is knowledgeable about the physical, pharmacological, and psychosocial principles related to the provision of nursing care.

Applies principles in the implementation of patient care.

Plans care using a wide data base and in accordance with the patient's needs.

Evaluates the effectiveness of nursing care delivered.

Cares about the patient.

Knows her own strengths and weaknesses.

Is self-directed in seeking learning.

Actively participates in nursing organizational activity.

Expands and improves nursing practice.

These are very broad conceptions of "what a nurse is." Probably none of you have a self-concept quite this broad. However, it is likely that many of the conceptions you have are specifics of the above broad categories. For example, you may see yourself as knowing the drugs your patients are on and knowing their implications and side effects. The school socialization process stimulated each of you to integrate various values, attitudes, and norms and to construct for yourself a new social self—nurse. This constructed self-concept guides and directs your behaviors as a nurse. Although the particular constructed self-concept is somewhat unique for each of you, there are some aspects of it that will be shared by almost everyone who fulfills the nurse role.

Associated with your concept of nurse is a given level of self-esteem. Although you may have a fairly high chronic self-esteem and a low opinion of yourself in a specific role, say the friendship role, this is usually associated with a specific point in time. For example, you may feel very bad about yourself because you let your friend down.

In most cases, if your chronic level of self-esteem is relatively low, it is unlikely that your self-esteem as a nurse will be high. If your chronic level of self-esteem is high, then the chances for high self-esteem as a nurse are considerable. Your level of self-esteem as a nurse is also dependent upon how the nurse socialization process went. If you achieved success in meeting the tasks put to you during your school years, and received favorable reactions from your instructors and peers, you probably have a relatively high nurse self-esteem. On the other hand, if you met with minimal success and had a lot of hassles with your instructors, you probably have a low level of self-esteem. The higher your level of self-esteem, the more competent you feel about doing the work of a nurse.

Your ability to perform as a nurse is determined not only by the self-concept and level of self-esteem that you had when you entered the work world, but also by a specific kind of adjustment that you must make after entering the work scene. This adjustment can best be described as a shift from the role of a beneficiary who had a choice to that of a provider who has less choice. Let us explain in more detail.

In school, when you were being socialized into the role of the nurse, you paid tuition to engage the services of those who were qualified to prepare you to become a nurse (the faculty). In essence, you paid for a service so that you might benefit from the expertise of those who were already nurses. If during the process you chose not to benefit, you were the one who suffered. For example, if you chose to cut classes, you missed a portion of learning, a portion of what you had paid for. You may have had to make up some time or work a little harder as a result, but this had little effect on anyone except yourself. Now that this period of socialization is over, the tables are turned. Someone is going to be paying you for your services as a nurse. You are no longer the beneficiary of someone else's service, but the provider of service. The employing organization and thus the patient are now the beneficiaries of your knowledge and expertise. You can no longer choose to take the service someone else is providing. As an individual receiving remuneration in the form of a salary and fringe benefits, you must appear on duty when scheduled, and you must perform a certain amount of service. By entering into a contractual agreement with an employing organization, you are subject to the legitimate authority of that employer[8].

One important aspect of the authority of the employing organization is its description of the behaviors expected of its employees. In your case, the employer indicates the expected behaviors of a nurse. Some of the typical role behaviors expected by nurse employing organizations throughout the country are as follows:

To plan and organize work and time effectively.

To know the duties of her position and to carry them out effectively. To interpret and use hospital policies in the exercise of her duties.

To perform technical procedures safely, accurately, and efficiently.

To relate to and maintain rapport with patients.

To maintain proper personal appearance.

To be dependable and punctual.

To be cooperative.

To establish priorities and to delegate work effectively.

To complete assignments on time and with minimal supervision.

To carry out directives and use appropriate lines of authority.

In listing the role behaviors expected of a nurse, the employing organization spells out its conception of the nurse role. If you compare your conception of the nurse role to the conceptions of the employing organization, you will find that there are some similarities and some differences. Both conceptions probably contain behaviors relating to maintaining relationships with the patient. However, you and the employing organization may give different weight to the importance of this behavior. In your conception of the nurse role, implementing technical procedures may be a minor nursing activity. In the work world, this is a very important aspect of the nurse's role. In terms of your conception, it may have never occurred to you to be concerned about completing your assignment on time as in school you always had plenty of time to do so. Now, your employer may hold the concept that it is highly important that you finish on time and yet, it is more difficult for you to do so. The more similar your self-conception and the demands of the employing organization, the less adjustment that is necessary. The greater the differences between your conceptions and those of the employing organization, the greater the adjustment.

In addition to the adjustment from the student or beneficiary role to the producer role, you must make other adjustments. Most of you have already begun work and are now faced with these adjustments. It is reasonable to expect that a change in orientation must take place as one enters the work world. But consider the effect that this change in orientation from a benefiter to a producer has on your conception of yourself as being self-directed, identifying and seeking out your own learning needs. Suppose you find that there are a number of skills in which you do not feel proficient. You have identified these as learning needs and would like to practice these skills as often as possible. You elicit the help of your fellow workers, who let you do all the catheterizations and start all the IVs that come up on your unit. At the moment that a co-worker tells you about a couple of IVs that need to be started, you have some patients who need ambulating and turning. What do you do? You can put off what needs to be done for your patients in the hope that it won't take too long to start the IVs; you can forget about starting the IVs and take care of your own patients; or you can arrange for someone else to care for your patients while you start the IVs. In deciding what to do, you must remember that you are primarily a producer of services now and that the patients have first claim. It is hard to make this adjustment, as you have been primarily a learner for quite some time. This doesn't mean that you must now cease to learn, but it does mean that learning must take a back seat to the work for which you are responsible. The adjustment you must make is to shift your concept of yourself from a learner who works incidentally (student nurse role) to a worker who learns incidentally (staff nurse role). Before you meet your own learning needs, you must take care of the needs of your patients or make arrangements for someone else to do so. You are now a worker. This is a simple hard fact that takes some getting used to.

Another factor in the adjustment process is the conceptions of the nurse role held by your co-workers. You may find that your conception of what a nurse is isn't theirs. The really important part of nursing—individualizing care, talking to and teaching patients and family—doesn't fit into the day's hectic schedule. Others seem surprised and/or disgruntled that you don't know and can't do the work that is expected of you. You can't organize care for large groups of patients very fast yet. A lot of the work that you see as really the work of the nurse must be delegated to others. You are expected to do technical procedures efficiently and you've never done a lot of them, or if you have, you've only done them once.

The experience is a shock. You expected to be a certain kind of nurse and you find that neither your employer nor your co-workers confirm your identity as that kind of a nurse. When a person holds to a certain value but receives no confirmation of that valued self from others, the individual perceives the situation as a threat[9].

The situation that you find yourself in affects both your self-concept as a nurse and the level of self-esteem that you feel for yourself as a nurse. Your self-concept, your identity as a nurse is confused and insecure. You may experience some of the feelings expressed by many new graduates in the shock phase of the reality shock process. You try to hang on to the conceptions which during school socialization were integrated into your self-concept as a nurse. You attempt to fight any change in these conceptions. At the same time, the work environment demands new conceptions. You experience a real struggle over your self-concept, your identity as a nurse.

This struggle is influenced by concurrent changes in your level of self-esteem. As you recall, there are three kinds of self-esteem: chronic, task-specific, and socially influenced. The current lack of confirmation of your self-concept as a nurse will affect your chronic self-esteem to the extent that your constructed social self (as nurse) is integrated with your more enduring and stable self-concept. The more thoroughly integrated it is, the greater the effect. However, the lack of confirmation is likely to have a greater effect on your task-specific and socially influenced self-esteem.

In the area of task-specific self-esteem, you find that you have many more tasks to do now than before. You are successful in a number of the tasks—giving medications, assessing the patient's needs, etc. However, there are other tasks that you aren't meeting with success. A lot of technical procedures come up, some of which you've never done before. You have to delegate work to others and you aren't exactly sure how to do this, or, worse still, what do you do when others do not accept the work you delegated. It's hard to get all the work organized and done within the allotted time. There isn't time to do much psychosocial work with patients and their families. Unable to do several tasks that you are called upon to do on a daily basis and lacking time to do some tasks that in the past contributed to your feelings of high self-esteem, you begin to feel less positive about your abilities. You tend to suffer from a decreasing task-specific self-esteem.

In the area of socially influenced self-esteem, there is also a decrease in the level of self-esteem. At a time when your self-concept is insecure and you are suffering from loss of self-esteem, the reactions of others affect you more[10]. What your co-workers have to say about you as a nurse is very important to you. The ratio of positive to negative comments may be heavily tipped to the negative side. (A longer discussion of feedback in the work setting can be found in "The Elusive Quest"). You may hear remarks about how slow and disorganized you are. Not infrequently you will hear, "You should know how to do that," or "Didn't you learn anything in school?" Thus, the reactions of others tend to decrease your feelings of competence and worth.

The upset in your self-concept and the lowered level of self-esteem make this a pretty rough time for you. To get adjusted, you must regain your stable self-concept and increase your level of self-esteem. The question that arises is: How? Should you ignore the demands of those around you and fight for the conceptions you learned in school? Or do you forget your old conceptions and take on an identity that is more congruent with the demands of the work world? Should you try somehow to form a new concept of a nurse—some combination of the two conceptions that seem to be at odds now? Perhaps at this time it would be useful for you to really look at your conceptions of yourself as a nurse, and at the conceptions of the employing organization.

### NURSE SELF-CONCEPT LEARNING ACTIVITY

The purpose of this learning activity is to help you express *in behavioral terms* your self-concept as a nurse and your perception of your employer's concept of a nurse. You can identify where the conceptions are similar, where they are different, and perhaps identify the behaviors that will form your reorganized concept of a nurse.

1.  Identify in behavioral terms your concept of a nurse and your perceptions of your employer's concept of a nurse.

    MY CONCEPTIONS OF A NURSE                EMPLOYER'S CONCEPTIONS OF A NURSE

2.  Identify the behaviors which are contained in *both* conceptions.

3.  Identify those behaviors that are part of *your conception of a nurse that you feel you absolutely must perform to be a nurse.*

4. Identify those behaviors in your employer's conceptions of a nurse which must be done in order that (1) you keep your job and (2) care can be delivered effectively to large numbers of patients.

KEEP JOB                          DELIVER CARE TO LARGE GROUP

5. Take a careful look at the behaviors contained in both conceptions—those that you feel you must do to be a nurse, and those that must be done to keep your job and to deliver care effectively to large numbers of patients. *These clusters of behavior provide a place for you to begin to examine and reorganize your self-concept as a nurse.*

The development of your self-concept as a nurse took time. It will also take time to reorganize your self-concept to include both those aspects of your present self-concept that you consider vitally important and those aspects of a nurse concept that your employer considers important. This reorganization is essential if you are to feel good about yourself as a nurse. Learning to make time to do the tasks that increase your sense of worth and becoming proficient at behaviors demanded by your employer will eventually increase your self-esteem as a nurse. The increase in self-esteem is needed if you are to continue to perform your duties as a nurse satisfactorily.

During this time of adjustment and reorganization of your self-concept as a nurse, you will be functioning as a nurse. Since behavior is an indication of one's conceptions of what a nurse is and does, perhaps a look at your current behaviors will provide you with additional insight into your self-concept as a nurse.

## CURRENT ROLE BEHAVIOR ANALYSIS

1. Analyze the behaviors that you do in an average work day. Do this by listing all of the major tasks that you perform in a usual working day. Indicate the amount of time that you spend doing each of these tasks.

| MAJOR TASK | BEHAVIORS INCLUDED IN THE TASK | TIME SPENT |
|---|---|---|
| Intershift Report | Listening, questioning, writing | 1 hour |
| Team Member Report | Deciding, delegating, transmitting information<br>Listening to Ms. Jones' complaints about assignment<br>End of day team report | 1¼ hours |
| A.M. Care for Mr. Smith | Endotracheal suction<br>Listening and talking to him<br>Planning for care | ¾ hour |
| Medications | Checking orders<br>Pouring and giving medications | 2 hours |
| Treatments | Blood pressure<br>Cath irrigation<br>IVs<br>Dressings | 1½ hours |
| Lunch and Coffee | Eating<br>Talking with other staff | ¾ hour |
| Passing Trays | Breakfast and lunch trays to patients | ¾ hour |
| Off Unit with Patient | Showing patient and his mother the Operating Room and Recovery Room | ½ hour |

| MAJOR TASK | BEHAVIORS INCLUDED IN THE TASK | TIME SPENT |
| --- | --- | --- |
| | | |

2.  **Review your list.** Cut the circle below into pieces to represent the portion of time spent doing each of the major activities. Indicate by placing a number in the pieces whether the behaviors associated with each major task are:

    (1) Just sufficient to get by in the job, producing minimal satisfaction in you.

    (2) Included in your conception of what you must do but not valued by employer.

    (3) Necessary to keep your job and deliver care to large numbers of patients, but not particularly valued by you.

SAMPLE

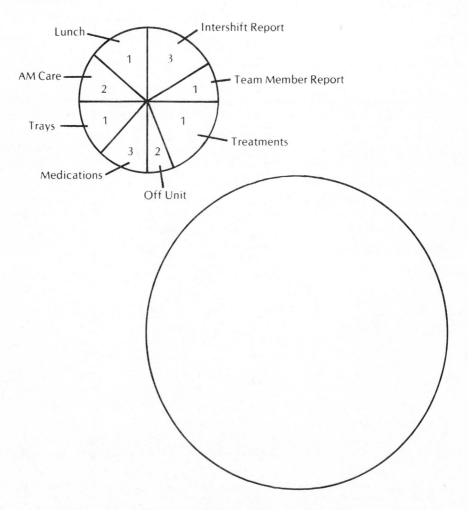

What does your Current Role Behavior Analysis reveal? If a large portion of the behaviors are rated 1, then you are probably meeting some of your job requirements, but satisfaction is likely to be low because you are doing just enough to get by. Consequently, you are not earning praise from your employer nor are you pleasing yourself, since you aren't doing things of major importance to you. If a large number of the behaviors are rated 2, then it is likely that although you are performing behaviors of importance to you, satisfaction is medium to low, for you find yourself at odds with demands of your employer. If a high proportion of the behaviors are rated 3, then it is likely that satisfaction is low because the behaviors most important to your conception of a nurse are not being performed. A balance of the three numbers probably indicates a favorable integration of the conceptions most important to you and to the employer, and your satisfaction is likely to be high.

The Current Role Behavior Analysis can tell you much more about your behaviors than whether you are satisfied with them. Remember the description of reality shock presented in an earlier module. In discussing the last phase of reality shock, called the resolution phase, we presented different modes of resolving the conflict between school and work values. If you examine your Current Role Behavior Analysis you can determine which mode of resolution of the school-work transition is now operating for you. If most of your behaviors are rated 1, then most likely you have chosen the "Rutter" approach to resolving the conflict. A 1 indicates you are doing just enough of what you believe to be essential to the role of nurse and just enough of what the employer believes to be the role of the nurse to get by. If most of your behaviors are rated 2, then it is likely that you are utilizing the "lateral arabesque" resolution style. If you continue to hang onto the conceptions of yourself as nurse developed during school, it is likely that in time you will flee the work scene. If most of your behaviors are 3s, it indicates that you've followed the resolution pattern of the "Organization Woman." Conceptions learned in school are abandoned so that you can meet organizational demands. A balanced behavioral picture is likely to indicate a bicultural mode of resolution—in which the school and work conceptions are integrated in a meaningful and useful way.

The adjustment you are now undergoing is not necessarily the direction you will continue to take in the future. However, if you are not made aware of the resolution mode you are using now, you may adopt a mode of conflict resolution before you realize its full implications. You have identified behaviors consistent with your conceptions of a nurse and behaviors demanded by your employer's conceptions of a nurse. You analyzed your current behavior to see where it fits into the schema of nurse conceptions that were previously identified. You may or may not be satisfied with your behaviors and the direction you seem to be taking. To determine if you will continue in the same direction, perhaps a further question must be asked.

Project yourself five years into the future and ask yourself, "How do I feel about the kind of nurse I have become and the contribution I have made to nursing practice?" This question will stimulate you to consider what kind of a nurse you really wish to be. This, in turn, can help you decide whether your current behaviors will allow you to become the kind of nurse you want to be, or whether some modification of those behaviors is needed. Only you can decide what your future course of action will be. If you are satisfied with the direction you are taking, then simply continue to develop your current behaviors. If you are dissatisfied with the direction you are taking, then you must modify your current behaviors. Let's look first at where you want to go as a nurse—your goals.

## GOALS

Goals refer to those things you wish to accomplish—for example, to become the kind of nurse you want to become. Goals give you some idea of where it is you want to go—what you want to do with your life as a nurse. Frequently, a new graduate who is working suddenly stops to take a look at what she has been doing and remarks, "Hey, what's going on here? What's this rat race all about?" This remark generally indicates either that the individual has no well-thought-out goals or that she suddenly realizes that she is not meeting the goals which she has.

Goals have two aspects—what it is you wish to accomplish and what you must do to accomplish the goals. *What you wish to accomplish* is a statement of where you are going. *What you must do to accomplish the goal* refers to the behaviors necessary to reach the goal. In order to meet your goals successfully, you must know clearly what your goals are and what behaviors are necessary for you to meet them. Let's take a look at your goals.

### GOAL ANALYSIS ACTIVITY

1. List your goals in Column 1 (on facing page). These do not need to be stated in any special terms; just describe what it is you wish to accomplish in your current work environment and in your career as a whole. In Column 2 list the behaviors you must enact to accomplish your goals.

2. Are the goals and behaviors consistent with your conceptions of the kind of nurse you want to be?

| COLUMN 1<br>(GOALS) | COLUMN 2<br>(BEHAVIORS NEEDED TO ACCOMPLISH GOALS) |
|---|---|
| 1. | 1. a. _____<br>b. _____<br>c. _____<br>d. _____<br>e. _____ |
| 2 | 2. a. _____<br>b. _____<br>c. _____<br>d. _____<br>e. _____ |
| 3 | 3. a. _____<br>b. _____<br>c. _____<br>d. _____<br>e. _____ |
| 4 | 4. a. _____<br>b. _____<br>c. _____<br>d. _____<br>e. _____ |
| 5. | 5. a. _____<br>b. _____<br>c. _____<br>d. _____<br>e. _____ |

3. To what degree are your goals currently being met? For each goal, describe to yourself some specific situation that indicates the goal is being met. Be as specific as possible. Next, use the following 7-point scale to rate the degree to which each of your goals is being met. On this scale, 1 indicates the goal is not being met at all; 7 indicates that the goal has been met.

Goals

1.

1  2  3  4  5  6  7

2.

1  2  3  4  5  6  7

3.

1  2  3  4  5  6  7

4.

1  2  3  4  5  6  7

5.

1  2  3  4  5  6  7

You have just completed an analysis of your goals and the degree to which those goals are being met. Now go back and look at the pie-shaped diagram that you did in the Current Role Behavior Analysis. Think about and answer the following questions to yourself.

a. Where do your major energies go? (These are the tasks which take most of your time)

b. Does the focus of your energies move you toward your goals? (Rate on a scale of 1 to 7 again)

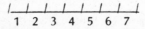

1  2  3  4  5  6  7

c. Are your behaviors in line with your desired concept of yourself as a nurse?

d. Are you satisfied with that desired self-concept—your goals?

This analysis will provide you with information regarding the congruence between your goal—your desired self-concept—and your current work activities. If you are moving toward your goal, if you are satisfied with your energy expenditure, and if you are satisfied with your goals, then your goals and behaviors are congruent. There is a high probability that you will achieve your desired self-concept. If you are *not* satisfied with all three aspects, your goals and behaviors may still be congruent. In other words, your behavior and goals may be in the same direction but you are not satisfied with them (negative congruence). If your goals and behaviors are incongruent, there are several possible conclusions:

1. Your behaviors are not moving you toward your goals and you are not satisfied with your behaviors; but you are satisfied with your goals.

2. Your behaviors are not moving you toward your goals but you are satisfied with your behaviors; you are not satisfied with your goals.

3. Your behaviors are moving you toward your goals but you are not satisfied with your behaviors; you are not satisfied with your goals.

There are other possible conclusions, but you probably get the point. If the behaviors and goals do not lead in the same direction, there is incongruence between the goals and behaviors, between the desired self-concept and the current behavior.

Generally speaking, if your goals and behaviors are congruent in a negative direction or incongruent, you will need to do something about either goals, behaviors, or both. Congruence is important in that congruent goals and behaviors provide a sense of satisfaction. Incongruence of the goals and behaviors can lead to dissatisfaction. Congruence in a negative direction can be as dissatisfying as incongruence.

In any case, whether the goals and behaviors are congruent or incongruent, you may decide to do something about either goals, behaviors, or both to bring you more satisfaction. It is you who must decide which component to deal with, and your decision is based on several factors. First, are you satisfied with your goals? Will the goals you have set for yourself lead you to the place you want to go? Can you realistically expect to meet your goals in any work environment? Are you satisfied with your behaviors? Do you enjoy doing what you are doing? Are there other things you would rather do if you had the choice? The answers to these questions will provide a base from which to decide whether to change goals or behaviors in order to produce more satisfaction.

Satisfaction can be judged on different planes. Satisfaction can be obtained from enjoyment of your work, rewards from colleagues and patients, and the feeling that your work serves a purpose. In addition, you can measure short-term satisfaction against long-range satisfaction. For example, your work may promote growth and change within you and contribute to the overall growth of the profession. But it may give you relatively little short-term satisfaction. You must decide, then, whether you want immediate or a more long-range satisfaction. It is possible that your work is giving you just enough immediate satisfaction to see you through while you work toward long-term goals. Or you may abandon long-term goals to engage in activities that bring satisfaction now—and never mind the future.

You must decide which type of satisfaction you want, as this will dictate whether your goals or your behaviors are changed when there is an incongruence. An incongruence between goals and behaviors that is corrected by a change in goals (to make them correspond with behaviors) will lead to immediate satisfaction—at least for a time. Incongruence corrected by a change of behaviors to make them correspond with goals is generally done with a view to long-term satisfaction. Thus, deciding which type of satisfaction you want will perforce help you choose whether to change goals or behaviors to acquire congruence. Since the type of satisfaction desired helps determine the focus of change, it is a good idea to look to the future. What is satisfying now may or may not be so in a year, two years, or even several months. Before you decide which aspect of your life to change—goals or behaviors—ask yourself this question: "In five years, when I look back over what I have done, how will I feel about my contribution?" This question will help you move the focus of your decision beyond current activities and will stimulate you to consider long-range satisfaction—doing work that promotes growth and change within you and effects growth and change in the profession and in the health care system.

"Work that promotes growth and change" challenges you to use your current abilities and to develop additional abilities. It may be that your work demands that you use all your talents and requires you to develop new talents. Or perhaps your work requires only a small portion of your talents and discourages the development of any new abilities not directly related to performance of your job. Putting into practice things you have learned in school would not only lead to growth for you but ultimately to growth and change in the profession and the health care system.

How can you tell if your work is challenging and growth producing? Ask yourself a series of questions.

1. Does the job require me to use all my abilities?
2. To what degree are my abilities used?
3. Does the job stimulate me to learn new skills?
4. When I think about going to work in the morning, do I look forward to the day with excitement, dread, boredom, pleasure, anticipation?
5. Am I bored and dissatisfied with my job more often than not?

6. When I look back over the past few months, do I feel good about the way I've been influencing the care given by others?

7. Given the situation, am I allowed to try new things so that I will *provide* care that I feel is the best for the patients?

8. Given the situation, what is the probability that I will be able to put into practice some of my beliefs about the way nursing ought to be practiced?

The answers to the questions will give you an indication of your present job's growth potential for yourself. Chances are that if you see that there are better ways of doing things, or if you see things that need some change, the potential for growth is present even if it now seems impossible to try anything new or influence others to try new things.

The growth-promoting potential is not only a factor to be considered when goals and behaviors are incongruent, but also when goals and activities are congruent. It may be that your goals and behaviors are congruent, and yet do not move you beyond "what is"—either "what is" in terms of your abilities or "what is" in terms of patient care. In this case, you may want to examine your goals and behaviors for possible revisions. Generally, goals and behaviors will be growth producing if they require you to go beyond things that you are now capable of doing. Of course, you must be careful not to reach so far that your goals exceed your potential abilities.

You must look at the abilities and behaviors required to meet your goals and compare them to your current abilities and behaviors. A decision to modify your current behaviors so that they are more in line with both your goals and your conceptions of a nurse or more in line with your employer's conceptions of a nurse requires more deliberative action on your part than does continuing in the same direction. The decision to modify your behavior requires consideration of two factors. What keeps me from performing the role behavior? And how am I going to begin performing the behavior?

There are any number of potential barriers that keep you from performing a role behavior. Some of the barriers are personal. Perhaps you are afraid of what others may think if you perform the behavior, or you haven't performed a particular behavior often enough that you feel comfortable about your ability to perform it. Other barriers may be situational. You may lack the staff or the time to perform a behavior. Once you identify the barriers, what can you do about them? You may be able to overcome your fears by saying to yourself, "Enough is enough. Let's get to it," and then start to perform the behavior. On the other hand, you may perform a behavior several times and really try to do it well but find that you just can't. For example, you may really work at helping patients get through an abortion experience, but no matter how hard you try, you just can't keep with it. You may have to concentrate on patients you can help and find someone else to work with abortion patients. You may have to set about developing behaviors and abilities that will help you achieve your goal. For example, you may realize that self-confidence is an ability that is very important if you are to achieve your goal of becoming a staunch patient advocate; but you are short on self-confidence. You must set out to build up your self-confidence. How? Well, for instance, by learning to ask questions in the proper manner. If you ask questions in certain ways, they not only destroy your self-confidence, but also influence the way that others treat you, which in turn affects your self-confidence. Let's say that a doctor comes up to you and asks you to help him with a lumbar puncture on two-year-old Johnny in ten minutes. You swallow hard and agree to do it, and then you think, "Oh, my gosh! I've never done one before. I've got to get help." You rush up to one of the more experienced staff nurses and say breathlessly, "I need help. Dr. Jones wants to do a lumbar puncture on Johnny and I've never done one. What do I do?" This approach destroys your own and others' confidence in you as a nurse; yet it is the approach most commonly used by new graduates. To help build up your self-confidence, learn to handle such a situation differently. Pause and think for a moment: "I've never done an L.P., but what do I know about it? And specifically what kind of help do I need?" Then go up to the experienced staff nurse and say:" Dr. Jones wants to do an L.P. on Johnny in ten minutes. I haven't assisted with one before, but I do know that in an L.P. the doctor takes a sample of cerebrospinal fluid. I know that I'll need a tray but I don't know how to order it up. I know that Johnny should be positioned in a fetal position on his side, but I don't know the order in which the doctor will want the equipment, nor what to do with the specimens after we're through." By asking questions in this manner, you will achieve two very important things. First, you will not destroy your self-confidence or others' confidence in your nursing ability. Second, you will let the other nurse know exactly what kind of help you need. And that has an added bonus. She's busy. She can give you the help you have said you need, and not waste your time and hers telling you things you already know. And most important, she will treat you with much more respect and with confidence in your ability. This, in turn, will increase your self-confidence. So, you see, a lot can be gained if you learn to ask questions in such a way that you do not undermine or destroy your own self-confidence.

When you encounter situational barriers, you must do the same sort of analysis, decision making, and questioning as you would do for personal barriers to goal achievement. For instance, you may find that you do not have enough staff to achieve some goal, and no matter what you do, it is impossible to get more staff. If you don't have enough time to perform the behaviors, perhaps you can make the time by delegating some tasks to others. The important point here is to identify the barriers and then work positively to overcome those barriers that you can do something about and forget those that cannot be dealt with. The difficulty arises in the tendency to accept barriers that are in fact removable. If there is any doubt, it is better to err by trying to remove the barrier and then learn that it can't be removed than to label a barrier as irremovable from the very beginning.

Identifying and sorting out both personal and situational barriers will allow you to focus your energies in such a way that goal attainment is possible. The following learning activity will help you do this.

### POTENTIAL BARRIER ACTIVITY

1. *Personal Factors:* Look back to your Goal Analysis Learning Activity. In Column 1 of this exercise, copy the behaviors you listed as necessary to achieve each of your goals. In Column 2, note the necessary behaviors that you already possess.* In Column 3, note the necessary behaviors that you do not yet possess to meet your goals. In Column 4, note behaviors that you possess that prevent you from meeting your goals.

COLUMN 1 (BEHAVIORS NEEDED)  COLUMN 2 (BEHAVIORS I HAVE)

COLUMN 3 (THOSE MISSING)   COLUMN 4 (BLOCKING BEHAVIORS)

The behaviors listed in Columns 3 and 4 are your personal barriers to goal attainment.

---

*If you need additional help in identifying traits and behaviors you do or do not possess, see the Trait Identification Activity at the end of this chapter.

2. *Situational Barriers:* Use the three-column chart below to answer each of the following questions.

   a.  Identify the goals you wish to attain.

   b.  Identify the barriers to the goals.

   c.  Identify actions necessary to remove the barrier and achieve the goal.

   d.  Star those actions that you can take at this time.

| GOALS | BARRIERS | ACTION NECESSARY |
|---|---|---|
|  |  |  |

For those actions that you have not starred, it is wise to ask yourself, why is the action unrealistic? It is well to remember that although the action may be unrealistic now, it may not be later on, and then the action can be taken. Or it may continue to be unrealistic, in which case trying it would only divert your energies from more productive activity.

You have identified the goals you wish to achieve, the personal and situational barriers that stand in their way, and the actions that you need to take to overcome those barriers. It is easy enough to say, "take the action necessary to remove the barriers" while one is sitting calmly and deliberating such action. It's quite a different story when you are faced with the barriers in the midst of your usual activity. The decision about what to do is yours. There is no magic formula for courage to act.

Perhaps the following considerations will help you change your behavior to achieve the goals you have set.

1. You, and you alone, are responsible for your behavior. It is up to you to decide what you are and want to be. If you decide to make some changes, it is your responsibility to make those changes happen.

2. Changes are more easily accomplished if stated in behavioral terms. It is difficult to accomplish generalized changes. For example, it is hard to change a lack of self-confidence into self-confidence. Self-confidence is evidenced by the behaviors you portray. Thus, if you list the behaviors indicative of self-confidence (poise; quick thinking), you can work toward concrete, specific actions that can increase your self-confidence.

3. Try on the desired behaviors. Making a behavior change is similar to being fitted for a dress. You put on the behavior and see how it fits. At first it may be uncomfortable—it just doesn't feel right. This doesn't mean you should throw it aside but rather that you try it again. Maybe you make a few modifications so that the behavior feels a bit more comfortable. You continue to try the behavior and modify it until it becomes comfortable or until it is evident that this change just is not going to work. The chief difference between trying on a dress and trying on a behavior is that it takes much longer to discover if a behavior fits well.

4. Make situational assessments of your behavior traits. Look at specific situations when the new behavior was enacted. Apply an assessment process to these situations to see how you are doing.
   a. Did you enact the behavior you wanted to?
   b. How comfortable was the situation?
   c. What must you do to make the new behavior more comfortable?
   d. Do you want to continue with the same behavioral action or to make some modifications?

5. Consider the consequences of the new behavior. When you try the new behavior what kind of response do you get from others? How do you feel about the new behavior? The key considerations here are: does the new behavior allow you to be yourself, move you toward your goals, and foster this self-movement without expense to others?

6. Assess the behavior in terms of your goals. Does the behavior you have taken on show promise of moving you toward your goals? The chief reason for taking on new behaviors is to help you become the person or nurse you want to be. If the behavior does not accomplish this end, then is it worth performing?

The adjustment required to reorganize your self-concept as a nurse so that those conceptions learned in school and those demanded by the work world may be integrated is difficult. It requires you to identify different aspects of the conceptions of the nurse role. It further requires you to identify those conceptions of the nurse role that are dictating your current behavior. In the final phase of the adjustment, you must decide upon your goals—your desired concept of the nurse role—and take action to adopt the role behaviors appropriate to that self-concept.

Most important, you should feel good about your concept of yourself—both as a person and as a nurse. Your level of self-esteem is directly related to the knowledge that you have succeeded at a task you set for yourself.

You must decide how to use your energies. You have examined your self-concept as a nurse, your goals and the behaviors necessary to achieve them, potential barriers to your goal attainment, and actions needed to overcome those barriers. You are unique and your direction will be unique. Taking steps toward becoming the kind of nurse you want to be will allow you to say with pride, "This is what I am; my life as a nurse has purpose and meaning."

### TRAIT IDENTIFICATION LEARNING ACTIVITY

This learning activity presents some trait descriptions and corresponding behaviors. All are traits that you may wish to develop more fully in yourself to achieve your desired self-concept, and you may find it necessary to change some of your behaviors in order to develop these traits. This is not a comprehensive list of traits or of behaviors corresponding to them. However, the list should provide you with an idea of the kind of self-inspection and analysis that will be helpful to you.

*Directions:*   Read the description of each trait and the behaviors listed. Decide which of the behaviors you possess, and think about related behaviors characteristic of you that may detract from the trait. Check your behaviors by placing the appropriate symbol (+ = you possess the behavior; **0** = you don't possess the behavior; − = you possess a behavior that detracts from the trait) in front of the behavior. For example, being tactful is one behavior related to the trait of self-control. You may possess the behavior (+), not posses it (**0**), or you may be tactless (−). List any additional behaviors you possess that are indicative of the trait described. By looking at your overall score on the behaviors indicative of each trait, you will get an idea of the extent to which you possess the trait. Then you can decide which traits you may or may not need to achieve your goals. If you want the trait, then you need to start performing the behaviors characteristic of the trait.

## 1: SELF-CONTROL

You are able to handle frustration and exercise tolerance in the face of uncertainty. Your actions are considerate of others but are governed by your own thought and judgments.

\_\_\_\_Tolerant of others' mistakes
\_\_\_\_Tactful
\_\_\_\_Deliberative action
\_\_\_\_Consider input of others but final decision my own

\_\_\_\_Keep cool
\_\_\_\_Control my temper
\_\_\_\_Self-starter
\_\_\_\_Think for myself
\_\_\_\_Voice calm under stress

## 2: COMPETENCE

You are capable, careful, and reliable. Responsibilities as well as consequences are accepted in the performance of your duties. You are an organized worker who knows what is expected and diligently completes assignments given.

_____Place self in situation where I can learn
_____Swift, sure action
_____On time
_____Assess outcome in terms of goals
_____Accurate in work
_____Know duties
_____Possess necessary skills
_____Delegate work to others

_____Plan work effectively
_____Function with minimal direction
_____Repeat performance until skill is obtained
_____Carry out assigned tasks on time
_____Request assistance when needed
_____Know and utilize alternatives
_____Task performance is consistent over time
_____Solve problems as they arise

## 3: STRENGTH OF CONVICTION

You have strong beliefs and values. You can defend your values and beliefs when necessary. You move ahead knowing your own abilities to make a decision or judgment. You can guide and convert others so that your beliefs become meaningful realities. You take risks to achieve your beliefs and goals.

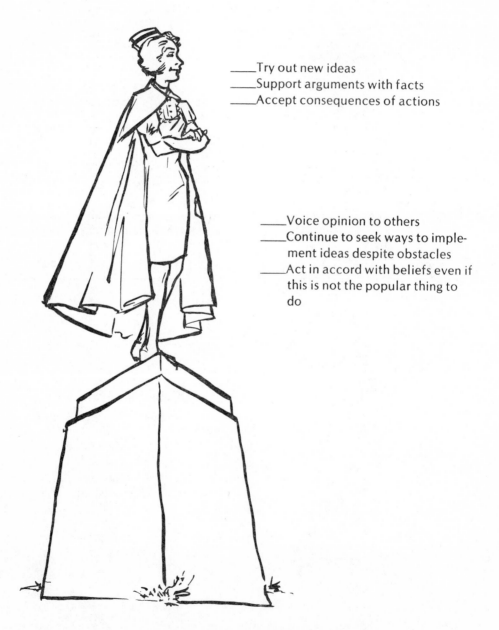

____Try out new ideas
____Support arguments with facts
____Accept consequences of actions

____Voice opinion to others
____Continue to seek ways to implement ideas despite obstacles
____Act in accord with beliefs even if this is not the popular thing to do

## 4: PERSEVERANCE

You believe in getting the job done and you persist against obstacles in order to accomplish what you set about. You are deliberative and purposeful in your actions. In projects there is a sustaining process through which you achieve a sense of completion.

____Emphasize meeting of deadlines
____Make several attempts before
     abandoning activity
____See job through to end

____Finish tasks regardless of time
     required
____Carry out tasks regardless of
     whether others carry out
     theirs

____Carry out activities despite
     difficulties

## 5: EFFECTIVE COMMUNICATION

You have the ability to express and convey a clear message. You can interact on a verbal and nonverbal level. You are sensitive regarding tone as well as content of verbal messages. You have the capacity to listen and are aware of the value of allowing others to re-state your message to validate its accuracy.

____Answer others promptly
____Express ideas clearly
____Initiate interactions
____Allow others to speak until finished
____Verbal and nonverbal communication are necessary
____Others can accurately re-state my message
____Co-workers can implement directions and tasks with a minimum of questions
____Acknowledge all communication
____Listen effectively, maintain eye contact and attentive posture

## 6: COOPERATIVE

You are agreeable about working with others and you are able to generate harmonious action from others. You respect and are concerned about people. Your attitude about being helpful is positive, so that you don't just go along but are dynamic in your approach to participation.

____Work willingly on unit projects

____Give help to others

____Give and get advice from others

____Accept new assignments

____Work overtime when necessary

____Acknowledge the success of others

____Concerned with goal attainment of others

____Do unassigned work without being asked

____Respond pleasantly when asked to help with tasks

____Offer new approaches to problems

### 7: SELF-CONFIDENCE

You know who you are and what capacities you have. You have the ability to live and adapt as necessary, to meet challenges, be objective, know your strengths and limitations. You are able to exercise judgment, creativity, and even meet the possibility of failing.

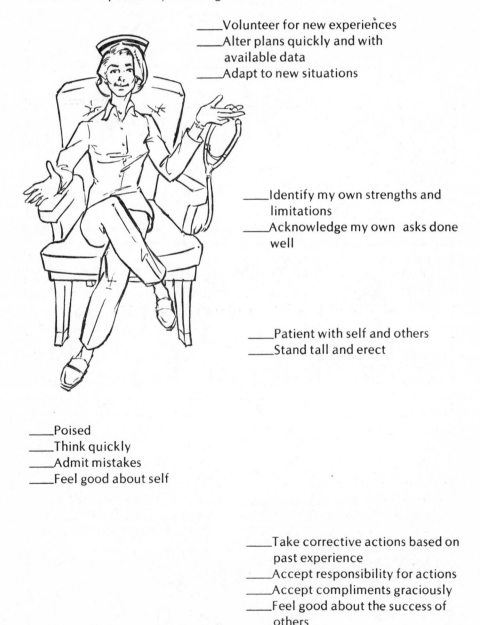

____Volunteer for new experiences
____Alter plans quickly and with available data
____Adapt to new situations

____Identify my own strengths and limitations
____Acknowledge my own  asks done well

____Patient with self and others
____Stand tall and erect

____Poised
____Think quickly
____Admit mistakes
____Feel good about self

____Take corrective actions based on past experience
____Accept responsibility for actions
____Accept compliments graciously
____Feel good about the success of others

## REFERENCES

1   James, W. *Principles of Psychology.* New York: Holt, 1890.
2   Cooley, C.H. *Human Nature and the Social Order.* New York: Scribner, 1902.
3   Mead, G.H. *Mind, Self and Society.* Chicago: University of Chicago Press, 1934.
4   Sullivan, H.S. *The Intersonal Theory of Psychiatry.* New York: W.W. Norton, 1953.
5   Kinch, J.W. "Experiments on Factors Related to Self-Concept Change," in J.G. Manis and
    B.N. Meltzer (eds.), *Symbolic Interaction: A Reader in Social Psychology.* Boston: Allyn &
    Bacon, 1972, pp. 262–268.
6   Schein, E.H. The individual, the organization, and the career: a conceptual scheme. *J.
    Appl. Behav. Sci.,* Vol. 7, No. 4, 1971, pp. 401–426.
7   Korman, A.K. Toward an hypothesis of work behavior. *J. Appl. Psych.,* Vol. 54, 1970, pp.
    31–41
8   Moore, W.E. "Occupational Socialization," in D.A. Coslin (ed.), *Handbook of Socializa-
    tion Theory and Research.* Chicago: Rand-McNally, 1971, pp. 861–883.
9.  Schein, 1971.
10. Argyle, M. and Rendon, A. "Self-Presentation and Competence" in Berkowitz, L. (ed.),
    *Advances in Experimental Social Psychology,* New York: Academic Press, 1967, Vol. 3, pp.
    79–98.

## BIBLIOGRAPHY

Cohen, A. "Some Implications of Self-Esteem for Social Influence" in C. Gordon and K. Gergen
    (eds.), *The Self in Social Interaction,* Vol. 1. New York: John Wiley and Sons, Vol. 1, 1968,
    pp. 383–390.
Dawis, R. V. and Lofquist, L. Personality style and the process of work adjustment. *J. Couns.
    Psychol.,* Vol. 23, No. 1, 1976, pp. 55–59.
Fitts, W. et al. *The Self Concept and Self-Actualization.* Nashville, Tenn.: Counselor Recordings
    and Tests, 1971.
Fitts, W. *The Self Concept and Performance.* Nashville, Tenn.: Counselor Recordings and Tests,
    1972.
Fitts, W. *The Self Concept and Behavior: Overview and Supplement.* Nashville, Tenn.: Counselor
    Recordings and Tests, 1972.
Greenhaus, J. and Badin, I. Self-esteem, performance, and satisfaction: some tests of a theory. *J.
    Appl. Psychol.,* Vol. 59, No. 6, 1974, pp. 722–726.
Jones, E. How do people perceive the causes of behavior? *Am. Sci.,* Vol. 64, May-June 1976, pp.
    300–305.
Reeder, L. G., *et al.* Conceptions of self and others. *Am. J. Sociol.,* Vol. 66, June 1960–61, pp.
    153–159.
Schein, E. H. The First Job Dilemma. *Psychol. Today,* March 1968, pp. 28–37.
Schneider, D. J. and Turkat, D. Self-presentation following success or failure: defensive self-
    esteem models. *J. Pers.,* Vol. 43, No. 1, March, 1975, pp. 127–135.
Thompson, W. *Correlates of the Self Concept.* Nashville, Tenn: Counselor Recordings and Tests,
    1972.
Turner, R. H. "The Self-Conception in Social Interaction," in Gordon, C. and Gergen, K. J. (eds.),
    *The Self in Social Interaction.* New York: John Wiley and Sons, 1968, 93–106.

# Module 4

# The Proving Ground*

## INTRODUCTION

It is not unusual for people to put themselves to a test, or for co-workers to test a newcomer. Although the content may change, to some degree, the process of testing out one's abilities is inherent in every new venture. This testing process performs a useful social function. By passing our own tests, we acquire identity in our own eyes, as well as an increase in self-esteem and self-confidence. This is particularly true when we are unsure of our self-image, as many new graduate nurses are when they first start working. In such circumstances, people need continual confirmation that they really are what they want to be and half-believe themselves to be[1]. Testing oneself provides such confirmation.

By passing the tests that others construct for us, we gain membership into an established work group. Membership carries with it the possibility of acquiring informal power, which is necessary if one is to influence the amount and quality of the group's work.

For new graduate nurses, the first job is a Proving Ground—a place to prove yourself, both to yourself and to your co-workers, a place to test out your abilities as a nurse. You have already proven your abilities as a student nurse and have successfully passed *out of* the role of student. This does not mean that you have successfully passed *into* the role of staff nurse.

After all of your investment of energy, time, and money in school, your first job is the chance to get some answers to some very important questions. Can I be the kind of nurse I have been taught to be? Just what kind of

*The contribution of Patricia Benner to the development of this module is gratefully acknowledged.

nurse will I be on an ordinary day? in an emergency? when I have to take care of a complex patient? when I have to plan the assignments of others? when others come to me for supervision and answers? Will others take my direction? How will I handle a disagreement with a doctor? How will I know if I should call the doctor at 3:00 A.M. or whether the problem can wait until morning? What does the staff expect of me?

## PURPOSE AND OBJECTIVES

These questions lead directly to the purpose of this module, which is: to help you recognize and analyze *your self-constructed* tests and the informal *other-constructed* tests in your work environment. The module's objectives are:

1. To identify the content and circumstances of *self-constructed* tests.
2. To develop strategies for identifying the content, circumstances, and basis for appraisal of *other-constructed* tests in the work environment.
3. To evaluate the criteria of this informal testing.
4. To point out some areas toward which self and other tests are focused.
5. To identify the perceptual distortions and measurement errors in informal testing.

Since entry into the work world involves the process of acquiring a new identity, an identity as a nurse, and since testing is part of this process, the issue is: how can you make this time of informal testing as successful and as comfortable as possible? By making the process of testing as visible and understandable as possible. If you know when and how you are being tested by yourself and others, then you can stop and take stock. What is the content of the test? What are the criteria for success? How will you know when you have made it? Is the test reasonable? Do the criteria and content of the test match your own values, or do others' values predominate in the testing criteria? Was the appraisal message communicated clearly? Was it accurately received? If the testing process is understandable and visible to you, you will be able to *choose* to pass the test or not, to decide whether to retain your old values or accept new values or compromises, instead of bending blindly to group expectations.

## FORMAL AND INFORMAL TESTS

Although self-constructed tests are usually informal, other-constructed tests may be either formal or informal. *Formal* other-constructed tests are identified by such terms as *probationary period, skills competency inventories, permanent payroll, certified for IV therapy,* or *return demonstrations* in orientation class. Such formal tests are rather easily dealt with because the criteria for passing them are spelled out.

On the other hand, *informal* self-and, especially, other-constructed tests are often very ambiguous. First, others may not be aware that they "test" the newcomer. Though they may indicate that they always "size up"the newcomer or that they can usually find out what kind of nurse she is going to be, the tests are constructed without the specificity of formal testing. Second, others often cannot spell out what the criteria for passing the tests are. For example, in one of the upcoming modules, "The Work Shoes Speak," you will find that one nurse aide said that she can "tell the difference between a new graduate and someone who is already a nurse." But *she cannot describe* exactly the behaviors of the "nurse who has arrived." In most cases, information about the criteria or content of the *informal* tests has to be gained from indirect questions and observations. Since the other person has never gone through the deliberate formal process of constructing the content and criteria of his test, he simply cannot tell you directly what it is.

Do you remember ever sitting down to an exam in school in which the questions were so vague and ambiguous that you asked, "What on earth is the teacher trying to get at? What does she want me to answer here?" You expected to proceed according to the rules of formal testing. You expected your instructor to have thought out the content and criteria of the test. Finding the questions vague and ambiguous, you were forced to resort to strategies used in response to informal testing. That is, you tried to figure out what kind of answer was wanted on the basis of who the instructor was, or what her pet subjects were, or the kind of material that was really "her thing." The same kind of strategy must be used in response to informal testing in the work environment. By developing and refining your questioning and observation techniques, you can make the content and criteria of the informal other-constructed tests visible and explicit so that you can choose to pass, avoid, subvert, or fail the tests, depending upon your own set of values and goals.

Both formal and informal tests are important for the newcomer in a work group. The formal testing is important because the newcomer must pass the tests in order to maintain a position in the organization. But informal testing is equally important, because it is the means by which fellow workers determine the acceptance, relative status, and potential influence of the newcomer[2].

Since formal tests are more easily dealt with, this module's major concern is informal other-constructed and self-constructed tests. The process of testing is the same whether it is other-or self-constructed, and consists of four components: content, circumstances, criteria, and appraisal. Each of these components will be discussed separately; however, in actual practice they are closely interrelated.

First, there is the *content* of the test. The content is the task or behavior to be tested. For a self-constructed test, the content may be things like, "Will I be able to get the needle into the vein?" "Can I handle myself in an emergency?" "Will I be able to understand all the doctor's order jargon?" For other-constructed tests, the content will vary, depending on who the 'other' is. For a nurse aide, the content might be, "Is this grad able to give all the sleepers by 9:00 P.M. so that all the patients are asleep by 9:30 or 10:00 P.M.?" "Does she give report on time?" For doctors, it might be "Does the nurse have all the pertinent patient information at hand when she calls?" "Does she know what's needed or what comes next in an exam or procedure?" For other nurses, it might be, "Can the new graduate function as a team leader?" "Is the emergency cart checked and the narcotic count correct when she's on duty?"

The content of other-constructed tests is based upon the values of the person constructing the test, while in self-constructed tests one's own values are tested. If the content of other-constructed tests is not specified, there is a good chance that the new nurse will fail because of value differences between herself and the tester. For example, when the new graduate is put to the test of caring for five or six patients, she will approach the test according to her perception of patient care, whereas the person who constructed the test will judge the new graduate's performance from her own perspective of what nursing care is. Since the two perspectives tend to differ the new graduate will have difficulty with the test. She will not perform as expected by others.

The *circumstances* of the test are the social context or the extenuating conditions under which the test must occur. For example, the test may involve starting an IV on an elderly person with fragile veins. The task of starting the IV is the content; the circumstances are that the task must be performed not only under ideal conditions, but also in situations that present a lot of handicaps to task achievement. A common self-constructed test among new graduates requires that they perform all the tasks necessary for a code situation in a *real* (not a pretend) emergency. A common other-constructed test is: Can the new graduate be a team leader on the weekend, when she is the only RN on? Or, for example, it might be acceptable for a nurse to talk fast and show a bit of anxiety after a truly large emergency, but it would not be acceptable and she would not pass the test if she did this after a minor emergency, such as a peripheral hemorrhage—even though that minor emergency might be a very new experience for the new graduate. Thus, the situational parameters of the test are the circumstances under which the test must be passed.

The third component is the *criteria* of the test. Criteria refer to the standards used in judging the content and circumstances of the test. The criteria constitute the most problematic component of the testing process. There are three primary questions to be asked about criteria: (1) How are the criteria derived? (2) What dimensions of the test are most important? (3) Will the criteria be based upon process or outcome?

In a self-constructed test, criteria emanate from two sources. One is the values the new graduate learned and used as a student. These values are likely to be unrealistic, failing to match the circumstances operating in the testing situation. For example, one new graduate's self-constructed test was that she give to the five patients assigned to her the same type of comprehensive care that she gave when she was in school. One of her criteria for comprehensive care was that she accompany her patient to the operating room. Because she had to remain on the unit to prepare another patient for the operating room, she failed her own test—she could not meet all her criteria.

In self-constructed tests, the other source of criteria is the staff nurse referent group. The new graduate often uses the standards of her co-workers as criteria for her own performance. This staff nurse referent group usually has had more experience, and has repeatedly performed almost any nursing task or behavior.

Research has shown that in the absence of explicit standards, and given a vague knowledge of their standing in a group, people will evaluate their own ability by comparing themselves with the person who is *best-off* in ability[3]. Thus, a new graduate, using the performance of others as a criterion for her self-constructed tests, will expect herself to perform in the same manner as the best staff nurse on the unit—and this without having the experience necessary to achieve the same level of expertise. Basing a test upon criteria derived from school and the staff nurse referent group is unfair and unrealistic.

In other-constructed tests, new graduates will be expected to perform and will be evaluated according to the level of expertise and the experience of the individual constructing the test. People tend to evaluate others on the dimensions with which they themselves are most comfortable. Thus, experienced nurses tend to evaluate the new graduate according to their own level of performance without consideration for the newcomer's lack of experience. Such tests are also unfair and unrealistic.

The second question in terms of criteria relates to the dimensions of the task that are considered most important. Every task has dimensions, and some dimensions may be more important than others. For example, in the test of taking care of five patients, you might be most concerned with the *comfort* of the patients as a result of the care, or the *speed* with which care was provided, or the *amount of help* required from others in giving the care. In ascertaining the criteria of a test, it is necessary to establish which dimension of the test is the most important to the person constructing the test. This holds true whether the test is self- or other-constructed.

The third question is whether the criteria will be based on process or outcome. When tests are looked at from a *process* point of view, one is concerned with the sequencing and progression of the various elements of the task or test. When tests are looked at from an *outcome* point of view, one is concerned only with the final results of the effort. In some tests, like tests of technical skills, most often it is the outcome that is judged. Did you get the needle into the vein? In other tests, such as when one's ability in an emergency situation such as a cardiac arrest is tested, it is usually process that is judged. Did the nurse follow correct sequencing and procedures in handling the situation? The constant shifting from one mode to another makes it difficult for the person being tested to know whether process or outcome is the important criterion for passing the test.

Outcome is the most frequent mode of criteria applied in other-constructed tests. When outcome criteria are used in technical skill tests, it is almost impossible for a brand new graduate to pass, since she will lack the speed and precision gained through repeated performance to accomplish the desired outcome.

The process mode of criteria predominates in the school setting, so this will be the mode that is most familiar to, and almost automatically used by, the new graduate. If you use this mode in your self-constructed tests, you have a pretty good chance of passing them. This is not necessarily true for other-constructed tests based on process criteria. Frequently, there is more than one process leading to achievement of an outcome, and the person constructing the test will evaluate the newcomer on the basis of the process he considers most appropriate. Thus, the newcomer may fail the test because she employed the wrong process.

The fourth component of the testing process is *appraisal*. The appraisal is a summary statement as to the outcome of the test—did you pass the test or not? In making the appraisal, the tester needs to consider two factors: (1) how much experience the newcomer has had, and (2) what, if any, message is to be communicated to the person who was tested. Although the amount of your previous experience must obviously play a part in the final outcome, you will not always find that it has been considered by the appraiser. To test you and compare your performance with that of others who have had more experience with the content and circumstances of the test is grossly unfair, but it is done. Your performance should be evaluated by comparing you with others with the same amount of experience. The appraisal or final message that is communicated to you is a factor of crucial importance and one that is frequently overlooked in the informal, other-constructed Proving Ground tests we are talking about here. It is not simply a matter of communicating "you passed" or "you didn't pass"; what is more helpful is communicating to you the reasons, the criteria, for your pass or failure. More often than not, you will find that in other-constructed tests, the appraisal message will be communicated to you indirectly and non-verbally and will contain a variety of messages—you did not pass the test, you are incompetent, you didn't learn anything in school; or you did a fine job (but there is no message telling you what you did to win such praise).

Now, all this is not meant to frighten you, but rather to give you a realistic view of the testing process and why it is that the end result, the appraisal message, might be very confusing and upsetting to you. It's intended to help you understand why it is that you may think you're doing fine, that you passed an other-constructed test, until you get the indirect or nonverbal message that you didn't. In all likelihood, the content and circumstances of the test were not clear, and you probably did not know that you were expected to perform as well as a graduate two years out of school (sources of criteria); that the primary consideration was your speed, not the comfort of the patient (dimension tested); that it was the final outcome that was being judged—not whether you did all the steps correctly (process- vs. outcome-based criteria). But don't despair! You may think it's terrible that others judge you this way, and that they shouldn't do it. . . . Well, maybe so, but that's the way it is. What can you do to help yourself in these testing situations so that you get an even break?

Before considering what you might do to make the testing situation clearer, let's ask ourselves why it is necessary to clarify such testing situations? Why should you analyze self-constructed and other-constructed tests? The answer is that by analyzing them and figuring out the content, criteria, and circumstances of both your self-constructed tests and other-constructed tests, *you* will become the *master* of the testing situation. Such analysis will increase your freedom to establish your identity as a person and as a nurse, to pass with honors, to merely pass, to avoid a test (in some cases), or to fail and still maintain yourself in the system. If you analyze them, you can take the tyranny out of both self-constructed and other-constructed tests. Once you know the content, criteria, and circumstances, *you* can evaluate the test:

1. Is the test reasonable?

2. Do the content, criteria, and circumstances make sense in terms of my value system?

3. How can I alter the content or criteria or the circumstances of the test?

As a first step in developing the ability to figure out the content, criteria, and circumstances of tests, read the following excerpt from a new graduate about an other-constructed test.

> Well, there was this kind of code blue situation. In this room where the mother is delivering by C Section, and there were all these monitors, and gas analysis machines, CVP, you know . . . and the baby was in some sort of difficulty—had respiratory, cardiac, or whatever. The other nurse, the older staff nurse who was on with me, left me alone with this situation! . . . And I was just brand new! . . . I didn't know what to do. Seven doctors were with the baby, and the baby was really zonked and they were all asking me for things at once. And I was handing them things and taking care of things really fast. The baby turned out to be OK after the first two hours. . . And I think I learned that . . . my greatest satisfaction was that I could react so fast. I was proud of it and the doctors were proud of it. But it was like being tested. . . . And that staff nurse, well, I would say that she was almost negligent, leaving me alone in a situation like that. I think she expected that I wouldn't make it, that I would get yelled at, and be deflated some. I think she thought that in a crisis situation I would fall apart. That's what I think they were all discussing. But I didn't fall apart. I passed the test and I was *proved* in a crisis situation. That really boosted my morale a lot.

Now, see if you can answer the following questions.

1.  a) What was the nurse being tested on? _____

    _____

    b) Who constructed the test?_____

    c) Under what circumstances did the nurse have to pass the test? ___

    _____

    d) What were the criteria for passing?
       (1) Source? _____

    _____

    _____

       (2) Important dimension? _____

    _____

    _____

       (3) Process or outcome? _____

    _____

    _____

    e) What was the appraisal? _____

2.  If this nurse wanted to check out whether she passed or not, what
    would she look for, or how might she approach the other staff
    nurse?

    _____

    _____

    _____

    _____

3.  This new graduate expresses anger toward the older staff nurse for
    leaving her alone in that situation. What is another possible ex-
    planation of the older staff nurse's behavior?

    _____

    _____

    _____

    _____

After you have answered the above questions, you may want to compare
your answers with the ones given on the following page.

1.  a) Not really clear, but had something to do with helping the doctors resuscitate the baby.

    b) Another staff nurse.

    c) Had to do it rapidly.

    d) (1) Had to do it as well as an older staff nurse with more experience.

    (2) Meeting the doctors' needs for equipment rapidly enough to prevent them from yelling.

    (3) Hard to say for sure. Outcome was important—baby was OK. No indication that correct process was a consideration.

    e) Passed the test.

2.  "That was a new experience for me. I think I did all right with the medications, but I could have been better organized getting the equipment that would be needed. For a first experience like that, how do you think I did?"

3.  With seven doctors in the room, the new graduate was not alone and did not have major responsibility for the welfare of the infant. The older nurse may have judged that it was better to leave the new graduate with the seven doctors in that situation while she remained out on the floor alone with the other patients where she would be the person primarily responsible.

    Another possible explanation: The older staff nurse may have been reluctant to destroy the new graduate's confidence in herself by replacing her in the situation. She may have thought that if she did this, the new graduate might think that the older staff nurse didn't trust her.

OK, now let's look at a self-constructed test. In the following excerpt, a new graduate describes such a test.

I had this patient and she was really sick. She had an abdominal incision open all the way down to her intestine which was draining. She had a hyperalimentation line that went directly into the aorta, so she had to have a pump because the pressure was so great. She was on a certain kind of pump that I was not familiar with at all, and at the beginning of the day, it was explained to me. . . . But the tubing had to be changed. Someone helped me change the tubing. I'd been in there a long time, so I left and took a half-hour break. When I came back I noticed the IV volutrol hadn't changed and it was going backwards and was pumping in reverse. I just really got nervous . . . I had been in there all morning trying to get things done and I really felt responsible because I should have stayed, and made sure the pump was working properly. I shouldn't have taken the break. I got some people to help me and we worked with her because she would have had to go back to the OR. We finally ended up breaking the clot that was in there and she seemed okay.

But I went home with a really bad headache that day and it really affected me very much—my confidence. . . . When I went back the next day I had the same patient and I was determined that I was going to get myself more organized. I was going to finish everything on time, and I was going to do it right. And I was. I was able to get all the tubing needed ahead of time, so that I didn't have to rush through anything. I was able to get it done right and I really felt good about that. It gave me a lot more confidence in myself.

1.  What was the content of this test that the nurse constructed for herself? _____

    _____

2.  Under what conditions did she have to pass the test? _____

    _____

3.  What were the criteria?

    a)  Source?_____

    _____

    _____

    b)  Important dimension? _____

    _____

    _____

    c)  Process or outcome? _____

    _____

    _____

4.  What appraisal did the nurse make? _____

After you have answered the above questions, you may want to compare your answers with the ones given below.

1.  Not clear, but apparently it was just giving the care needed by this patient.

2.  Not stated, but presumably the same conditions that existed the day before. Also, it appears that she had to give the care alone in order to pass her test.

3.  a)  It would seem that the nurse is using her performance of the day before as a basis for comparison, although she also seems to have in mind some internal standard. This internal standard was probably developed from observation of other more experienced staff nurses who had cared for this or similar patients.

    b) Organization and doing it within a specific time period.

    c) Process. She had to do it right—whatever the correct process meant to this nurse.

4. I passed. I did it.

If you would like some additional practice at identifying the content, criteria, and circumstances of self- and other-constructed tests, try some of the following excerpts from interviews* in which new graduates talk about whether they can become the kind of nurse they want to be on their first job. See if you can identify the *content, criteria,* and *circumstances* of their tests.

**Excerpt 1**

The hospital I work in is small. I work at night. We have pediatrics all the way up to geriatrics. I pass the meds, give assignments, do treatments, etc. I was very frustrated at first, and I get disgusted now at times when we are busy, because we have less staff than the day or evening shift. However, I feel I am getting a well-rounded experience. Although we have an IV nurse, she has taught me to start IVs and watched me start a couple. I enjoy working at this hospital.

*Content:*

*Criteria:*

*Circumstances:*

---

*These interviews are from a study on the work-entry of new graduate nurses in San Diego and Imperial Counties, conducted by Patricia and Richard Benner under the auspices of the Coordinating Council for Education in Health Sciences in Imperial and San Diego Counties, with a grant from the California committee on regional medical programs from the regional medical programs service, Health Resources Administration, US Department of Health, Education and Welfare grant #5G03 RM 00019-04 and 06.

## Excerpt 2

I tend to act as a patient advocate because this is my training and I believe in it. Patients deserve to be treated as individuals and they have a right to make choices in their care. We have a great many women having therapeutic abortions on our floor and there are value judgments made by some staff. I find myself taking a patient advocate position and trying to work with staff to help them be less judgmental. I love my job—it's a unique challenge.

*Content:*

*Criteria:*

*Circumstances.*

## Excerpt 3

My unit is too slow. The surgeries aren't major enough. There isn't enough medicine in it for me to become competent. If I want to work in ICU, I need more learning experiences.

*Content:*

*Criteria.*

*Circumstances.*

After you have determined the content, criteria, and circumstances for the three interview excerpts, compare your analysis with those given below. This will provide you with some verification and validation of your ability to identify content, criteria, and circumstances of self-constructed tests.

### Excerpt 1

The *content* of this new graduate's test seems to be that she be able to perform a broad range of nursing skills, such as passing meds, doing treatments, etc. She views herself as a generalist rather than a specialist at this point. She values learning technical skills, particularly IVs. The excerpt does not give information about her *criteria* for performance.

*Circumstances:* This graduate does not view working under conditions of short staffing as being part of her test. In other words, she expects herself to perform well when there is adequate staffing.

### Excerpt 2

*Content* is her ability to actualize patient care values—particularly patient advocacy—in a practice setting.

The *criteria* are unclear, but it appears that it is important to this graduate to be a patient advocate in a conflicting environment—one in which she herself can change the attitudes of others.

*Circumstances:* A certain amount of conflict and challenge. If everyone agreed with her, then she would not be able to test herself.

### Excerpt 3

The *content* of this graduate's test is caring for patients with major surgeries and complex medical needs.

Her *criteria* are to demonstrate competence in caring for a number of patients with multiple therapeutic needs.

For *circumstances,* this graduate wants a fast-paced unit which will prepare her for ICU nursing.

The following excerpts are from nursing service persons talking about the informal testing of newcomers. See if you can identify the *content, criteria,* and *circumstances* of these other-constructed tests.

### Excerpt 4

The aides are very critical of the RNs. The ones who have been working for a long time realize that an RN has a lot more to do than sit at a desk charting. If the RN will get up and go when the aide needs her, it helps. I say respect is earned, not passed out, because you have RN after your name.

*Content:*

*Criteria:*

*Circumstances:*

**Excerpt 5**    (In response to the question: Describe important qualities that you look for in a nurse:)

> Calmness, maturity. I think a lot of it is time. In most hospitals, however, new graduates need help and they need it *now* . . . the staff get frustrated and the pressure goes back to the new graduate. She has to show confidence, she has to show her team members her knowledge so that they can respect her.

*Content:*

*Criteria:*

*Circumstances:*

**Excerpt 6**

> The new graduates have to prove themselves here, not only a new graduate, any new staff member on the unit. We have one doctor who will stand over your shoulder and watch everything, he glares, and just gawks . . . and that puts the kids under quite a bit of strain. Some of them learn to handle it after it has happened two or three times. They really feel like: "This doctor thinks I'm a complete idiot." Then, if they question him, they begin to find out that they've gotten on the good side of him. Then, the more they show interest, the more he responds to them, and the next thing you know he's calling them by name, etc. They've won their point, and they're respected.

*Content:*

*Criteria:*

*Circumstances:*

After you have finished identifying the content, criteria, and circumstances of the other-constructed tests, compare your analysis with the ones below. You will note that the content and criteria are quite ambiguous in some of the excerpts. This is characteristic of informal tests. In the next section of this module, strategies for making content, criteria, and circumstances explicit will be explored.

### Excerpt 4

*Content:* A demonstrated willingness to respond to aides' requests for help.

*Criteria:* An RN who is respected will always respond to requests for help if she is sitting at the desk.

*Circumstances:* The test becomes pass or fail, if the nurse is sitting at the desk.

### Excerpt 5

*Content:* Personality, style, calmness. Demonstrated self-confidence and use of "knowledge.

*Criteria:* Must demonstrate the personal attributes of calmness and self-confidence.

*Circumstances:* Must demonstrate competence as soon as possible after being hired.

More information is needed in order to identify the behaviors that represent these attributes.

### Excerpt 6

*Content:* Ability to ask questions.

*Criteria:* Does not appear intimidated by unusual behavior of doctor.

*Circumstances:* Can pass the test under the stress of doctor's strange social behavior.

The analysis of the other-constructed tests which you have just done points out the importance of and need for developing strategies to make the content, criteria, circumstances, and appraisal message of informal testing visible, explicit, and therefore manageable. Not only is it frustrating to be unable to pass a test that you would like to pass, it is less than satisfying to pass a test and not know why or how you passed it. In fact, there may be tests that you wish to avoid, but avoidance is not possible unless the tests are visible to you. The next section tells you how to build strategies for making informal tests visible and explicit.

First, let's look at how to make self-constructed tests visible. You might think that you need not worry about this; since it is you who is constructing the tests, you can assume that they will be fair. You may assume that you will construct tests that you have a reasonable chance of passing. Well, this might not be so. Before you assume that your own tests are reasonable guidelines for your performance on your first job, consider the following questions. What is the content of your tests? What are the sources of your test items? Does the content of your tests agree with what you value in patient care? Or have you accepted other people's values in constructing your tests?

To help you identify the content of your self-constructed tests, try one or both of the following:

**First Alternative.** Think about some situation at work that was particularly satisfying to you. Many times, situations that are particularly satisfying are ones in which we face up to and pass some test. Now, list the competencies that you portrayed in that situation. (You may wish to write them out on paper.)

If you performed the previous exercise, skip the next paragraph and go on.

**Second Alternative.** List the competencies you expect yourself to have when you become the kind of nurse you want to be. If you have difficulty listing competencies you want to have, think of a nurse you admire—one that you consider an excellent nurse. Then list the attributes, qualities, or competencies that cause you to rate this nurse as excellent. (You may wish to write these out on paper.)

The competencies listed in either of the previous exercises probably represent the content of your self-constructed tests. They are characteristics you admire and value. Evaluate them by answering the following questions:

1. How many competencies relate to psychosocial or interpersonal helping aspects of caring for patients or patients' families?

2. How many competencies relate to managerial aspects of nursing? (For example, giving report; team leading; remembering doctors' orders or lab test rules.)

3. How many competencies are knowledge and skills related to specific disease entities?

4. How many competencies relate to use of time?

5. How many competencies relate to manual or procedural skills?

6. How realistic is it to expect yourself to gain the competencies on your list within three months? Within six months? Within one year?

7. How realistic is it to expect yourself to gain the competencies given the work group's expectations of you? Given the working environment? The patient care load?

8. Are there competencies you have already mastered which might disappear from lack of use and practice if you master all the competencies on your current list?

This exercise was designed to make you aware of the content of your self-constructed tests. This content may or may not be what you want it to be. This will be discussed in later programs.

Although there is no necessary correspondence between the content of *your* self-constructed tests and those of other recent graduates, you may find it interesting to make the comparison. In a national survey of 196 recent graduates working in 13 large hospitals in the United States, the following goals (p. 119) were listed as "High in Importance" by over 50 percent of the sample. Our goals are a reflection of our values, the things that are important to us. So it is highly likely that these are the areas around which these new graduates built self-constructed tests. You too will probably construct your tests around your goals and values.

Now that we've looked at strategies for examining the content of your *self*-constructed tests, let's try to examine the content of *other*-constructed tests. Some of the strategies used for making your self-constructed tests visible will work for other-constructed tests as well. For example, if you find out who your various co-workers consider to be their "ideal" or "most successful" nurse, then further questions of them will elicit the attributes that make that nurse "successful" or "ideal." The purpose of your questions is not to enable you to become everyone's model, but rather to help you learn what your co-workers expect of *you*. Only by learning their expecta-

| Rank | Stated Goal | No. and Percent Listing Goal as High in Importance | |
|------|-------------|------|---------|
| | | No. | Percent |
| 1 | To test out my speed, ease, and competence in functioning as a staff nurse | 146 | 74.5 |
| 2 | To see if I am competent in technical skills and procedures | 146 | 74.5 |
| 3 | To try out my interpersonal skills in working with patients and families | 140 | 71.4 |
| 4 | To try out my organizational skills and time management ability | 134 | 68.4 |
| 5 | To see if and how well I would function in emergencies | 111 | 56.6 |
| 6 | To test out some of my ideas about improving patient care | 108 | 55.1 |
| 7 | To see how well I can plan and give care to large groups of patients | 101 | 51.5 |

tions can you exert some control over the amount of influence these expectations will have on your behavior. If you choose *not* to live up to certain expectations, *not* to pass certain tests, you will be able to interpret your behavior to others from *your* point of view while at the same time understanding *their* point of view.

It is necessary to check out both the registered nurses and the auxiliary staff regarding the "ideal nurse." One group may choose a nurse different from the other, or the two groups may choose the same person but for different reasons. To check out only one group of co-workers leaves a gap in your understanding of the various work group values present on a unit.

Another way to ascertain the content of other-constructed tests is to ask various persons on the unit what things they consider it important for a team leader to do. It is also a good idea to gather information about the expectations and values of your co-workers from people who have worked on the unit, but who are no longer working there. They may be more candid. Further, this cuts the number of questions you have to ask your co-workers.

In the nationwide survey mentioned earlier, 305 head nurses and supervisors working in the same hospitals as the 196 recent graduates were asked to rank order the goals that they thought new graduates should achieve. The results were the following listed from one to seven in order of importance:

| Supervisor Ranking | | New Graduate Ranking |
|---|---|---|
| 1 | Organizational skills and time management ability | 4 |
| 2 | Planning and giving care to large groups of patients | 7 |
| 3 | Developing speed, ease, and competence in functioning as a staff nurse | 1 |
| 4 | Competence in technical skills and procedures | 2 |
| 5 | Getting along well with co-workers | 10 |
| 6 | Making effective assignments and delegating tasks effectively | 8 |
| 7 | Functioning well in emergencies | 5 |

You will notice that the rank ordering of the goals is not the same for the two groups. However, since tests are structured around one's goals and values, it is highly likely that the areas high in the supervisor's list are the areas in which your head nurse and co-workers will build tests for you.

Once you have identified the major content of the tests that you will probably construct for yourself and that others are likely to construct for you, you are ready to identify and evaluate the circumstances, criteria, and appraisal of the tests. The techniques and strategies for doing this are the same whether the test is self- or other-constructed; the only difference is who is asked the questions.

Let's look first at strategies for identifying and evaluating the circumstances of self- and other-constructed tests. (This will be done in the context of self-constructed tests—just turn the questions around to use them for other-constructed tests.) To begin this analysis, start by examining your list of competencies (from page 117) in relation to the following questions. Are the content and criteria of your test related to certain circumstances or settings? For example, must your test be performed during an emergency or on a particular type of patient, or in a particular type of unit? Does your test require a certain degree of independence or autonomy before you can pass? Most important, will your present situation allow you to put your self-constructed test to a test?

The third step is to identify the criteria you have set up for judging your test. What are the sources of your criteria? What dimensions of the test are most important? Are the criteria based on process or outcome? How will you know when you have achieved mastery on the content items of your self-constructed test? To do this, take a moment and think about the evidence that you would accept as "proof," or as an indication that you have "passed your test."

Now, let's evaluate the criteria that you have just described to yourself. To help you do this, answer the following questions:

1. Is successful performance related to ability to:
   provide the same kind of care you did in school?
   provide the same kind of care as others on the unit?
   perform technical tasks as if you had done them several times before?

2. Is successful performance related to ability to perform:
   certain levels of quality of care?
   certain patient care goals?
   within a specific time limit?
   under stress?
   without supervision or assistance?
   in addition to doing a number of other activities?

3. Is successful performance related to ability to:
   achieve certain approaches or processes related to patient care (for example, nursing care plans, team conferences, primary nursing)?
   pass all the meds by 1:15 P.M.?
   do five baths in three hours?

4. Do your criteria fit your goals or values related to patient care?

After determining the criteria used in the test, you need to appraise the outcome of the test.

1. Did you pass the test or not? For what reasons?

2. If the appraisal message was "not pass," what specific performance or behavior caused you to not pass? Were the criteria for performance reasonable?

3. Are you getting messages that because you failed in a specific behavior you have failed as a nurse or as a person?

4. Does your failure in this test truly detract from (or negate) the other qualities or characteristics you possess as a nurse?

The final step in the appraisal strategy is for you to acknowledge the accuracy or inaccuracy of the appraisal on specific behaviors while also acknowledging those behaviors that you do well.

To ascertain the criteria for passing other-constructed tests, determine what evidence the other would accept as "proof" of your passing the test. Obviously, the easiest and most accurate way of finding out this information is to ask directly. However, this is fraught with problems, largely because the person constructing the test is not conscious of and cannot clearly articulate the criteria. Try instead to get answers to the following questions. From these answers, you will be able to deduce the criteria for passing other-constructed tests.

1. When I perform this task what is most important? The result? (outcome?) The correctness of procedure, or steps, leading to the result? (process?)

2. What's really important in doing this? Speed? Comprehensiveness? Getting everyone involved? If I have to sacrifice one for the other, which do you think has highest priority?

3. Am I expected to do this alone? With or without supervision?

4. Does this task take precedence over other things I've been assigned . to do, or that I usually do?

After deducing the criteria that seem to be operating in the other-constructed test, you should be much more able to decide whether you want to pass the test or not. If you do want to pass it, try to; then appraise the outcome by using the questions outlined above for self-constructed tests. If you choose not to pass the test, you should explain your decision to the other—describing what you perceive the test and the criteria for passing to be, and why you chose not to accept the challenge.

The last section of this module is concerned with helping you to identify some of the perceptual distortions and measurement errors in informal testing. If formal testing is imperfect and imprecise, informal testing is even more so and must be categorized as fickle and rose-colored at times, harsh at other times, and sometimes even ridiculous. Making a test visible or explicit does not make the content reasonable, nor the criteria or circumstances just. It only makes it more manageable. It is not possible to list all the perceptual distortions of informal testing here, but a few examples are in order.

### PERCEPTUAL DISTORTIONS OF SELF-CONSTRUCTED TESTS

When you are testing yourself, acquiring mastery and identity in a new situation, you are prone to take feedback from others about your performance more seriously than if you were not testing yourself. This can be particularly problematic if the feedback is conflicting (that is, different people give you very different opinions), or if it does not fit your own view of your performance. Under nontesting circumstances, you can shrug off such conflicting feedback more easily. But under testing conditions you require resolution of conflicting views; you need reliable and usable information about your performance. You are seeking it and you are sensitive to it. This sensitivity may cause you to give *too* much weight to feedback that is not valid. Someone may comment on your performance without understanding the content or rationale for your actions. Since you are very sensitive to feedback, under testing conditions, it is wise to take extra effort to validate peoples' observations so that you are not using misinformation to judge your performance. Also it is reasonable to set limits on *what feedback* you will accept and under *what circumstances* you will consider information on your performance valid or reliable. For example, people may fall prey to the testing distortion of rating all performances alike. Thus, if they see you on a disorganized day, they may consider you to be generally disorganized, until they receive evidence to the contrary. If they judge one performance as excellent, then they are apt to judge future performance as excellent. If they judge one performance as poor, they are apt to judge other performances similarly, unless you can intervene and change their perception.

Sometimes, testing may take the form of a trial by fire, and there may well be times when you choose not to pass the test, or to barely pass it. For example, consider the following test described by one new graduate:

> In the beginning of my second month I was asked to work on the weekend by myself. I don't know why I was asked; there were plenty of nurses at that time. And I don't know why I accepted; I guess I just thought that I should make myself appear more self-confident. . . . We all talked about my being alone Saturday. In fact we were over at one nurse's house the night before for a drink, and we were laughing and talking about it. A couple of nurses said that they would call me the next day to see how I was doing. I had two orderlies and an LVN scheduled to work with me. And everyone said, "Wait til you meet this LVN!" I had never worked with her before, but she had a reputation for being impossible to work with. . . .
>
> The day started off badly. I was panicked! The report even started out bad because I was so scared, and I told the LVN before the report was finished. The ward was really busy that day. We had one active GI bleeder, and there was a man who was hallucinating and who was constantly getting out of bed. When I was pouring my meds this man came up and tried to strangle me! Several doctors were standing around and they pulled him away. After that I called the nursing office, and they sent up an orderly just to watch this one patient. Then the phone kept ringing. Two of the nurses called and asked me how I was doing. I really didn't have time to talk so I just said that I was busy and that I had to go.
>
> It was just a horrible day and I kept thinking: "Only three more hours . . . only two more hours . . . if I can just make it through." Toward the end of the shift the man who was hallucinating disconnected the blood tubing on the patient's bed next to him. When I went to change the tubing I ended up spilling the blood all over my uniform. That just finished up the day for me! I don't know if the nurses treated me differently nonverbally or whether they acted differently afterwards, but I felt braver. That's what changed. I figured that after I had lived through that day I could live through anything. I felt braver.

Do you think the above test was reasonable? Would you have chosen to pass it or not? How would you have handled the situation if you decided that you did not want to accept the test? What information might you have found out before accepting the weekend duty assignment that might have given you a better chance of passing the test and ensured that the patients would get reasonably adequate care?

## THE PROVING GROUND

There are no absolute answers to the above questions. Each individual must decide for herself. The important principle is that you must evaluate the test and the testing conditions. If they are unfair or unwarranted, you can devalue or discard them simply by not allowing them to define your identity or to be an evaluation of your performance.

Informal testing seems to be functional both on a personal level and on a social level. Therefore, it is doubtful that it *will* or should go away. Self-constructed tests give you information as to where you are in relation to where you want to be. Other-constructed tests tell you something about where the group wants you to be, and they also serve as membership or passage rites into the group. When you pass a group's informal tests, you move further along on your way to membership in that group, with all the rights, privileges, and obligations of membership. By analyzing the informal tests, you can pass them and gain membership without *dropping* your own values and identity. Once you are a member of the group, you are in a position to influence the group's informal testing.

In this module, "The Proving Ground", strategies for identifying both self-constructed and other-constructed tests in the work environment have been presented. Criteria for evaluating the informal tests have been discussed, and some of the perceptual distortions and measurement errors in informal testing have been described.

The purpose of this discussion has been to make the time of testing as constructive and growth producing as possible. The question is not whether newcomers *should* be tested but whether the tests are constructive and whether the new graduate has a good chance of passing the tests. Self- or other-constructed tests that strip you of your sense of worth and self-confidence are both unkind and wasteful. If you do not pass a test, it is a personal loss for you as well as for the patient and the health care system. Learn and adopt strategies to make both self-constructed and other-constructed tests visible and understandable. In this way, you can interpret your behavior to others, you can retain your own values, and/or you can choose new values or compromises rather than bending blindly to group expectations.

## REFERENCES

1. Argyle, M. and Rendon, A. "Self-Presentation and Competence," in L. Berkowitz (ed.), *Advances in Experimental Social Psychology*, Vol. 3. New York: Academic Press, 1967, pp. 79–98.
2. Dornbusch, S.M., and Scott, R.W. *Evaluation and the Exercise of Authority.* San Francisco: Jossey-Bass, 1975.
3. Friend, R.M. and Gilbert, J. Threat and fear of negative evaluation as determinants of locus of social comparison. *J. Pers.*, Vol. 41, No. 3. September, 1973, pp. 328–340.

## BIBLIOGRAPHY

Benner, P. and Benner, R.V. *The New Graduate: Perspectives, Practice and Promise.* LaJolla, California: The Coordinating Council for Education in Health Sciences for San Diego and Imperial Counties, 1975.

Erikson, E.H., *Childhood and Society.* New York: W.W. Norton, 1970.

Gergen, K.J. and Wishnov, B. Others' self-evaluations and interaction anticipated as determinants of self-presentation. *J. Pers. Soc. Psycho.*, Vol. 2, No. 3, 1965, pp. 348–358.

Kinch, J.W. "Experiments on Factors Related to Self-Concept Change," in J.G. Manis and B.N. Meltzer (eds.), *Symbolic Interaction: A Reader in Social Psychology.* Boston: Allyn & Bacon, 1972, pp. 262–268.

Kramer, M. *Reality Shock: Why Nurses Leave Nursing.* St. Louis: C.V. Mosby, 1974.

Kramer, M. and Schmalenberg, C.E. The first job—a proving ground. Basis for empathy development. *J. Nurs. Admin.*, Vol. 7, No. 1, 1977, pp. 12–20.

Schein, E.H. The first job dilemma. *Psych. Today*, Vol. 1, No. 10, 1968, pp. 28–37.

Schneider, D.J. and Turkat, D. Self-presentation Following Success or Failure: Defensive Self-esteem Models. *J. Pers.* Vol. 43, No. 1, March 1975, pp. 127–135.

Shrauger, S. and Patterson, M.B. Self-evaluation and the selection of dimensions for evaluating others. *J. Pers.*, Vol. 42, No. 4, December 1974, pp. 569–585.

Shibutani, T. "Reference Groups As Perspectives," in J.G. Manis and B.N. Meltzer (eds.), *Symbolic Interaction: A Reader in Social Psychology.* Boston: Allyn & Bacon, 1972, pp. 160–171.

# THE ELUSIVE QUEST

# Module 5

# Why is the
# Quest Elusive?

**INTRODUCTION**

As a new graduate nurse employed in a health care facility you have probably spent a great deal of time searching for the elusive answer to the question, "How am I doing?" Your thinking may have gone along these lines:

> Sometimes I wonder if anyone knows what I am doing! . . . That's probably not true. When I goofed and took the orders off the chart and sent the wrong slip to the lab and X-ray, I was told pretty quick that I did something wrong. . . . No one has sat down and had a conference with me since I left school. . . . How can I learn where I need to shape up if no one tells me? Maybe they are telling me but I just don't get the message. . . . I think I'm not hearing what I need to hear. . . .

What you're looking for is feedback. This program is about feedback. It attempts to show you how you can get an answer to your question, "How am I doing?" in the work setting. We will look at several dimensions of feedback: (1) your expectations of what it should be, (2) the various forms it takes in the work setting, (3) how to obtain what you need to know about your performance in the work setting, and (4) principles for providing feedback to others.

**EXPECTATIONS—SCHOOL**

Your past experiences are largely the source of your current expectations. In school, evaluation was usually a structured and formalized procedure. At the end of each clinical experience, your instructor held an evaluation conference with you. Predetermined criteria in the form of specific course objectives and clinical assessment tools guided you and your instructor in the evaluation. In addition to such conferences, there was other less structured, but ongoing feedback coming through to you on the clinical areas. You could predict with almost 100 percent accuracy that each time you performed a new procedure or wrote a care plan you would have a conference or receive written comments evaluating your work. This feedback ritual, as well as comments like, "Now tell me what you did," or "How could you have done that better?" were standard. Not long into your educational program, you began to expect feedback at certain intervals and occasions.

You could anticipate not only *when* you would receive feedback, but also the *kind* of feedback you would receive. In school, feedback tended to be "particularistic," that is, your instructor provided you with feedback on a specific skill or technique. For example, you received a complete rundown on how well you carried out sterile technique. The fact that your instructor actually observed you performing different activities allowed her to provide this firsthand, specific information to you. If you will reflect on the feedback you received in school, you will see that it basically fell into four classifications: positive (all good), negative (all bad), balanced (a mixture of positive and negative), and ambiguous (message or meaning unclear). The classification of feedback into one of these four categories is based on content, mode of delivery, or both. Sometimes what is being said is very positive but the way it is said cancels out the meaning of the words. At times, the opposite is true. The content is negative but the way it is said makes the content seem positive. Perhaps, presentation of samples of common feedback techniques utilized by nursing school instructors will help clarify this classification of feedback. As you read the techniques, some will probably sound familiar.

## Technique #1 SUPER NURSE

"Excellent! Very well done! I couldn't have done it better myself." You get all As or Bs on papers handed in, and your care plans receive comments like, "well done" and "very creative." You quickly get the message that you are very good and have little need to improve. Obviously, this is very positive feedback.

## Technique #2 BRUTAL BUT FRANK

"If you don't shape up and get that sterile technique right, you aren't going to make it." This is not a commonly used feedback technique, but one does see it occasionally. It is totally negative and is used primarily to scare the best out of you. . .and it is usually quite effective!

## Technique #3 THE QUARTERBACK SNEAK

"Well, I must say we have had an interesting six weeks. I imagine you are quite anxious to hear how you have been doing." (Oh boy! Here it comes! The instructor certainly picked the right word: ANXIOUS!) The content of the feedback can be positive or negative, but the withholding of the information for so long and the somewhat negative method of delivery tends to generate either profound relief or a negative rather than positive feeling.

You are relieved that you are finally getting some feedback, but because it has been held back so long, you have not been aware of ways in which you might have improved on your performance. This type of feedback is generally unsatisfying and ambiguous, particularly during the long period before the quarterback sneak. During this time, you were probably forced to rely on unclear, diffuse, nonverbal messages to get some clue as to the evaluation of your performance.

## Technique #4 MIRROR, MIRROR ON THE WALL

"Now tell me, how do you think you did?" Being humble or not wishing to have someone else tell you all the things you didn't do well, you begin to blurt out all the things you think were lacking in your performance. The instructor, not wanting you to feel totally crushed, tells you all the things she thinks you did well. Between the two of you an evaluation of your performance is compiled. This is balanced feedback, with you and the instructor providing the pros and cons.

## Technique #5 THE SANDWICH

"Now let's take a look at what you have been doing." (The *"let's"* is often a clue that she will talk and you will listen.) "Your organization was good, your sterile technique was excellent, but you really should be more conscientious about draping the patient. You did a fine job of cleaning up and your interpersonal communication was okay." The "but you should" is tucked in neatly between two layers of positive feedback. You have to lift up the edges of these two slices of bread to take a look at the meat and catch the negative comment. The net result is a semblance of both positive and negative feedback. However, the positive feedback is much greater than the negative, thus preventing this technique from being completely balanced.

**Technique #6 YES SIR! CAPTAIN, SIR! MA'AM! SIR!**

"Let's have a rundown of that procedure. You did this, this, and that well, and you need to work on this, this, and that." The technique seems more like a machinegun drill than an informative conference, but you *do* have a clear understanding of what you need to do. This is a balanced feedback technique, as you generally receive both kinds of information in this staccato mode of delivery. The mode of delivery may detract somewhat from the positive content.

These six feedback techniques are the ones used most frequently by instructors in schools of nursing. As you read the examples, you probably noticed that there are more positive and balanced feedback techniques than there are negative or ambiguous techniques. Positive, balanced, structured (or predictable) timing, first-hand character, specific nature and evaluation criteria are the qualities of the feedback in the school setting.

**EXPECTATIONS—WORK**

The feedback process in the work setting is quite different from that in the school setting. Until now, you probably have not had much experience with the kind of feedback provided in a work setting, and you have little or no experience with how to deal with it. As a student, you may have heard or seen some of the feedback provided by or to individuals in the work setting, but it didn't count much to you personally. Now, this feedback counts because it affects your concept of yourself as a nurse, your performance evaluation, and your ability to hold onto your job.

In the work setting, there are few predictables regarding feedback for the newcomer. A formalized time structure for evaluation usually does exist. However, it is not always operational. For example, many new graduates are told upon employment that a three-month evaluation of their progress will be performed—but it has now been seven months since you started and you still haven't seen any evaluation. The criteria to be used for the evaluation are often unknown to you. You received a job description, but it may not be very specific about your duties and responsibilities and even less specific about the actual behaviors to be performed.

As time goes by, a feedback pattern emerges. When you do something wrong, someone tells you P.D.Q. Eventually you conclude that when you are not being told about your mistakes, you must be doing all right. Logical; but not necessarily true. Sometimes the "degree of wrongness" or the "size of a mistake" determines whether you will be told about your error.

In the work setting, not only is the predictability of feedback different from school, but also the nature of the feedback differs. The feedback is primarily "global" in nature; the head nurse (or others) may comment, "You're doing a good job," but provide no specifics to clarify or support their general, global statement. Since a head nurse may not actually see you perform, she relies on other staff members to provide her with information. Her use of secondhand information contributes to the global nature of the feedback she gives you.

### Technique #1 NO NEWS IS GOOD NEWS

You come to work, do your thing, and go home. Absolutely nothing is said about your performance. This technique is widely used not only in health care facilities but in many other work settings. It is most often a form of positive feedback. When the silence is broken, you are usually in trouble for doing something wrong—therefore, no news is good news. However, you are never absolutely sure that "no news is good news." Therefore, this technique is ambiguous.

### Technique #2 THE FROWN

The eyes glare, the brows gather darkly, the posture stiffens, the teeth grit. She bears a striking resemblance to the "Big Nurse" of One Flew Over the Cuckoo's Nest[1]. The message seems to be that you or someone isn't doing well. If ever there was a time when looks could kill, this is it! There is no possibility of misinterpreting the message. It is negative feedback for sure! However, is the message meant for you or someone else? The uncertainty about whether this feedback is directed at you makes this technique ambiguous.

The feedback you receive at work falls into the same four basic categories as that in school: (1) positive, (2) negative, (3) balanced, and (4) ambiguous. Let's look at some of the techniques used in the work setting to provide you with feedback. (Please note: the techniques about to be presented are not specific to any one person. Feedback may come from the head nurse, supervisor, staff nurses, or other personnel on the unit.)

### Technique #3 THE SNAPBACK

You: "I really think that it would be a good idea to call Mr. Jones' doctor and have a conference this afternoon. Mr. Jones is having a hard time getting used to the idea of having 'his leg amputated'."

Head Nurse: "You can't even get your work done and get off the unit on time and you want a case conference?!"

The message is quite clear. You're not "cutting the mustard." This is, of course, negative feedback on your work performance, but the exact nature of what you have done wrong is unclear.

### Technique #4 THE BLUDGEONING (parallels BRUTAL BUT FRANK)

"You forgot to take the orders off the chart on Mrs. Smith last night; you didn't mix the IV properly; and your meds are not on time. I just can't understand this."

Clear, concise, and to the point. You are having difficulty in a number of work areas. You have an itemized list of your faults and you need to do something about them. The message is loud and clear, and (if you had any doubts) it is purely negative.

## Technique #5 THE HIDDEN AGENDA

"This all needs to be done by three o'clock."

There you stand with a really tough and heavy assignment. The thoughts tumble through your head. "What have I done to deserve so much work? And the toughest patients on the unit to boot! Boy, is she out to get me! I'm going to show her I can do it!" This is one of those ambiguous situations. To you, it looks like you are being punished for Heaven knows what. To the head nurse, this may well be a way of saying, "Hey, you are doing a good job. You can handle more difficult assignments and situations."

## Technique #6 WHAT NEXT??

"I never know if the patients are going to get their baths or not. I never know which doctor will be after me next because there are visitors in the rooms when there are no visiting hours. When the supervisor comes down the hall, all I can think of is, 'What this time?'"

Despite the apparent verbal and nonverbal expressions of exasperation, there is no indication that your overall performance is either good or bad. The verbal comments seem to indicate that some things you are doing are causing the head nurse difficulty, yet there is no indication that you should stop doing what you are doing. Of course, there is also no direct message that you should continue. Clearly, this message is ambiguous. You don't know if you are being told to stop doing what you are doing, or that although what you do creates some difficulty, it is all right to continue doing it. It is difficult to know what to do with this type of feedback.

## Technique #7 SO, WHO CARES??

Your evaluation reads: "Your organizational skills are very good. Your patients are off to surgery on time and prepared well. Your charts are in order and you are finished with report and off duty on time." From the head nurse's point of view you are doing well. From your point of view, the evaluation is telling you things you already know, and things you are not particularly looking for in an evaluation of your performance. You want to see something in it about your care plans, your direct patient care, which you feel is quite individualized—and what did you get? Miss Efficiency Plus. So, who cares?

The head nurse may see this type of evaluation as a very positive one. For you, it lacks comments on things you consider very important. This type of feedback leaves you with mixed feelings—relieved and pleased that all is going well and yet thinking, "So what?" However, the message and intent of the feedback are positive.

These are a sampling of the techniques used in the work setting to provide you with feedback. As you reflect on the techniques that were presented, you will note that the feedback tends to be heavily weighted toward the ambiguous and negative types. For the most part, it seems that you only hear when things are going poorly, and the rest of the time you are not really sure how you are doing.

The change from a direct, specific, and predictable feedback system to one that tends to be indirect, global, and unpredictable makes it difficult for you to be certain about how you are doing in the work setting. You must begin to identify how others in the work setting are providing you with feedback, just as you learned to identify the modes of feedback used in school. Because the feedback does tend to be indirect, global, and unpredictable, it is more difficult to perceive exactly what the "message" is in the work setting.

The following Feedback Identification Exercise may help you become more aware of feedback in the work setting. It may heighten your awareness of the feedback techniques utilized by your co-workers.

## FEEDBACK IDENTIFICATION EXERCISE

The purpose of this exercise is to capture the essence of the style or manner in which your co-workers provide you with feedback. Identifying the usual feedback techniques of your co-workers will allow you to establish realistic feedback expectations for yourself in your work setting. Observe the head nurse and others on the unit. Then either write the answers to or think about the following questions:

1. Is the content of the feedback given to others and to yourself usually positive, negative, balanced, or ambiguous?

2. What is each person's style or technique of giving feedback?

3. Does the combined content and technique generally yield positive, negative, balanced, or ambiguous feedback?

You may wish to complete this exercise now or continue on to the end of this section before you complete it.

## FEEDBACK DIFFERENCES: WHY DO THEY EXIST?

Differences between school and work feedback do exist. There are three main reasons for the differences: (1) value systems, (2) institutional role expectations, and (3) behavioral reward systems. Each of the three factors will be discussed separately.

What one chooses to give feedback about is reflective of one's values—what one considers to be important enough to act upon. In a later section of this book, "Walk A Mile In My Shoes," we will present an in-depth discussion of values. At this point, we'll only briefly describe why value systems create differences in feedback.

One of the major organizing values prevalent among instructors in schools of nursing is the delivery of comprehensive, individualized patient care. Thus, instructors generally provide feedback on matters related to individualized care. You probably received comments on your care plans and nursing histories—the more detailed, creative, and individualized, the better. In caring for patients, you were expected to meet their every need. You were to provide the TLC, the physical care, the medications, and the teaching, as well as taking care of the doctor and the chart. Most of the feedback you received in school evaluated your ability to deliver comprehensive, individualized care to each patient. This feedback was a logical result of the values of the instructors.

Head nurses have quite a different value system. The predominant value of the head nurse is the delivery of the best possible care to all the patients on the unit. This does not generally translate into comprehensive, individualized care for each patient. The head nurse is concerned about your abilities to manage personnel and emergencies as well as patients. You are expected to be neat, prompt, composed, responsible, and cooperative in the delivery of care. It is necessary that you delegate care and not do it all yourself. Because of the concerns emanating from the value system of the head nurse, you will find that most of the feedback you now receive is related to the efficient delivery of care to large numbers of patients. Thus, the differences in the value system of the instructor and of the head nurse result in different kinds of feedback.

Differences in feedback also result from institutional role expectations. In any organization, there exist certain role positions such as those held by the head nurse or faculty member. The organization has formal expectations of any individual who happens to occupy the position. These formal expectations take the form of job descriptions, rules, regulations, and guidelines. In addition to these formal expectations, there are informal expectations in the form of norms. These norms are the informal standards of conduct that develop within a group and guide the actions of its members. Instructors and head nurses are guided by both formal and informal role expectations in the performance of their duties. However, the expectations guiding the respective groups are different.

Both the formal and informal standards guiding the instructor emphasize providing students with feedback. The institution requires that the instructor provide grades and, if necessary, that she justify those grades. Furthermore, norms among instructors call for the use of evaluation tools, and prescribe just how and when these tools are to be utilized. For example, a group of nursing instructors will frequently determine the standards a student must achieve in passing medications before she is allowed to proceed in the instructor's absence. An instructor must inform the student of her progress (i.e., provide her with feedback) in this aspect of her learning so that the student will know whether she should call the instructor when she needs to give medications.

The instructor is also guided by the formal and informal expectation that she help the student become a nurse. Achievement of this goal necessitates feedback to the student. This goal takes precedence over other tasks an instructor may wish to accomplish. For example, an instructor may plan to go over some nursing care plans that students have written while she is supervising her students in the clinical area. However, as she gets started, one of the students calls to have her assist with starting an intravenous infusion. The instructor puts off her own goal to assist, observe, and provide the student with feedback. Although care plans are important, they are not as important as the instructor's given task of assisting the student acquire the skills of a nurse.

Contrast the expectations for the instructor role with the formal and informal expectations of the head nurse role. The organization wants the head nurse to manage the unit in such a way that the maximum staff effort is put forth to provide the best possible care for the patients within the institution's rules and regulations. Within the scope of the head nurse's role expectations is the provision of a yearly evaluation on her staff. The evaluations may be more frequent for new staff members. The norm established by the head nurse peer group is that required evaluations be done, but between evaluations, little emphasis is given to providing staff members with ongoing feedback. However, there is an informal expectation that if a staff member is making mistakes or errors, then she must be given feedback to correct the problem.

Just as the instructor is guided by her institution's expectations, so too the head nurse is guided by the expectation that she will manage her unit in such a way that all the patients get the best possible care. In order to meet this expectation, a head nurse must accomplish certain tasks. She has responsibilities to other departments, to the unit staff, to the patients, and to nursing administration. The head nurse has rounds to make, orders to check, and shift report to do for the supervisor. In case of difficulties, the head nurse is available to assist you and other staff members. However, the expectations of the institution do not allow the head nurse to give you the amount of time and attention that the instructor gave you. Performance of her own duties prevents her from giving you as much attention as you got from your instructor, and thus she has less opportunity to provide you with feedback.

Another set of role expectations influences the provision of feedback—student role expectations and staff nurse role expectations. The student is expected to learn. In order to learn, the student must receive appropriate feedback from instructors. The role of the staff nurse requires that you provide care to patients in accordance with your job description. The institution expects you to *know* the parameters of your work and to know how to do it. This expected competence removes the necessity for frequent feedback. Because the student is learning to acquire competence, she needs frequent feedback on the progress she is making.

In addition to institutional role expectations, the behavioral reward system operating in an institution also affects feedback. People tend to do those things that bring positive rewards or sanctions and to avoid those things that bring negative rewards or sanctions. For example, an instructor who is brought before the school grievance committee by a student to protest a grade on the basis of lack of feedback and opportunity to improve will most certainly receive negative sanctions from faculty peers as well as from the school administration. To avoid this in the future, it is likely that the instructor will increase feedback to students. On the other hand, an instructor who meets the formal and informal expectations of peers and students will likely receive positive evaluations and perhaps a promotion or raise in salary. The desire for rewards makes it probable that the instructor will continue to give feedback. Thus, the possibility of either positive or negative behavioral sanctions increases the probability of feedback.

The principle of behavioral rewards holds in the work setting, but there are few formal or informal expectations in relation to providing feedback. Low expectations for a behavior decrease the probability of recognition for that behavior. As the probability of recognition for a behavior decreases, so too does the probability that the behavior will occur. Thus, less feedback is provided in the work setting.

Differences in *amount* of feedback are not the only differences between school and work. The feedback you receive in the work setting tends to be less specific, more indirect, and less predictable than that you received in school. The techniques used to provide you with "the message" are different. There are a variety of reasons for the differences. The three reasons discussed here were the different (1) value systems, (2) institutional role expectations, and (3) behavioral reward systems.

In and of itself, the difference in the two feedback systems is not a problem. A problem occurs when one moves from one system to the other. The new system is unfamiliar and hard to understand. In order to obtain the needed feedback, the newcomer must learn the new feedback system. "Why Is The Quest Elusive" has pointed out the differences between the school feedback and the work feedback systems. Understanding these differences is a first step in learning about the type of feedback you are now encountering. The next two modules will show you what the new feedback looks like, and how you can identify the feedback being given, as well as how you can obtain feedback from others and provide others with feedback.

**REFERENCE**

1.  Kesey, K. *One Flew Over the Cuckoo's Nest*. New York: Viking, 1962

# Module 6

# Disguises of the Quest

Once upon a time in the land of Fuzz, King Aling called in his cousin Ding and commanded, "Go ye out into all of Fuzzland and find me the goodest of men, whom I shall reward for his goodness."

"But how will I know one when I see one?" asked the Fuzzy.

"Why, he will be *sincere*," scoffed the king, and whacked off a leg for his impertinence.

So, Ding the Fuzzy limped out to find a good man. But soon he returned, confused and empty-handed.

"But how will I know one when I see one?" he asked again.

"Why he will be *dedicated*," grumbled the king, and whacked off another leg for his impertinence.

So the Fuzzy hobbled away once more to look for the goodest of men. But again he returned, confused and empty-handed.

"But how will I know one when I see one?" he pleaded.

"Why, he will have *internalized his growing awareness*," fumed the king, and whacked off another leg for his impertinence.

So the Fuzzy, now on his last leg, hopped out to continue his search. In time, he returned with the wisest, most sincere, and dedicated Fuzzy in all of Fuzzland, and stood him before the king.

"Why, this man won't do at all," roared the king. "He is much too thin to suit me." Whereupon, he whacked off the last leg of the Fuzzy, who fell to the floor with a squishy thump.

The moral of this fable is that. . .*if you can't tell one when you see one, you may wind up without a leg to stand on.* *

---

*From the book, *Goal Analysis* by Robert F. Mager, Copyright © 1972 by Fearon Publishers, Inc. Reprinted by permission of Fearon Publishers, Inc.

As a new graduate searching for feedback, you may find yourself in the same predicament: "You can't tell one when you see one." You may not be equipped with the skills to identify and interpret the feedback you receive about your performance. You look for feedback, but it isn't there in a form that you recognize, so that frequently you may not even see it. To recognize the feedback that is being provided, you need to begin to look from a new perspective. A look at the various providers of feedback and the forms that feedback often takes in the work world will help you gain this new perspective.

Feedback can be broken down into its component parts. To do this, you should ask, "Who are the providers?" "What do they provide?" "When do they provide it?" "How does it come" "How can I tell one when I see one?"

## PROVIDERS OF FEEDBACK

Let's begin by determining who are the providers of feedback in the work setting. Virtually everyone you deal with in the organization can and probably does provide you with feedback. Those with whom you work most closely, of course, provide the most feedback. These are the physicians, your head nurse, other staff nurses, the aides, the orderlies, and the patients. It is from this constellation of individuals that you can obtain your feedback. No single individual can be labelled *the* provider of feedback as the instructor was in school. The head nurse will probably be the major person to provide formal feedback, but ongoing feedback comes from all sources.

What do these sources provide in the way of feedback? The kind of feedback they provide will vary according to their expectations, status, and authority. For example, the feedback given by physicians is different from that provided by aides. The best way to examine the feedback provided is to look at each provider separately.

### The Head Nurse

The head nurse, more than anyone else, replaces the instructor as the individual responsible for providing formal feedback. Most head nurses comment primarily on your efficiency and organization, your ability to take responsibility, get the work done, and handle things well in crises and emergencies. The head nurse is concerned with your ability to manage large numbers of patients, personnel, and technical tasks. In addition, she frequently provides feedback in the area of hospital policies and procedures.

### Physicians

Without a doubt, physicians provide feedback. Usually, their feedback is related to the physical and technical aspects of patient care. For example, the physician provides feedback on how well you are following through with his medical plan of treatment. In addition, the physician provides feedback on his view of your competence as a nurse. Your interpersonal relationship with the physician gives him an indication of how you are filling the role of a nurse as he sees it.

### Staff Nurses

Staff nurses are literally a gold mine of feedback about your interpersonal behavior. They give you constant messages about your acceptance on the unit. They can also provide feedback on technical skills, but their feedback is concerned mostly with their perception of your competence and acceptability as a nurse.

### The Aides and Orderlies

This group provides feedback on your performance of technical tasks and procedures and on how fairly they feel you treat them. There is also feedback on how you do things in comparison with others on the unit and how well you are carrying your share of the work load.

### The Patients

Patients provide feedback about you as a member of the organization and about you as an individual. Because you are the individual in the organization closest to the patient, praise or criticism about other departments, such as X-ray, lab, or dietary, or about physicians, is often leveled at you. The remarks may not relate directly to you or to matters under your control, but you are the hospital staff member the patient most often sees.

The patient also gives you feedback about you as a particular nurse providing either "good" or "bad" care to him. In both areas, the feedback usually reflects how comfortable the patient's hospital stay has been.

These are five major groups providing feedback. Obviously, there are others who provide some limited feedback. Each group provides a special kind of feedback content. However, in such areas as competence, it seems as if everyone has something to say to you!

### WHEN TO EXPECT FEEDBACK

In the work setting there is no specific time when you can expect feedback. The best rule is: *Be prepared for feedback at all times.* There are, however, certain times when you are more likely to receive feedback. These are:

1. Immediately following a change of shift report
2. Immediately following a report to the head nurse
3. While making rounds with a physician or immediately following the head nurse's rounds with a physician
4. When you ask questions

5.  Whenever you suggest performance of a procedure or duty different from the usual way of doing things
6.  When you make out patient care assignments
7.  When you ask others to do something for you
8.  When you give overt, direct feedback to others

### WHAT DOES FEEDBACK LOOK LIKE?

Feedback comes in a variety of verbal and nonverbal forms in the work setting. Earlier, several forms (the frown, the hidden agenda) of feedback were described. Feedback can take many other forms as well. These forms of feedback seem to cross the lines of all provider groups and are not particular to any one group. Let's take a look at some of them.

#### Grumbling

This consists of chronic complaints that are never aimed specifically at you, but which always make you feel uneasy. Some such comments follow:

"Why do *I* always get the toughest assignments?" "Are *you* my team leader today?" "We sure seem to be having a lot of trouble with the surgical patients today." "I don't suppose we will have more than one coffee break today." "Sure can't count on any help with my patients today." "The desk is always so much harder to handle when I have new graduates as team leaders." The litany could go on, but you probably have a feel for the "under the breath" discontent of the staff transmitted in the above statements. Often, this is the way staff tell you that you are not managing your share of the work properly and you aren't giving them fair work assignments.

#### Questioning

Both negative and positive feedback is transmitted through questions. There may be a steady flow of questions about your performance: "Well, did you...?" "Can I help you with...?" "Does Mr. Smith need...?" "When was the last time...?" "Are you sure that's right, I've never seen it done that way before." You feel as though everyone is keeping track of what you are doing and that this reflects the staff's doubts about your abilities. On the other hand, they may ask for your help: "How do I go about...?" "I'm having a problem with Mr. Gray, could you...?" "What should I do about this?" Questions of this type usually indicate that others see you as knowledgeable and able to help.

#### Requesting

In this form, feedback can be either positive or negative. You may have physicians requesting that their patients be cared for by you, or head nurses transferring or assigning patients to your team. You may find patients requesting you or your team to care for them. After you have been off a day or so on another assignment, patients may comment that they missed you. Team members may request to remain on your team. This is all very positive and a good indication that the individuals you work with, as well as those you care for, see you as competent and capable.

Special requests may have the opposite meaning. You may find physicians asking that their patients not be cared for by you, or head nurses always giving you the team with patients requiring the least amount of care. Patients may request not to be assigned to you or comment that they have never had such poor care. Team members may request other teams or manipulate the schedule so that they never have the same lunch or coffee break schedule as you. Obviously, this is negative feedback.

There is another type of special request that is positive feedback on your performance. Your co-workers may ask you to do things that you are particularly good at. You may be asked to check on a patient whose catheter is plugged because you always seem to have success with such problems or you may be asked to talk to a patient's family because they are having difficulty adjusting to the patient's disease. This is pretty clear feedback that you are recognized as having strengths in these areas and are respected by the staff.

### Cluing

When this begins to happen, you will probably feel that you are really finding out what is going on. The staff begins to provide you with inside information about the unit. A staff nurse gives you the word about "which doctors you call on nights and which you go ahead and give the med and they'll cover you in the morning." Other staff members explain which of the rules and policies are followed and which are ignored or bent a little. By letting you in on the "back region" of the unit, the staff indicates that it accepts you as part of the unit group. If cluing is absent, it may mean that they do not think you fit in with the group.

### Doing

By "doing," we mean that other staff members perform tasks for you. For example, a patient on your team needs a nasogastric tube and another staff member goes to insert the tube even though you indicate that you will do it. Or a patient on your team has an IV running and you bring in the next bottle to be hung and leave it on the bedside stand until it is time to hang it. When you come back to the room to hang the bottle, another staff member has brought in a bottle and changed it already. "Doing" is a very difficult form of feedback to interpret. Are others telling you that your ability is questionable, that you aren't doing the tasks at the appropriate times, or are they just trying to be helpful? Usually, if any feedback is intended, it is negative.

### Redoing

In this situation, you are going about your work and you change a dressing or make a bed and right after you have completed the task, another staff member comes along and redoes it. This may well be feedback that you have not done the job correctly or to their satisfaction.

### Planting

One of the providers who cannot tell you directly that you have done a good job or a poor job tells another person about your performance. The provider handpicks an individual who she is quite sure will see to it that you hear the news. Although this is generally positive, it can also be negative feedback.

### Side-Stepping

Again we have an individual who cannot bring himself to provide direct feedback to you. However, he is a little less subtle than the "planter." This individual makes sure that you are within earshot, then comments loudly to someone that you are doing either a good or a poor job. For example, a head nurse tells the supervisor what a good job the new graduates are doing, knowing that you are in the chart room and can overhear her comment. The key component here is that you are in a position where you cannot miss the feedback.

### Displacing

The head nurse, knowing that you have been caring for Mrs. James, says to you, "Dr. Jones commented on the sloppy dressing Mrs. James has on. Is there something you can do about it?" In this situation, the head nurse agrees with the doctor but cannot verbalize her agreement and provide you with direct feedback. Therefore, she uses the doctor as the main feedback agent. This constitutes displacing. If the head nurse did not agree with the doctor, she probably would not convey the message to you, or when she did convey the message, she would let you know that she did not agree. This can be a way of providing positive as well as negative feedback, depending on the situation.

### Telling

An example is probably not needed here. A provider tells you directly what he thinks of your performance.

### Respecting

This refers to the dispositional stance you perceive in your co-workers. Do they treat you as an equal? An inferior? When people talk to you, do they seem to enjoy it or do they talk to you only because they have to? Do people feel free to ask questions of you and you of them? All of these items can be indicative of the amount of respect accorded you by co-workers. These items also reflect the "give and take" of your relationships with others. It is the "give and take" that indicates respect. Such "give and take" occurs, for example, when a physician waits to make rounds with you because you and he can discuss his patients—it does *not* occur when a physician who always likes a nurse on rounds with him goes alone if you are the only nurse available.

### Assigning

Assignments can be an indication of how well you are performing. For example, if you are assigned to patient care and then switched to the functional assignment of giving meds, it may indicate that you are considered more efficient at giving meds than doing patient care. The feedback is not necessarily based upon the quality of your patient care, but rather on the amount of time it takes you to perform the task.

### Ignoring

When you ask a co-worker, "How am I doing?" she can respond by praising you on how well you are doing or by ignoring the question. If there is an outpouring of praise, sit back and relax, you are doing well. If she ignores the question, or changes the subject, you could be in trouble. The ignoring response may mean, "I have nothing good to say, so I won't say anything."

### Hearing

At times in report or at coffee, a provider will comment on another's behavior or actions. "That isn't appropriate to this report." or "Don't tell me she's trying to change the P.M. routine." This can provide you with feedback on acceptable and unacceptable behavior without you ever having to enact the behavior yourself.

In this discussion of some of the forms in which feedback is presented, most of the examples involve the head nurse. It must be emphasized, however, that no form of feedback is specific to any single group of providers. Various groups of providers may use the same forms of feedback.

These are not all the possible forms that feedback can take, nor are all the behaviors described always intended as feedback. A number of you are probably quite paranoid at this time, thinking about all the feedback you have received and were unaware of. You are probably trying to fit different verbal and nonverbal messages from others into the various feedback forms. It is important that you begin to be aware of others' behavior and their possible messages. But remember, not every behavior described here as a form of feedback is necessarily intended as feedback. If every behavior described is not always feedback, how will you know when and if it is feedback?

**HOW TO IDENTIFY FEEDBACK**

You can identify feedback by systematically observing, storing, and sorting knowledge about an individual's pattern of behavior and about the circumstances in which the behavior occurred. A process useful in identifying feedback behavior involves the following steps:

1. Observe the behavior and the circumstances in which it occurred.
2. Remember the behavior.
3. Recall the behavior and the circumstances when you see the behavior again.
4. Extrapolate the recurring theme of the behavior and circumstances.
5. Find the meaning of the recurring theme.

The process will be described in detail. It is difficult to do at first, but it becomes easier with use.

### Observing the Behavior

There are two concepts embodied here, cue sensitivity and perceptual vigilance[1]. To improve your ability to observe behavior, you need an understanding of these two concepts.

*Cue sensitivity* refers to the ability to select out of the total configuration of stimuli available, those which have inferential meaning for the way someone else is structuring reality. Whenever you are interacting with another, that person does and says things that are important to him. You must learn to identify these things and make accurate inferences about what they mean to the other. Accurate interpretation of behavior increases your chances of obtaining important feedback. It sounds easy, but the problem is that the meaning things have for *others* is not necessarily the meaning they have for you. For example, when the head nurse says, "I ordered the cath tray for you," she may well be saying, "You are not doing your job properly." When she says it, you may not get that meaning at all. To you it is something she did for you that wasn't really necessary. You would have done it later, but it was nice of her. The point is that unless you look at what the other person is *really* saying, you may miss the feedback that is being provided. Therefore, when you interact with others, you must ask yourself, "What might this mean from the other person's point of view and what does it mean to me?" If there is no apparent significance in the behavior, tuck it away in the back of your mind for the time being. One of the benefits of this approach is that the time spent analyzing an event for meaning imprints the event in your mind. If a similar event occurs again you will be more likely to remember it.

The other concept, *perceptual vigilance*, refers to a willingness to accept incoming stimuli without making value judgments on them. In other words, it means being open and objective about the stimuli. This is very difficult. When we observe, we look for those situations and behaviors that will confirm what we expect or want to see. Perceptual vigilance calls for attention to the full range of stimuli, with as little distortion as possible. Perceptual vigilance can be maximized by being very descriptive.

When you are involved in an encounter, carefully observe what happens. Afterwards, describe the situation to yourself. What did the actors look like? (facial expression, gestures, body posture?) What did they say? (their words, not your interpretation of their words?) What was the quality of the voice? (slow, fast, sharp, smooth?) What were the *feelings* you heard? What happened *preceding* the encounter? How did you feel after the encounter and what made you feel that way? Where did the encounter take place? Describe in as much depth and detail as you can all the elements of the encounter. If you look at the situation in this way, the scope and objectivity of your observations should increase. Increasing the scope and objectivity of your observations, as well as taking the other's meaning into consideration, will prepare you to perceive meaning in behavior.

### Remembering the Behavior

Remembering behavior is necessary if you are to make meaning out of your observations. Your associations on your unit are long-term. Many times feedback messages are so interspersed with other material that the connections are not immediately apparent[2]. It is only when a phrase or behavior is repeated that it takes on meaning. For example, the head nurse mentions that she ordered supplies for you. If she does this just once, it may mean nothing, but if, on another occasion, she tells you that she ordered supplies for you, something is going on. If you forget that you were told the same thing once before, then the second time around holds no meaning for you. You have missed the head nurse's message. The message contains feedback about her expectations of your performance. You cannot afford to miss too many of these messages. It contributes to the head nurse's frustration and also to yours — she cannot understand why you are not getting the message and you don't know what she is driving at. It is vital that you learn to commit to memory the general behavioral patterns of your co-workers.

### Recalling the Behavior and the Circumstances

This requires bringing back into conscious awareness the behaviors and circumstances that you have observed and committed to memory. You find yourself saying, "Oh, I remember hearing that before," or, "This seems to have a familiar ring to it." When you recall the behavior, reconstruct the previous situation that was similar to the present encounter. Then you need to analyze the present situation as outlined in the section, *Observing the Behavior.*

If the present encounter does not seem familiar, you should reconstruct past encounters and compare it to them. There may be times when the relationship between events is not apparent until they are carefully compared to one another. For example, a nurse aide tells you that Mr. Jones needs something for pain. About twenty minutes later, as you are going to him with the medication, she again says that Mr. Jones is in pain. Two weeks ago, the head nurse told you that she ordered the cath tray for you. These events do not seem related; they do not even involve the same actors. However, both actors are giving you a similar message. The message from both parties should tell you that there are expectations as to *when* you are to perform certain tasks. The aide wants you to know that when she says someone has pain, you are to respond immediately. The head nurse is letting you know that when you use supplies, you are to reorder immediately. Both messages contain feedback about the *time sequence* of your action. Such encounters may occur on the same day, or they may be weeks apart, and unless you reconstruct and compare them, you will miss the similarities between them. It is just as important that you reconstruct and analyze situations when there is *no* ring of familiarity as when there *is* a ring of familiarity.

Recalling the behavior and circumstances allows you to reconstruct those things you have seen and remembered. This prepares you to move on to the next step in the process—extrapolating the recurring themes of the behavior.

### Extrapolating the Recurring Themes of Behaviors and Circumstances

The process of extrapolating recurring themes is begun by using your descriptive analysis of various incidents to compare the incidents on all dimensions and then note the similarities. You can construct a column describing each incident and then compare the columns. The easiest way to understand the process is to do it with the examples provided about the nurse's aide and the head nurse.

When you have the two (or more) events described, you can ask questions. The questions you should ask are the following:

1. Were the main actors the same or of the same status?
2. Were their nonverbal expressions the same? In what ways?
3. Who were the other actors?
4. What were their reactions?
5. Was the subject matter of the comments the same or similar? In what ways?
6. Were the individuals commented about the same or similar? (i.e., Mr. Jones is a patient; I'm on staff)
7. Were the events precipitating the encounter the same? In what ways?
8. Did the encounters take place in similar areas?
9. Were the feelings expressed the same? In what ways?
10. Were my reactions the same? In what ways?

| QUESTIONS | COLUMN A | COLUMN B |
|---|---|---|
| The actors? | Nurse aide | Head nurse |
|  | Face grimly set | Intent, not smiling |
|  | Hands on hips, back straight, feet firmly planted on floor | Sitting, legs crossed |
| Voice quality? | Fast and sharp | Quiet, pointed |
| Any other actors? | No | No |
| Reaction of other actors? | — | — |
| What was said? | "Mr. Jones is in pain" | "I ordered the cath tray for you" |
| What preceded the encounter? | Twenty minutes before, she said Mr. Jones needed pain med | I had taken cath tray from supply cupboard, done cath, and did not re-order supply. |
| Where did encounter take place? | In hall on way to Mr. Jones' room | At nurses' station desk |
| Feelings heard? | Irritation and anger | Matter of fact reporting, no anger or distress |
| My reaction? | I don't know what she's so miffed about. I came as soon as I finished with Mrs. Lee | Hey, that was kind of nice. It wasn't necessary; I would have done it later on |

If you ask these questions about the situations outlined, you can see that the similarity lies in the precipitating event. You did not respond immediately to the aide's request for Mr. Jones' pain medication; you did not re-order the cath tray immediately after taking one. In both situations, a lapse of time is apparent. By comparing the two events, you can see that you were being given feedback about appropriate time sequence. You have extrapolated recurrent themes from observed situations.

### Finding Meaning of the Recurring Themes

To find the meaning of the extrapolated themes, you must have some knowledge of the persons involved in the situation and of the functioning of the unit. You need a baseline of data with which to compare what you are seeing and hearing to detect meaning. The data base is gathered over time through use of the four steps we have discussed. As you get more and more information, things begin to fall into place. It is this "falling into place" that lets you make meaning of the behavior and events that you see.

Let's look at a way to facilitate this process of linking emerging data and themes. The best way is to ask a series of questions of the baseline data. Let's take the situations analyzed previously and ask the questions that will help you find the meaning of the recurring themes.

1.  *What is the theme or issue that I have identified?*

The issue as identified in the aide-medication situation was the time sequencing of your behavior. The same issue was apparent in the head nurse supply situation. So, the recurring theme is, "What is the appropriate time interval for responding to specific events?"

2.  *Are there any rules, regulations, or norms on this unit already in existence which can tell me how to respond to or handle this kind of situation?*

There are no rules regarding how quickly you give a pain medication when it is requested, but you do know that staff members usually give the medication as soon as it is requested. So there is a norm for when to give the medication. Regarding supplies, there is a rule that says you are to reorder supplies as you use them.

3.  *If norms and standards exist, what is their history? Where did they come from and why?*

It is likely that if you know of the existence of norms and their history, you will follow them. Often, they are not known to you. The norm about giving medication as soon as it is requested developed because people forgot to give the medication if they did not respond immediately and the aides caught flak from the patients if the medication did not come immediately. This resulted in some very unhappy aides and equally unhappy patients. So nurses decided it was best to respond immediately. The rule regarding immediate replacement of supplies could possibly have resulted from an incident at another time when an IV needle was needed for a cardiac arrest and supplies had not been replaced. The lack of that IV might have resulted in the loss of a patient's life. Since that time, the rule for immediate replacement of supplies has been in effect.

4.  *Did my actions violate or ignore the norms?*

There is no question; in both instances violations occurred.

5.  *What are the consequences of my actions for myself? For the other actor?*

The consequences for myself are two-pronged—those resulting if I *do* respond immediately and those resulting if I *don't* respond immediately If I do respond immediately, the aide is happy, the work I was doing may take more time, and the patient gets quicker pain relief. If I don't respond immediately, the aide is unhappy, the work I was doing is completed sooner, and the patient waits for pain relief. If I respond immediately, the consequences for the aide are that the patient is satisfied and she may continue her work. If I don't respond immediately, the patient is unhappy and the aide must ask again for the medication.

In the head nurse-supply situation the consequences are that it will take me a few minutes longer to get back to the patient if I order now, and the head nurse will remain satisfied with my performance. If I don't reorder immediately, it will take me a few minutes less to get back to the patient, and the head nurse will be dissatisfied with my performance.

6. *Which of the consequences of my actions are more harmful?*

In the aide-medication situation, if I respond immediately, I have an aide who is happy and thus more likely to cooperate with me in the future, and a patient who is relieved of pain and thus more able to rest and recover. The only negative feature is that my work is interrupted. On the other hand, if I don't respond immediately, the aide will be less willing to cooperate with me in the future and the patient's recovery may be slowed. The positive feature is that my work is complete. When I weigh the consequences, the more harmful ones seem to result if I don't respond immediately. In the head nurse-supply situation, if I respond immediately, the reordering is complete, the head nurse can continue with her own work, and I'm a little bit slower getting back to the patient. If I don't respond immediately, the supply is not reordered, the head nurse interrupts her work, and I'm quicker to get back to the patient. Of course, the head nurse may also be quite unhappy and the performance evaluation may say something about my disregard for rules. You weigh the consequences; decide which is more serious.

7. *Is this the usual pattern of behavior for myself? For the other actor?*

Any unusual behavior on your part or on the part of others is indicative of something. Whether the behavior is indicative of feedback or personal difficulties can only be determined by further investigation.

8. *If the behavior of either person is unusual, what might be contributing to the unusual behavior?*

Factors that could be contributing to the unusual behavior might be pressure on the aide from the patient, pressure on the aide because of personal problems, pressure on you to get your work done, etc. You need to stop and take a look at what these factors might be so that you can understand the meaning of the feedback, if in fact any feedback is intended.

9. *Have you ignored or assaulted the important beliefs of the other person in this situation?*

It may be that you have disregarded the important beliefs of the other. For example, it may be important to the aide to help keep the patient comfortable, since this brings rewards from the patient. When you don't respond immediately, you disregard what is important to the aide. The same is true with reordering supplies. If the head nurse believes that her unit should always be prepared for an emergency so that things run smoothly and the patient does well, you disregard her beliefs by not replacing the supplies.

10. *What are the possible interpretations of the behavior?*

List all the possibilities suggested by the answers to the previous questions.

    a. You have violated a norm.

    b. Your behavior is different and you are getting feedback that this behavior is not as acceptable as your usual behavior.

    c. Your behavior is the same, the other's behavior is different; she must be having a bad day.

Once you have the answers to the questions and have drawn conclusions as to the possible meanings of the behavior, you have several options.

    1. You may choose to operate on the conclusions you have drawn.

    2. You may elect to check out with the other person the correctness of your conclusion.

    3. You may check out your conclusions with another individual on the unit.

    4. You may choose to gather more data about the person to validate your conclusion.

Of course, electing to operate upon your own conclusions is the riskiest of all options. You continue to operate without any feedback about (1) how well you have interpreted behavior and (2) what the behavior was really meant to convey to you. All the other options involve eliciting additional feedback. This will be dealt with in the next module of this program.

It takes time to familiarize oneself with the feedback identification process presented here. A feedback identification exercise is included to enable you to practice the process. A note of caution—not all behavior is meant to convey feedback to you. The idea of the feedback identification process is to make you alert and sensitive to the behavior patterns of others so that you will not miss important feedback when it is sent your way.

### FEEDBACK IDENTIFICATION EXERCISE

For the next couple of weeks, observe and describe two or three encounters in which you are involved. Utilize the feedback identification process to analyze these encounters for feedback. Blank process worksheets are included to assist you in this analysis.

The feedback identification exercise completes this module on the forms that feedback can take. In this discussion, we looked at the providers of feedback, what they provide, when they provide it, how it comes, and how will you know it when you see it. With this information, you should find yourself better equipped to recognize feedback in the work setting.

The next module of this program will deal with: 1) strategies for eliciting feedback so that inferences and interpretations that you make about the behavior of others may be validated; and, 2) strategies for providing feedback to others in a constructive way.

**FEEDBACK IDENTIFICATION EXERCISE**

COLUMN A                    COLUMN B

The actors

Voice quality

Any other actors

Reactions of other actors

What was said

What preceded the encounter

Where did encounter take place

Feelings expressed (heard)

My reaction

---

1. Were the main actors the same or of the same status?

2. Were their nonverbal expressions the same? In what ways?

3. Who were the other actors in the situation?

4. What were their reactions?

5 Was the subject matter of the comments the same or similar? In what ways?

6.  Were the individuals commented about the same or similar?

7.  Were the events precipitating the encounter the same? In what ways?

8.  Did the encounters take place in similar areas?

9.  Were the feelings expressed the same? In what ways?

10. Were my reactions the same? In what ways?

---

1. What is the theme or issue that I have identified?

2. Are there any rules, regulations, or norms on this unit already in existence which tell me how to respond or handle this kind of situation?

3. If norms and standards exist, what is their history? Where did they come from and why?

4.  Did my actions violate or ignore the norms?

5.  What are the consequences of my actions for myself? For the other actor?

6.  Which of the consequences of my actions are more harmful?

7.  Is this the usual pattern of behavior ror myself? For the other actor?

8. If the behavior of either person is unusual, what might be contributing to the unusual behavior?

9. If the behavior is unusual, have I ignored or assaulted the important beliefs of the other person in this situation?

10. What are all the possible interpretations of the behavior? (Just list all the possibilities suggested by the answers to the previous questions.)

**REFERENCES**

1. Weinstein, E. "The Development of Interpersonal Competence," in D. Goslin (ed.), *Handbook of Socialization Theory and Research*. Chicago: Rand McNally, 1969.
2. Dittman, A.T. *Interpersonal Messages of Emotion*. New York: Springer, 1972.

# Module 7

# Eliciting
the Elusive

There is something I don't know
   that I am supposed to know.
I don't know *what* it is I don't know,
   and yet am supposed to know,
and I feel I look stupid
   if I seem both not to know it
   and not know what it is I don't know . . .

I feel you know what I am supposed to know
but you can't tell me what it is
because you don't know that I don't know what it is.*

## WAYS OF GETTING AT WHAT YOU WANT TO KNOW

There are times when we find ourselves not knowing what others apparently
think we do know or should know. We then search for a way to find out
what we need to know. This module deals with finding out what you want to
know, (i.e., eliciting feedback) and with providing feedback to others in a
constructive way so that they can *use* it.

There are several options available when you don't know exactly what
message a person's behavior is meant to convey. Option 1, operating on the

---

*From *Knots* by R.D. Laing. © 1970 by Pantheon Books, a division of Random House, Inc., New
York. Reprinted by permission.

available information, precludes the need to elicit more information. The other options permit you to find out what you may need to know. These options are:

To check things out with another individual on the unit

To check things out with the other person involved

To gather more data

### Checking Things Out with Another Individual on the Unit

Any time you find yourself not knowing what message another's behavior is meant to convey, you can ask a third party. You can use a direct or an indirect method to obtain feedback. The direct method means just that— come right out and ask what the behavior means. For example, when the nurse aide responds angrily to you because twenty minutes pass before you give pain medication to her patient, you could find another staff nurse, relate the situation to her, and then ask, "What was going on?"

The indirect method is more subtle. You provide a third party with enough information so that they can respond, but you do not ask for an opinion. For example, feedback about the meaning of the nurse aide's behavior could be obtained indirectly by commenting to another staff nurse, "Boy, is Lucy having a bad day! It took me twenty minutes to get Mr. Jones his pain medication, and she really snapped at me!" The other staff nurse may respond by saying that you should have gotten the medication there sooner or that the aides are used to having people respond immediately to their requests. It may seem silly to check out a situation by the indirect method. Sometimes it is. But let's look at the other two options for eliciting information, and then discuss the advantages and disadvantages of the direct and indirect methods of eliciting feedback.

### Checking Things Out with the Other Person Involved

This is essentially similar to checking out information with a third party. The only difference is that you deal with the party involved. The advantage of this option over the other is that it should give you more accurate information, since you are seeking feedback from the other person. If you want to be as sure as possible that your feedback is accurate, you should ask the primary source.

Again, you have the choice of using direct or indirect means. The direct method is carried out by approaching the other individual and saying, "Look, this is what I observed this morning. I get the idea that you are trying to tell me something but I'm not sure what and I would really like to know." With the indirect method, you sort of beat around the bush trying to get an idea of what is going on. It sounds like this. "How are things going today? . . . Need any help with anything? . . . Having any problems with anything?" The idea is to provide an opening that allows the other to come out and tell you what it is they may be trying to give you feedback about. Of course, you take the chance that you may not get at the situation you are trying to find the meaning of.

### Gathering More Data

This option is a combination of all the other options. You decide to operate temporarily on what you know so that you may make more observations, check things out with a third party, and then finally check out with the individual involved. You could really call this the "look before you leap" approach. A one-time behavior that seems to be telling you something about your performance is hard to interpret accurately. It could be simply that the aide is having a bad day, and there is no intention of communicating that you are not performing up to expectations.

Using this method to determine whether you are performing up to others' expectations is data banking. You do an analysis of the behavior, as was outlined earlier. You continue to make observations of similar situations until you feel you have an adequate number to say, "Okay, this is what seems to be operating."

The next step is to check out your inference with a third party. This is done in the ways just described. If your inference is validated, you check it out with the person involved. If the third party does not validate your inference, drop back to data banking to find out which of the two inferences is correct. Now, you are ready to check things out with the individual involved.

You may approach this as we have already mentioned on page 165 (checking things out with the other person involved). But with this method of gathering more data, there is an even more subtle way of doing the check. Given that you are fairly certain what the feedback is, you may check out your inference by re-enacting the situation in two different versions. For example, the next time the aide tells you that a patient needs medication, repeat your prior performance. Note her reaction. Another time, stop everything and give the medication immediately. Note her behavior. If you meet with the same kind of anger on the repeat performance, but you find that an immediate response elicits approving behavior, you can be fairly certain of the feedback being provided.

Now comes the question: Why bother to use the indirect method? Wouldn't it be simpler to ask outright what you want to know? It may be simpler to ask, but it is not always possible and frequently it's highly impractical.

The direct method is best suited to those situations in which the other party and yourself are interpersonally on a collegial basis. This does not mean that the two of you are on the same level within the organizational hierarchy. It only means that each party is secure in her own role and that give-and-take about each other's performance is possible. This kind of relationship implies that neither party is afraid to let the other know that she has weaknesses that need to be worked on.

The indirect method is most appropriate in situations where either yourself or the other party is threatened by providing feedback. The threat may exist for any number of reasons. Someone may fear what might happen to them or what you might think of them. If such situations exist, the direct method may not work. If you directly ask the person what was happening, he or she may say that nothing was meant by the incident. Maybe there was no meaning; maybe there was. The denial may leave you still feeling that some feedback was intended, but you have no way of finding out what message was intended. The indirect method allows you to gather sufficient data so that you can approach the other individual, state your observation, and explain your inferences. This removes the pressure from the other to spell out the feedback intended. Sometimes it is difficult for others to tell you about negative factors in your performance; if you have already inferred their message yourself, it is easier for them to discuss it. The truth of the matter is that the direct approach may yield the information you want but it may not allow the two of you to continue to have a comfortable working relationship. Thus, for our purposes it is not a workable solution. The basic premise is that it is better to take the extra time to get at what you want to know than to create a rift in ward relationships.

You may wish to practice eliciting feedback about your performance. The Final Quest exercise is included to help suggest performance areas about which you might wish to elicit feedback.

### THE FINAL QUEST

1. In what areas have you received feedback from your co-workers?

2. In what performance areas have you not received any feedback?

3. In what performance areas would you like to receive feedback from your co-workers?

4. Select an area in which you have not received or would like to receive feedback and construct a plan designed to elicit the feedback.

Up to this point, this program has dealt with answering the question, "How am I doing?" We have discussed differences in expectations between the school and the work setting. And we have presented examples and explanations of techniques used by others to provide feedback, forms that feedback may take in the work scene, and methods for eliciting desired feedback.

Graduate nurses have another question about feedback: "How do I provide feedback to others in a way that the other individual can accept and use the feedback?" The remainder of this program will focus on principles for providing feedback to others[1,2].

*Principle 1*: Describe behavior instead of providing interpretations, inferences, or blanket evaluations.

Often, when giving feedback to others, one says, "That was really inappropriate behavior," or "You're really well organized." These statements are interpretations or inferences about the meaning of some behavior. They are a form of feedback, but without supporting behavioral data, they are not particularly useful. So also with evaluations. Evaluations are value judgments about the behavior of the individual receiving the feedback. Inferences and interpretations often have value judgment connotations, although sometimes they are more subtle than the evaluation statement: "That was good." Negative value statements not only tend to make an individual defensive, they also tell the individual very little about those behaviors to which you are referring. Of course, there is always a question whether the inference or interpretation is correct. Thus it is better to describe the behavior and allow the individual to draw her own inferences or else describe the behavior *first* and then share the inferences that you have drawn. In the following example, this principle is used in providing feedback. One staff nurse is speaking to another.

> This morning you and the doctor came into Mr. Rey's room, discussed the tests that were to be done and then left the room. As you left, I heard the doctor express his concern that the low hemoglobin and platelet count might possibly delay surgery. Mr. Rey also heard the comment and asked a great many questions about why this would delay surgery and how come this problem existed in the first place. (Observation). He seemed quite apprehensive. (Inference.) It seems to me that if the patient is not to know about some particular problem, it is not appropriate to continue with a discussion of that kind within earshot of the patient. (Interpretation.)

A description of the behavior allows you to make your point: the behavior was inappropriate. At the same time, it does it in such a way that even if the other disagrees about the appropriateness of the behavior, she can follow the logic of your interpretation.

*Principle 2*:   Be specific about what was said and the sequencing of events.

In order to preserve the meaning of behavior, you must be clear and exact, and you must preserve the chronological sequence of events. For example, the previous feedback excerpt specified when the event took place and the entire chronology of events. How meaningful would this feedback be if the speaker had been vague about when it happened, what patient was involved, and whether the patient heard the remarks? The nurse would have no way of knowing about the events that happened after she left the room, and this probably isn't the first time that a doctor and nurse have continued to discuss a patient as they walk out of a room. So the specifics and chronology of an event make the feedback clear. Since it is difficult to remember the specifics of an event for long periods of time, this principle implies the necessity of providing feedback as soon after the event as possible.

*Principle 3*:   Focus feedback on behavior that can be changed.

The main reason for providing feedback in a work situation is to modify or change an individual's behavior. Therefore, it makes sense to focus on behavior that can be changed. There are times when co-workers' personal characteristics annoy us. You may not like the way someone looks or talks. But there isn't too much that can be done to change some things, and there is no point expending a lot of energy giving feedback about these things. In nursing, we tend to spend a great deal of effort trying to change co-workers' attitudes. We don't like the attitudes of some of the people we work with and we try to provide feedback about those attitudes until they change. Attitudes can be changed, but it takes time. Most often, attitudes will not be changed as a result of verbal feedback. Rather than focus on the attitude, focus on behavior. For example, some nurses dislike caring for alcoholic patients and their attitude is reflected in the way they address the patient, and in the amount of time they spend providing care to the patient. You can provide such a nurse with feedback by telling her, "The tone of your voice when speaking to an alcoholic patient is sharp, and you always address the patient as 'hey drunk'." It is possible to modify an individual's behavior so that she uses the same tone of voice with alcoholics as with all other patients and she addresses the patient by name. However, you might never change her attitude of dislike for alcoholic patients. Remember, the main reason for providing feedback is to help the individual receiving the feedback—rather than to give emotional release for your own anger or frustration. With this in mind, perhaps you will focus your feedback on behavior that can be changed.

*Principle 4*:   Time your feedback according to the moods and needs of the persons involved.

Feedback provided at a time when an individual is emotionally upset or has other matters on his mind is usually wasted. For example, if someone has just had a first-time experience with a dying patient and you would like to provide the person with feedback on how she handled the situation, you should wait until she has recovered from the incident. Or if a behavior occurs at 9 A.M. and you want to discuss it with the individual immediately, but find she has five more patients to care for and procedures that have to be done, you should perhaps delay the feedback until later in the day.

*Principle 5*:   Give feedback with appropriate attention to environmental factors.

It is important to choose the appropriate place to give feedback. The primary factor in choosing a place is privacy. You need a place where others will not hear or interrupt the feedback process.

*Principle 6*:   Validate feedback data with others.

Communication can easily be distorted. It is important that the accuracy of the feedback being given and received is checked out. Two aspects of feedback are validated: (1) Are the inferences being drawn from observed specific behaviors accurate? (2) Is the feedback being perceived accurately? To validate your inferences, you should describe the specific behaviors, present your inference, and then check out your inference.

> I've noticed that for the last three days, you make numerous trips down the halls. When x-ray or physical therapy comes for your patients, they aren't quite ready to go. You are missing coffee breaks, late for lunch, and late getting off duty. It seems to me that all these things indicate you are having trouble getting organized. I want to check out with you if my inference is correct and you need some help.

It's important to validate inferences, because if you want to provide help and guidance, both you and the other need to begin at the same point. If an inference is incorrect, your suggestions are of no value. In the above example, if the cause of the behaviors is lack of familiarity with the patients because the team leader assigns different patients each day, then working on organization will help a little but won't really solve the problem.

The second validation necessary is to make sure that your listener understood your feedback message. You need to determine if what you said is what was heard. The idea is to have the other person tell you the content of the message they received.

*Principle 7:* Describe the feelings that the behavior generates in you.

Motivation to change behavior and the amount of available information can be increased if the feedback giver describes the feelings that a particular event generated within him. Information about how behavior affects you broadens the individual's knowledge about others' responses to her behavior. Without this information, one cannot know and thus cannot decide if this is the kind of reaction one wants to produce or not. For example, if you share with your head nurse the feedback that when she is off the unit so much you become angry because you can't get any help from her, she has a lot of information about how her absence affects you. Perhaps if you feel that way, other staff do also. This may motivate the head nurse to lessen the amount of time that she is off the unit.

The use of these seven principles can increase the effectiveness and acceptability of the feedback you provide to others. At first it is difficult to use the principles, but practice can help you become proficient with them. By learning to provide effective and acceptable feedback, you may be able to prevent others from struggling with "The Elusive Quest."

## REFERENCES

1. Johnson, D.W. "Building Self-Actualizing Relationships," in D.W. Johnson (ed.), *Contemporary Social Psychology*. Philadelphia: J.B. Lippincott, 1973.
2. Fitts, W. *Interpersonal Competence: The Wheel Model*. Nashville, Tenn.: Counselor Recordings and Tests, 1970.

## BIBLIOGRAPHY

Barnlund, D. *Interpersonal Communication: Survey and Studies.* Boston: Houghton Mifflin, 1968.

Dittman, A.T. *Interpersonal Messages of Emotion.* New York: Springer, 1972.

Fitts, W. *Interpersonal Competence: The Wheel Model.* Nashville, Tenn.: Counselor Recordings and Tests, 1970.

From, F. *Perception of Other People.* New York: Columbia University Press, 1971.

Gergen, K.J. and Wishnov, B. Others' self-evaluations and interaction anticipated as determinants of self-presentation. *J. Pers. Soc. Psychol.*, Vol. 2, No. 3, 1965, pp. 348–358.

Goffman, E. *The Presentation of Self in Everyday Life.* New York: Doubleday, 1959.

Haney, W.V., *Communication and Organizational Behavior,* 3rd ed. Homewood, Ill.: Irwin, Inc. 1973.

Johnson D.W. "Building Self-Actualizing Relationships," in D.W. Johnson (ed.), *Contemporary Social Psychology.* Philadelphia: J.B. Lippincott, 1973, pp. 49–64.

Kadushin, A. Games people play in supervision. *Soc. Work*, Vol. 32, July 1968, pp. 23–32.

Kramer, M. *Reality Shock: Why Nurses Leave Nursing.* St. Louis: C.V. Mosby, 1974.

Laing, R.D. *Knots.* New York: Vintage, 1970.

Mager, R.F., *Goal Analysis.* Belmont, Cal.: Fearon Publishers, 1972.

Munson, E. and Kiesler, C.A. The role of attributions by others in the acceptance of persuasive communications. *J. Pers.*, Vol. 42, No. 3, 1974, pp. 453–466.

Myers, G.E., and Myers, M.T. *The Dynamics of Human Communication: A Laboratory Approach.* New York: McGraw-Hill, 1972.

Shrauger, J.S. and Lund, A.K. Self-evaluation and reactions to evaluations from others. *J. Pers.*, Vol. 43, No. 1, 1975, pp. 94–108.

Shrauger, J.S. and Patterson, M.B. Self-evaluation and the selection of dimensions for evaluating others. *J. Pers.*, Vol. 42, No. 4, 1974, pp. 569–585.

Stewart, J. *Bridges Not Walls: A Book About Interpersonal Communication.* Reading, Mass.: Addison-Wesley, 1973.

Turner, R.H. Unresponsiveness as a social sanction. *Sociometry*, Vol. 36, No. 1, March 1973, pp. 1–19.

Veninga, R. Interpersonal feedback: a cost-benefit analysis. *J. Nurs. Admin.*, Vol. 5, No. 2, 1975, pp. 40–43.

Watzlawick, P., et al. *Pragmatics of Human Communication: A Study of Interactional Patterns, Pathologies, and Paradoxes.* New York: W.W. Norton, 1967.

Weinstein, E. "The Development of Interpersonal Competence," in Goslin, D. *Handbook of Socialization Theory and Research.* Chicago: Rand McNally, 1969.

Wilson, S.R. Ability evaluation and self-evaluation as types of social comparisons. *Sociometry*, Vol. 36, No. 4, 1973, pp. 600–607.

# WALK A MILE IN MY SHOES

## INTRODUCTION

Values are an individual's conceptions of what is important or desirable. They are cultural products. Values, or shoes as we are calling them in this program, are transmitted to the uninitiated by those in positions of authority and influence. There are two major transmitters of values in the subculture of nursing—faculty in schools of nursing and head nurses in the work setting. Do these groups transmit to the neophyte nurse the same values about nursing? The answer is a resounding "no."

The subculture and values of nursing as taught in schools of nursing all across the country in all kinds of nursing programs are quite different from the nursing values that are transmitted to neophyte nurses in work settings all over the country. There is more uniformity in the values of nursing taught and practiced in schools of nursing in Birmingham, Chicago, New York City, and Pocatello, than there is in the values held and fostered by a hospital and a school of nursing located directly across the street from one another and under the same control and auspices. A research study by Smith illustrates this point.

In Smith's study, designed to determine the extent to which role values of head nurses and nurse educators were alike or different, performance evaluations of staff nurses written by head nurses and of nursing students written by nurse educators were randomly drawn from hospital nursing service and school of nursing files [1]. A total of 52 staff nurse evaluations and 56 student evaluations were used in the study. Content analysis was done on the two sets of evaluations and the results showed very clearly that faculty and head nurses value different traits and behaviors. Head nurses valued leadership behavior, directiveness, obedience, conformity, cooperation, friendliness, composure, and appearance significantly more than did faculty. Faculty valued such traits as sensitivity, emotional supportiveness, guidance, intelligence, and use of cognitive skills more than did head nurses. Both groups highly valued independence and self-reliance, but independence meant different things to the head nurses and faculty. The head nurses valued nurses who could perform independently with self-confidence, poise, and initiative, while to faculty, independence meant the ability to judge their relevance of observation, to make decisions appropriate for the nursing needs of patients, to be self-sufficient in meeting nursing needs, and to be resourceful.

Since nursing faculty and head nurses have different conceptions of nursing, the new graduate is likely to experience some stress and confusion between what she was taught to value in school and what she finds is valued in the work setting. Not only is there a difference between school and work values, but also, within the work setting itself, it is quite probable that various groups of workers (aides, orderlies, nursing supervisors) will operate according to different value systems. For example, head nurses often say they wish time would "stand still" so they could get everything done. They value time as a commodity—it permits them to get work organized and get as much as possible completed. In contrast, nurse aides often say they wish time would "fly" so they can get off and go home. For them, time is something to be occupied or filled so that it passes quickly. Because the work setting presents so many value systems different from the ones you learned in nursing school, you would be wise to take a close look at your own values and those of the people around you.

This program, entitled, "Walk a Mile in My Shoes," is about values and value systems. Its overall purpose is to help you become as interpersonally competent within the nursing work subculture as you were in the school subculture. Perhaps you were not as interpersonally competent and effective in school as you would have liked to be. Although not its major purpose, this program may help you raise your basic level of interpersonal competence so that you can function well in all subcultures. It is assumed, however, that you were at least minimally competent in the school subculture. By gaining interpersonal competence in the work subculture, you will be able to acquire sufficient informal power to enable you to make your work environment not only a pleasant, livable place, but also a place in which you can perform quality nursing care and influence others in the performance of quality care. As a first step toward interpersonal competence in the work subculture, you must learn what values are all about and the relationship between values and behaviors. That is the objective of the first module, entitled, "A Look at Shoes in General." The second module, entitled, "Work Shoes and School Shoes," will introduce you to two value systems relative to the work of nursing. We'll examine how each of these value systems hangs together and provide you with a guide for action toward some of your co-workers.

Aides, orderlies, LVNs and head nurses will speak directly to you in the third module. Entitled, "The Work Shoes Speak," this module presents some of the values expressed by the various groups of workers, and how these values fit into the systems we looked at in the second module.

The fourth and final module will focus directly on you. Entitled, "Putting Your School Shoes to Work," its goal is to help you identify your own values and value system, and to help you put your values about nursing into practice while at the same time accepting and respecting the values of your co-workers.

**REFERENCE**

1.    Smith, K. "Discrepancies in the Value Climate of Nursing Students: A Comparison of Head Nurses and Nursing Educators." Doctoral Dissertation, Stanford University, 1964.

# Module 8

# A Look at Shoes in General

Walk a mile in my shoes,
Walk a mile in my shoes,
And, before you abuse, criticize and accuse,
Walk a mile in my shoes.

If I could be you and you could be me for just one hour,
If we could find a way to get inside each other's minds,
If you could see you through my eyes instead of your ego,
I believe you'd be surprised to see that you'd been blind.

Walk a mile in my shoes,
Walk a mile in my shoes,
And, before you abuse, criticize, and accuse,
Walk a mile in my shoes.*

The lyrics to this popular song suggest that before you abuse, criticize, and accuse, you spend some time within the subculture or value system of the other person, and see his world as he sees it. Values are reflected in behaviors; they are the means by which other people introduce us to their world or subculture. To be able to practice nursing as you want to, perhaps as you've been taught in school, it will be necessary for you to learn to walk a mile in the other guy's shoes, to learn and understand his value system. In this way you will be better able to nurse more effectively yourself, as well

---

*From the song "Walk A Mile In My Shoes," written by Joe South, Copyright © 1969 by Lowery Music Co., Inc. International Copyright Secured. All Rights Reserved. Used by Permission.

as to exert influence on the nursing practice of others in your work environment. This module will take a look at values in general.

The objectives of this module are:

1. To define values, their characteristics, the process of valuing, and the relationship between values and attitudes.
2. To examine the major ways of changing values.
3. To identify the verbal and behavioral clues of values.
4. To clarify two important principles relative to values.

Let's begin by defining what a value is, and then we'll look at the differences and similarities between values and attitudes.

In a very practical sense, a value is some interest or concern of ours that has withstood the test of time and criticism. A value is a criticized interest. Any of our interests are candidates for becoming values. If you look at values in this way, you will find that they have two characteristics. First, values precipitate action. Any of us can have a verbal interest—one that we talk about a lot—but it's just talk. Values express themselves in behavior: things we like, we do, and we do them as often as we can. Second, each of our interests is very sensitive to our other interests. We judge the worth of any one of our interests in terms of its relationship to our other interests—not by some fixed standard, but according to our own particular pattern of interests. Values are not isolated commodities; they come with strings attached. The question really becomes, "Is *this* worth enjoying, considering all that I must do or give up to get it?"

If someone wants to determine what things or experiences you value, he will need to watch you and see how much time and effort you invest in them. A truly valued experience may happen once by chance, but the real indication of its value to you is the pains you take to repeat it.

## PROCESS OF VALUING

Let's now look at the process of valuing—that is, of weighing your interests and deciding which ones will become a value.

The *process of valuing* is a four-stage process.

1. First, you must make a judgment. Is X worth enjoying—for example, is reading history worth enjoying; are nursing care plans worth doing?
2. The second step in the process is to look at the antecedent preparations and at the consequences of two or more candidates for value, and compare them on the basis of the antecedents and consequences they share in common. For antecedents—time, money and effort are the ones that are usually shared in common. In some instances, particularly for interests that you have not yet tested out,

you will have to imagine the consequences and at least some of the antecedent preparations required.

3. The third step in the process is to do what interests you and test out the consequences predicted. Compare them to the consequences you predicted for other interests. How do you feel about the relationship that you thought would occur. Sometimes anticipation is better than realization.

4. The fourth step in the process is to decide whether you derived as much satisfaction as you anticipated. The question is: Was it satisfying, all things considered?

Perhaps an example here will illustrate valuing as a process of criticizing our interests. Let's say that on a particular weekend, you have two interests, both of which you consider to be worth enjoying—you'd like to go to a particular symphony and you'd like to go camping. You can't do both, so it will be a bittersweet package—you have to forego one in order to get the other. Now, both of these interests share certain antecedents in common. In addition to time, there is also money—money for the symphony tickets versus money for camping gear. Preparation of clothes might be another antecedent in common. There are also some antecedents which are not shared. For example, going away camping for the weekend would require the collecting and packing of gear and closing up the house which would not be required in going to the symphony. In looking at the consequences of engaging in both interests, there may be some things different and some things in common; it depends upon the individual. Let's say that you identify the consequences of going to the symphony as follows: 1) It's a consummatory event, i.e., satisfying in and of itself—pure enjoyment in the ecstasy of the music; 2) the pleasant company of your husband without having the children along; 3) growth in your ability to appreciate good music, and 4) the opportunity of possibly meeting other people who also enjoy the symphony. For camping, you identify the consequences as: 1) a close family togetherness; 2) opportunity for fresh air and exercise; 3) meeting other families who enjoy camping; 4) seeing the children grow in their understanding and appreciation of nature.

Now, the next step in the process is to test out your interests and see whether what you thought was going to happen is what actually happened and whether it was as satisfying as you thought it was going to be. Also were the antecedent preparations you made sufficient? OK, let's say that you decide that you desire the consequences of camping more than the consequences of going to the symphony, so you go. You find out that instead of two hours it took over six hours to make the preparations to go camping; it turned out to be a beautifully sunny weekend as you had predicted; however, your enjoyment of the out-of-doors was markedly dulled because you got poison ivy and started itching. And then the sunnier the day got, the more you itched, and you discovered you had not packed anything for relief of itching. Moreover, when you got home, your friends told you that you had missed the best symphony performance of the year.

Now, you obviously won't make your judgment as to which of these interests is a value of yours based solely on one experience. But if you act on these interests several times and find that the antecedents and consequences repeat themselves, then you are in a position to make a value judgment. And if I watch you, I will see which of these criticized interests you have put into your value system. You have judged that something is satisfying to you, all things considered.

## RELATIONSHIP BETWEEN VALUES AND ATTITUDES

Let's turn now to a consideration of the relationship between values and attitudes. Because the terms *values* and *attitudes* are frequently used interchangeably, and because they do have some characteristics in common, it is well to differentiate between them. You will recall that a value was defined as a criticized interest—a preference based upon a consideration of the investment required and the return you will get on that investment. A value is a cognitive apprehension of the worth of an interest; it becomes a value when we act upon this interest in some systematic and patterned fashion.

An attitude is a predisposition to act in a positive or negative way toward persons, objects, ideas, or events[1]. Like values, attitudes provide direction; they prepare you to respond to your environment in predetermined ways. Attitudes and values are alike in that both represent preferences; however, *values are preferences based upon conceptions of what is desirable, whereas attitudes need not be based upon such conceptions*[2]. Attitudes are reflected in such words as *like* and *dislike*; they specify the relationship between you and some object. Values are reflected in such words as *good* and *bad*; they specify the relationship between objects as you apprehend their worth at present. You may have a positive attitude toward nursing care plans, but when you criticize them as an interest in relation to other interests (coffee breaks, getting technical treatments done, doing your charting, getting off duty on time) you may decide that they are worth less to you than some other interests. You may have a positive attitude toward them, but you do not really value them.

Both for yourself and for others, it is absolutely necessary to differentiate between values, and attitudinal liking or preference for something. Oftentimes we assume that, because something is in our value system, it is also in the other individual's value system, when it may not be at all, or what is more usual, it might be in the attitudinal system, but not the value system. When an interest is a part of a person's value system, we expect that the interest will be translated into behavior. We are then in for a rude awakening when we find out it wasn't a value at all but only in the attitudinal system. We get into difficulty in communicating with one another, in trying to motivate others toward some common goal, when we misinterpret attitudinal noises or expressions for statements of values.

Attitudes and values share several characteristics in common which would be helpful to consider:

1. Both values and attitudes have direction—either we are positively or negatively attracted toward some object, or we see the object as having more or less worth than another object or interest of ours.

2. Both have intensity. This characteristic is concerned with how strongly the attitude is held, or how important the value is when compared with other values.

3. Both attitudes and values are acquired or learned through a process of discrimination and generalization.

4. Attitudes and values are consistent and stable over time; we tend to act and react with regularity.

5. Attitudes and values are integrated into complex systems; they are usually interconnected with one another and form clusters.

These characteristics should be kept in mind when we consider how to go about changing attitudes and values.


## CHANGING ATTITUDES AND VALUES

We often try to direct others—be they patients or staff—toward some goal or motivate them to change in some way. If you, a new graduate, want to try to put some of your school ideals into practice, you will need to work through and with both the attitudes and values of your co-workers. Thus, it is important that you know how to go about changing their attitudes and values.

There are two types of change that can be produced, and three ways of bringing about change. Let's look at types of change. First, there is congruent change, in which the attitude is changed from a plus direction to a more plus direction. This kind of change is always easier to produce than is the second type—incongruent change, that is, a change from a plus to a minus direction or from a minus to a plus direction. Obviously, this is much more difficult to bring about than is congruent change. The more important a belief is to someone, the easier it is to get him to believe it more strongly (congruent change). The more extreme, internally consistent, and want-serving the attitude or value is, the easier it is to bring about a congruent change and the harder it is to bring about an incongruent change.

Attitude or value change is brought about through one or some combination of the following three methods:

1. Exposure to additional information. This is the most commonly used method of effecting value and attitude change. It is the basis of TV

commercials and all patient instruction. However, it has been shown to be the least effective. Factors to be considered in this method include:

a) Whether exposure to the information was solitary or in a group. It is easier to ignore information that does not fit our attitudes and values when we are exposed to it alone rather than in a group.

b) Whether a private or public commitment is made. The chances of bringing about a change in attitude toward caring for alcoholics is greater if the entire ward staff receive and process information relative to care for alcoholic patients, and make a public commitment that they are going to individualize and dignify the care of such patients, than if such a commitment is a personal resolution.

c) The credibility and attractiveness of the communicator. Does the person who is trying to induce change know what he is talking about? Does he have a good track record? Attractiveness is also very important. Quite often, even if an individual is credible, we will not listen to information from him because we are turned off by his personal unattractiveness. This does not mean that this is the way it should be; it simply is. Many of the things that the long bearded hippie types were saying in the 60s were not listened to because people perceived beards and unwashed bodies to be unattractive. Often, the new graduate has difficulty because she hasn't been around long enough to build up credibility, nor does she have a record of successes that support the information she is trying to present.

d) The group affiliations of the communicator. What group you belong to—old timers versus newcomers, your racial group, diploma versus baccalaureate nurses—will make a difference in the audience's receptivity to your information.

e) The medium through which information is communicated. Often, the most effective way of transmitting information is through word of mouth. Other media frequently used in nursing include log books, blackboard, Kardexes, and the like.

f) The form and content of the information. In this area, results from numerous research studies can guide us with a few principles. Communicating information as to the *use* of something is more effective than emphasizing the why or rationale. If you are trying to produce a congruent change, a one-sided presentation (i.e., presentation of only the positive aspects) will produce the most change in the shortest time. If you are trying to produce an incongruent change (i.e., you suspect or know that the other nurses are against what you are proposing), you need to present both or all sides of the argument. In any event, the desirable features of what you are communicating should always precede the undesirable. High intensity or strong emotional appeal is not as effective as minimal or moderate appeal. People get hung up in the emotion and don't hear what you have to say. Finally, your presentation will be much more effective if you draw conclusions from the information, instead of letting the group draw its own conclusions.

2. A change in group affiliation. This is the basis for much of what we do in nursing when we urge patients to join ostomy clubs, new voice clubs, oncology groups, and the like. As a person moves from one group to another (for example, from school to work) he feels pressured to accept the attitudes and values of the new group. Simultaneously, the pressure of the values, attitudes, and norms of the old group begin to diminish.

Your status in the group, the kind of reception you encountered when entering the group, the value you place on your membership, and your perception of the legitimacy of group norms will help determine whether attitudinal and value change will be produced in you.

In school, emphasis and rewards are given to planned, deliberative nursing care for two or three patients, but in the work setting, the new graduate feels pressure to conform to the ward unit's norms: give efficient, rapid, fragmented care to large groups of patients.

3. Enforced modification of behavior through control of important rewards and sanctions. Enforced modification may be produced through intimate contact, coercion by authority, or through the internal discomfort aroused when an individual publicly says or does something counter to his private attitudes or values. When an individual is forced into a behavior that runs counter to his values or attitudes, he will experience internal dissonance or incongruity. This produces a lot of discomfort so that sooner or later if the individual continues with the behavior that runs counter to his thoughts or beliefs, he will change cognitions so that they are more in line with the behavior, and an attitude or value change results. For example, as a team leader, you may find yourself saying and expecting your team members to get all their task activities done although this means that teaching and listening activities with patients are ignored. You might even say: "When you get your work done, then you can do those extra things." If these words and actions are counter to your values, they will produce discomfort. To diminish or reduce that discomfort, you will change the way you think so that your attitudes or values come into line with your words and behaviors.

### VERBAL AND NONVERBAL CLUES

In the preceding sections we have looked at what values are, how they are developed, their relationship and similarity to attitudes, the characteristics common to both, and some of the ways in which attitudinal and value change can be most effectively brought about. Let's consider now some of the verbal and behavioral clues to values. If we are to walk a mile in the other guy's shoes we must be able to hear and to recognize his values and attitudes. It should be clear that if you hear someone say "I really like to take care of post-op hysterectomies", that this individual is expressing a favorable attitude toward caring for that kind of patient. If they say "I love taking care of Mrs. Smith," they are expressing a positive attitude toward Mrs. Smith as a person. I once had a student tell me that she liked best taking care of post-partum patients up until the time of the first voiding and that that was the kind of nursing job she wanted. This, I would say, is an extremely well focused attitudinal liking!

The verbal clues of values are not as easy to recognize as are those of attitudes. The first clues will be use of the terms, *ought, should,* and *must.* "I know I *ought* to spend more time with Mrs. Jones..." "You really *should* teach patients about their disease condition and their medical and nursing regime before they go home..." "You *must* get all the vitals done and recorded before the doctors make rounds." These are clues to values, but until you look further, you really don't know whether they are truly criticized interests or just potential values. Unlike attitudes, values must have a behavioral component. If you say, "I really *should* do nursing care plans or nursing histories," but do not, in fact, do them. This is the real insight into the fact that nursing care plans are not a value of yours. This is not meant as a criticism, or an ignoring of the reality constraints. It simply is a statement of fact. We do what we value. Behavior is more revealing than any verbal proclamation. An example will easily illustrate this point.

You have two friends who proclaim their love for good music. When you visit the apartment of one friend, the music greets you as he opens the door. Record jackets are lying around all over the living room. On more than one occasion, he has passed up a movie with you so that he could save money to buy a new stereo. Your other friend also says that he really enjoys listening to good music. But when you visit him, the TV is on to a soap opera; his beautiful stereo stands quiet, covered with dust. You see or hear no evidence of music. Which of these two friends would you say really values listening to music? Obviously, it's not enough for someone to say he values something; we must look at his behavior to see what he truly values. Furthermore, it is not behavior that is enacted just once that we should look at, but rather behavior that is repeated.

Both attitudes and values are organized into interconnecting systems. These systems are balanced and sustained when they are receiving new information that is congruent. Congruent information, such as reading that birth control pills are not harmful when we already have a positive liking for "the pill" and consider them to be worthwhile for their purpose, reinforces our attitudes and values and is relatively easy to assimilate. When the information coming in is not congruent with our value system, it produces a great deal of strain and stress on the whole system. The more the information challenges a value of high intensity and high priority, the greater the likelihood that feelings of intense distress, frustration, hostility, and anger will be produced.

During nursing school, you built up a complex matrix of values around patient and nursing care. This value system probably focused on complete, comprehensive patient care, family involvement, continuity of care between hospital and home, individualization of patient care, and so on. All these interests are congruent and interrelated, and they fit together very nicely. Upon entering the work scene you were probably suddenly exposed to the necessity of taking a complete patient care assignment. You may suddenly have found yourself so caught up in the "do-dos" of patient care that you had little, or no time to talk with the patient about his "want-wants." You may have found that you were so busy organizing and coordinating the care for many patients that you have no time for a one-to-one supportive relationship with a single patient. Increasingly, you find your interest in giving psychological support to patients interfered with by the necessity of doing a little for everybody instead of optimum for a few. Because values are organized into systems, a threat to a single value of central importance easily becomes a threat to the whole system, throwing many parts of it, as well as your self-system, out of kilter. As you begin to reorganize your value system, you will find that more and more of it needs revision. Until it is revised, you feel tension and inner turmoil (the latter results when the various parts of the system are not congruent). For example, because you must perform certain physical-care tasks, you may find you cannot talk and listen to patients, an activity you value. Pretty soon you realize that talking with patients is no longer a value, but only a value candidate ("I really should sit and listen to Mrs. Jones, but I have to get these temps done and recorded."). To decide whether to re-establish it as a value, you must compare your interest in listening to Mrs. Jones with your interest in getting the temps done. You'll probably say that you're not really interested in getting the temps done, but it is something you have to do "because it's my job." Perhaps more honestly you'll say, "It's because I'll get into trouble if I don't do them," or, "It's because I want my head nurse to like me and think that I'm a good nurse." The point is that you have examined and criticized both interests and decided that you enjoy the consequences of "completing assigned tasks" more than you would enjoy the consequences of "listening to Mrs. Smith." Therefore, you reorganize your value system, and "completing assigned tasks" gains higher priority than "listening to patients." Our values are organized into systems, and when we change one part of the system, we generally need to go on to change other parts. If your interest in "completing assigned tasks" is given high priority, you will probably find that other interests opposed to this interest will have to be deprioritized.

In this module, we have begun to learn how to walk a mile in the other guy's shoes, to begin to understand and accept his value system. In discussing values and attitudes, we emphasized two major principles: (1) values must be reflected in behavior; and (2) values are organized into systems. Changes in one part of the system usually require changes in other parts.

**REFERENCES**

1.  McDonald, F.J. *Educational Psychology,* 2nd ed. Belmont, Calif.: Wadsworth Publishing Co., 1965, p. 308.
2.  McDonald, F.J., 1965, p. 374.

# Module 9

# Work Shoes and School Shoes

**Work Shoes:**

Whew! I've been going like mad since 7:00 this morning. Hope I get to stop and rest soon. But can't yet. Got to check on that GI bleeder that just came in, and that IV in 14 is about to run out. Wonder if that student could hang the new one. I bet not—it's not her patient and I don't dare ask her to do anything that's not for her patient . . . Oh, mustn't forget to order the home meds for old Ben—gosh, I'm glad he's going to his own place instead of getting shunted off into an old folks home . . . Wish I had some time to talk with him before he goes, to make sure he can care for himself OK . . . Better hurry—that's 16's light—she was having some trouble breathing before . . . . I can drop that cath tray off, on the way . . . . Now think a moment—if you plan, you can save some wear and tear on your old work shoes. Stick your head in and tell Mrs. Cole that her doctor called and he'll be in to see her this afternoon . . . . Oh, there's Jim; tell him about doing the male cath in 26 . . . . Oh, here's 20, check that CVP line. While you're at it, might as well take her BP.

**School Shoes:**

Gosh, I'm excited! And scared, too. Mrs. Mackey, my patient, is going to surgery today. Hope all goes OK with her and for me too. I think I'm all prepared and have everything down straight, but you just watch. Mary Lou is bound to ask me something I haven't thought of. Oh, good heavens, my care plan, do I have it or did I leave it in the dorm—oh, no,

186

here it is. Better move faster, polished white shoes, or you're going to be late, and you'll get the old frown from the head nurse. I sure don't see what she gets all uptight about when a person is late. What difference does it make? As long as I take good care of Mrs. Mackey and see that she gets everything she needs, I don't see why she gets mad if I'm a few minutes late . . . . Made it, report's just beginning. Let's see, Mrs. Mackey is on Team II so I can daydream for a while before they get to her . . . . Don't forget to copy that lab data from her chart for the case study report you're doing on her . . . . Oh, yes, and tomorrow I make my home visit on Charley. I think I'm all ready for that. Let's see, I've contacted the social worker and I've got him all set up with the homemaking service. Hope his social security check came through all right this month—I'll have to remember to ask him    Hmmm, I really ought to think about checking with Mrs. Mackey about her home arrangements. Hey, that patient they're talking about sounds kind of interesting. I haven't had any experience with leukemia patients before, and maybe if I ask to take care of her, I'll see what a bone marrow puncture is all about. Poor thing, she sounds so sick. I'd better listen closer . . . I might learn something new.

The world looks different when you're in work shoes than it did when you were wearing school shoes, doesn't it? I wonder why that is. Nursing is nursing, and it should be the same everywhere—but it isn't. What makes the difference between the kind of nursing you were taught to do in school, and what you're doing as a nurse now at work?

The answer to this question is what this module is all about. In this module, you will be introduced to two different value systems, work shoes and school shoes. You'll see that both systems are logical, internally consistent, and make a great deal of sense. You'll see what happens when a student, trained in one value system, becomes a worker paid to perform according to the other value system. Finally, we will examine the affect of resistance on task achievement and analyze the relationship between resistance and the two value systems.

## PART TASKS AND WHOLE TASKS

Let's start by focusing on a task, a job to be done. There are two possible ways of doing any task. You can do the whole task, or the job can be split up, so that you and other workers each do a part of it.

If you are going to do the whole task, one thing you need is complete knowledge of the work to be done. If you're going to do only part of the task, then you need only partial knowledge. Translated into patient care, this means that if you're going to take care of the whole patient, give comprehensive patient care, you need to know everything that goes into the total care of that patient. You need to know about the medications, the technical procedures, physical hygiene, teaching, and so on. If, on the other hand, you're going to give only part of the patient's care, you need only partial knowledge.

If you need complete knowledge to do a task, you have to acquire it over a long period of time in an organization apart from the employing organization. An employing organization cannot afford to support you while you acquire complete knowledge. If you need only partial knowledge, you can often acquire it in on-the-job training such as that provided to nurse aides. If the organization provides on-the-job training, it has the *right* to require that workers do their job the way they were trained to. Thus, knowledge acquired in on-the-job training is very particularistic. "At this hospital you chart *this* way." That's only fair, isn't it? And logical? If, on the other hand, you're going to acquire complete knowledge in an institution apart from the employing organization, you must be taught general principles, applicable in a variety of situations. The knowledge is more universalistic and may not have the immediate usefulness of knowledge acquired in on-the-job training, but it can be used in a wider range of situations.

When a task is broken down into its component parts, with various workers performing parts of it, there should be someone to coordinate their work. Figure 1 shows all individual workers, each doing part of the task—one is doing treatments, one is talking with the patient, another is planning with the patient's family, and one is taking the patient to X-ray and so on. Although it doesn't necessarily happen, it is highly desirable if somebody coordinates and puts the patient care back together again. This person is generally someone who has more complete knowledge and has the

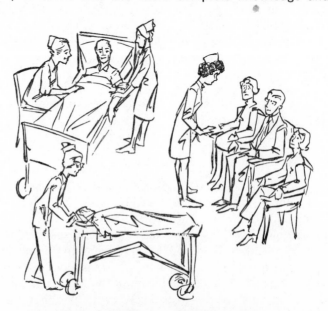

**FIGURE 1. PART-TASK SYSTEM OF WORK**

authority and status needed to supervise part-task trained workers. This, of course, implies a hierarchical control structure. (See Figure 2.) Now, in Figure 3, you see the whole-task view with one nurse doing the total job. If

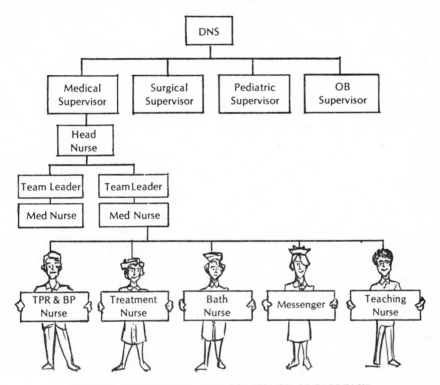

**FIGURE 2. HIERARCHICAL CONTROL STRUCTURE (PART-TASK)**

**FIGURE 3. WHOLE-TASK SYSTEM OF WORK**

all workers perform the total task, there is no need for supervisors or coordinators; that is, the hierarchical control structure is replaced by a peer control structure. (See Figure 4.)

If you have a situation in which you have a group of workers each doing a segment of the task, you must also have some kind of external coordination—someone to direct traffic, to say, "Okay, Mrs. Jones will go down to X-ray now, then when she comes back she'll have her treatments and medications, and then discharge planning in the afternoon and so on." (See Figure 5.) Somebody has to direct the flow of the activity making up the total task. This is external coordination and it's usually done on the basis of

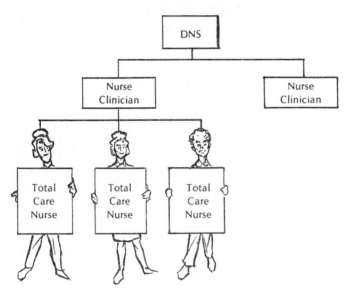

**FIGURE 4. CONTROL STRUCTURE (WHOLE-TASK)**

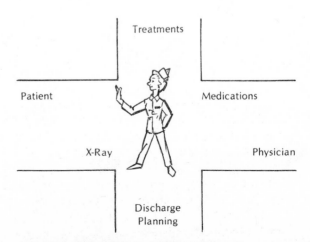

**FIGURE 5. EXTERNAL COORDINATION (PART-TASK)**

**FIGURE 6. INTERNAL COORDINATION (WHOLE-TASK)**

**FIGURE 7. EXTERNAL STANDARDS OF PERFORMANCE (PART-TASK)**

time efficiency. On the other hand, if you as the worker are going to do the total task of patient care, you can internally coordinate when you're going to do what. You can decide for yourself, "I'm going to give the medications now, then I'm going to bathe the patient, then I'm going to ambulate him and so on." (See Figure 6.) You internally coordinate these activities and make the decisions, generally, on the basis of some established goal—hopefully a patient-centered goal—at least the potential for such is there.

In addition to external coordination, the part-task system also has external standards of adequate job performance. A worker who is doing only a segment or component of the total task will in all likelihood repeat this same task very frequently, say, taking temperatures or giving medications. She therefore has the opportunity to develop tremendous skill and speed in the performance of the task, and work output can quite easily be judged in terms of the number of units completed. For example: "Janis is a terrific nurse. When she's on meds, all the patients get their meds on time and no one has to wait." Janis' work output is being judged solely on the repetitive task of administering medications. For many part-task jobs, external controls and standards, usually in the form of rules, regulations, policies and procedures, are set up and are used as the external criteria against which one's work output is judged. (See Figure 7.) These external standards might also take the form of norms which grow up within a group, and which specify exactly how much work is reasonable to expect—how many bed baths, how many temps should get done, etc.

When a worker is performing the total task, internal rather than external coordination makes sense and is usually the order of the day. For example, total patient care requires a unique and highly individualistic combination of the various components of care. Productivity is not evaluated on the basis of rapid and repetitive performance of any particular sub-task but rather on the skill and judgment used in combining sub-tasks. Work output is evaluated in terms of the correctness of the procedures used and judgments made. A nurse who is passing medications all day is judged on the basis of units of work accomplished. A nurse who is giving total patient care is best judged on her ability to assess and plan for meeting the total care needs of the patient; on her ability to coordinate such sub-tasks as bathing and ambulating the patient; and her ability to perceive and meet his need to talk, instruct him on his medications, clarify and interpret the physician's remarks relative to diagnostic tests, etc. The standards of performance in this system are much less clear, and it is more difficult to measure performance. Standards of performance are usually communicated as norms or codes of ethics, and are taught during the long training period. As the worker acquires complete knowledge during the long training period, she internalizes the norms, or standards, so that she knows when she's done a good job teaching the patient or turning the patient postoperatively, or when she's done a good job listening to a patient or coordinating the various elements of care. (See Figure 8.)

The whole-task and part-task systems have implications for hiring standards and employee loyalty. In the part-task system hiring standards can be lower than in the whole-task system, because prospective workers are assessed on a much narrower range of competencies. The part-task system is more vulnerable to breakdown, but broken down parts are more readily and easily replaced. For example, if an aide does not show up for work, the part of the task assigned to her (like taking TPRs) will be glaringly omitted, but another aide can be floated into the unit to replace her. The whole-task system is much less vulnerable to breakdown because each worker controls all facets of the task and can make immediate adjustments to compensate

**FIGURE 8. INTERNAL STANDARDS OF PERFORMANCE (WHOLE-TASK)**

for any minor breakdown. For example, if the whole-task nurse finds that the bed scales will not be available for half an hour, she can make immediate adjustments in her plan of care. However, when a major breakdown occurs, as when two nurses giving complete care do not show up for work, the broken down parts are not easily replaced. If a part-task-trained worker is floated in to cover for a whole-task worker, the system is very vulnerable to error, because the part-task-trained worker will not have all the knowledges and skills needed to do the complete task.

The location of workers' loyalty is different in the two systems. Part-task workers develop loyalty to the employing organization because it trained them in the knowledge necessary to do their job. These workers know that their knowledge is often specific to that one institution, so that their mobility is limited. The whole-task trained worker tends to develop loyalty to the discipline or to her knowledge base, because this knowledge transcends any particular place of employment and provides her with lateral and upward mobility.

So far, we have analyzed the whole-task and part-task systems. We have seen that each system has an inherent logic in terms of the preparation of the worker, the place of this preparation, the kind of knowledge learned and used, the structure for the control of work, the coordination of the work, how the quality and quantity of work output is evaluated, and the kind of loyalty that will tend to develop. Finally, we should examine the relationship of these systems to the terms *professional* and *bureaucracy*.

Summarized below are the characteristics of the part-task system and the characteristics of a bureaucracy. Note the striking similarity.

| Part-Task System | Bureaucracy |
|---|---|
| Partial knowledge | Division of labor based on functional specialization |
| Short training period | Well-defined hierarchy of authority |
| Specialized skills learned on the job | System of rules covering the rights and duties of occupants of positions |
| Particularistic in nature | A system of procedures for dealing with work situations |
| Coordination by some official removed from the workers | Hiring and promotion on basis of technical competency |
| Hierarchical control and authority structure | |
| External standards through rules and regulations | |
| Evaluation through work output | |
| Loyalty to the organization | |
| An organizational layer whose major purpose is to maintain the organization | |

Now, let's do the same thing for the characteristics of the whole-task system and the characteristics of a profession.

| Whole-Task System | Profession |
|---|---|
| Complete knowledge and skills | Body of knowledge having an intellectual component |
| Long training period | Knowledge base acquired through long prescribed training |
| Skills learned in separate educational institutions | |
| Universalistic in nature | Development of training facilities controlled by professional group |
| Internal coordination | Autonomy and responsibility in the use of special competence |
| Peer control and authority structure | |
| Internalized standards; norms; code of ethics | Decision making governed by internalized standards |
| Evaluation through process rather than output | Adherence to a set of norms or code of ethics |
| Loyalty to an occupation or discipline | Adherence to service ideal |

Because the part-task and whole-task systems have characteristics corresponding to those ascribed to a bureaucracy and a profession, respectively, the terms will be used interchangeably. When we use the word *bureaucracy* or *bureaucratic*, we are talking about a worker or a work system functioning on a part-task basis.

Nursing care organized on a "functional" basis, with one nurse doing treatments, another doing medications, another worker giving baths, a worker assigned to nourishments, another to transporting patients, etc., is a bureaucratic system of work. To a large extent, team nursing as it functions in many hospital and public health organizations is in reality a functional or bureaucratic system of work. A nursing system in which each nurse gives complete nursing care to all the patients in her charge would be a professional system of work. And herein lies the problem. In 99.9 percent of the schools of nursing in this country, students are taught nursing according to a whole-task or professional system of work. When these students graduate and begin to work, most of them find nursing organized on a bureaucratic or part-task system. (See Figure 9.) The discrepancy between what is taught in nursing schools and how nursing is organized in the real world is what produces "reality shock." Although you can find some systems of work organization that approximate the total care approach learned in school —for example, primary nursing or the nursing assignments typical of Intensive or Coronary Care Units—most nursing work is organized according to the part-task system.

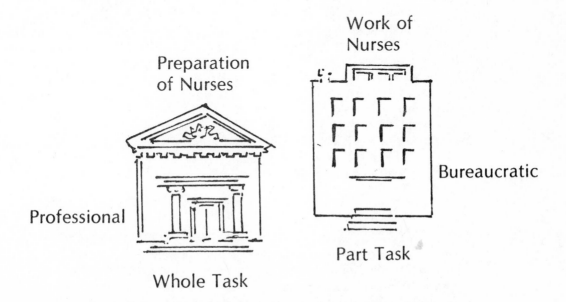

**FIGURE 9. SYSTEMS OF WORK ORGANIZATION**

It might also be noted here that this phenomenon between prospective workers in a field being trained in a whole-task or professional system and then having to work in a part-task or bureaucratic system is not unique to nursing. It has been and will probably continue to be encountered by all kinds of workers: social workers, teachers, physicians employed in clinics, scientists working in industry, intellectuals employed by labor unions, to mention but a few. The problem and the resultant conflict are so widespread that we're forced to ask, "Why?" Why were you given one view of the practice of nursing as a student, only to find that the work situation demands a different system of work organization? The answer is relatively simple. The whole-task approach is a good way of teaching what optimum health care is all about. It is probably the best way of demonstrating the impact of the health care system upon the individual and his family, of showing the interrelationships between the various components of care. If this be so, then why isn't nursing in the work world organized that way? The answer to this question revolves largely around economics and availability of resources. The part-task, bureaucratic system started in modern times with the industrial revolution and is very efficient and economical. Remember, it is based on the principle of breaking a task down into its component parts and then training workers to acquire the limited knowledge they need to execute their part of the task. Because the worker repeats the same task over and over again, he becomes highly skilled at it, and work output is accordingly very high. The whole-task system is much more costly. The longer training period, the higher job standards and qualifications, the system's great vulnerability to massive breakdown—all these contribute to higher costs. There is also the question of availability of resources. If all of nursing service were organized according to the whole-task approach, it would require an all RN, or all whole-task trained working force; there would be no jobs for nurse aides, orderlies, and LVNs. It is doubtful whether our society could afford to educate and employ enough registered nurses.

At this point you might be saying to yourself, "There's a missing link somewhere! If nursing care can be given to patients more economically on the part-task bureaucratic system, why are nurses educated to give care according to a whole-task professional approach, even if that approach does provide students with an excellent way of learning what optimal nursing and health care is all about?" Well, you're right: there is a missing ingredient.

### ACTIVE AND INERT TASKS

To find it, let's look again at some task that we want to accomplish. There are two possible outcomes to task execution: the desired outcome, (See Figure 10.) what you want to accomplish; and the actual outcome, (See Figure 11.) what you do in fact accomplish. The difference between these two is the margin of error. (See Figure 12.) With different tasks, we're willing to tolerate different margins of error. If you're going to shoot a man to the

**FIGURE 10. DESIRED OUTCOME**

**FIGURE 11. ACTUAL OUTCOME**

**FIGURE 12.**

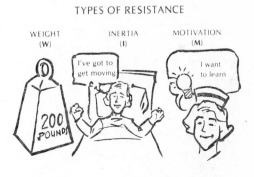

**FIGURE 13. TYPES OF RESISTANCE**

moon, you're not willing to tolerate a very great margin of error between the desired outcome and the actual outcome. But if you want a two-year-old to dress himself, you had better be willing to tolerate some error between actual and desired outcome.

What causes error in task execution is resistance. For any task, a certain amount of resistance must be overcome. If you are going to get out of bed in the morning, there's the resistance of inertia. If you're going to pick up your purse, there's the resistance of weight. If you want to teach a diabetic patient about his diet, there's the resistance of lack of motivation to learn what may happen if he doesn't accept the disease. (See Figure 13.)

Now, there are several features of resistance that must be considered. First, there is the *amount* of resistance, the amount of weight, inertia or motivation. (See Figure 14.) But considering amount alone is not enough to get a true picture of resistance. There are two aspects to amount of resistance that must be considered. The first of these is *predictability* in the amount of resistance. (See Figure 15.) Is the amount known or unknown, i.e., is it *predictable*? For many tasks, the amount of resistance is predictable. We generally know how much energy is needed to overcome the inertia of staying in bed in the morning. When you go to lift something, its size and shape generally make its weight predictable. Knowing the amount of resistance that something will offer is what is meant by predictability. But there may also be *variability* in the amount of resistance. We usually expect that the amount of resistance will remain the same over repeated performances of a task. If you are giving an adult patient oral medications, you would expect that if he took the medications without much resistance at 2:00 P.M., he would do the same at 6:00 P.M. And if he did so on Monday, he would take the medications pretty much the same way on Tuesday. There is very little variability in the amount of resistance offered. The same could not be said if you were administering medications to a three-year-old child. On Monday, he may take the pills and swallow them right down. On Tuesday, he may spit them out at you. On Wednesday, he may pouch them and hold them in his cheek, and on Thursday, he may chew them up before choking on them. Administering medications to this three-year-old child is a task fraught with high variablity in the amount of resistance. (See Figure 16.)

Now, by analyzing tasks with respect to the predictability and variability in amount of resistance they present, we find that there are two kinds of

**FIGURE 14. AMOUNT**                    **FIGURE 15. PREDICTABILITY**

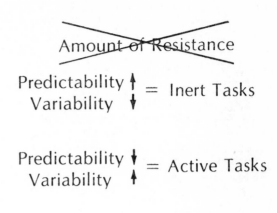

| | |
|---|---|
| **FIGURE 16. VARIABILITY** | **FIGURE 17.** |

tasks. *Inert tasks* are those presenting a predictable amount of resistance that does not vary much over repeated performances. Lifting a purse off the floor is an inert task. The amount of resistance is predictable, and it does not vary much from purse to purse. Lifting 50-pound dumbbells is also an inert task. The amount of resistance is very great, but it's known and predictable. Inert tasks are those that are routine and standardized.

*Active tasks* are those presenting an unpredictable and highly variable amount of resistance. Active tasks require decision making and judgment; they are nonroutine and generally cannot be standardized. (See Figure 17.)

Generally speaking, active tasks are most efficiently handled on the professional system of work organization; inert tasks are best handled on the bureaucratic system of work organization. Tasks in which the amount of resistance is predictable and unvarying are good tasks to train a worker to do over and over again. Speed and efficiency increase with repetitive performance of these tasks. On the other hand, active tasks, which present many variables, require workers who have complete knowledge, which permits them to make judgments and assess the amount of resistance likely to occur.

Increased error, cost, reality shock, and poor morale due to boredom result when we take active tasks and organize them on a bureaucratic system, or take inert tasks and organize them on a professional system. (See Figure 18.) And we do this all the time. Think for a moment. What are some inert tasks in nursing that are frequently done by whole-task trained workers? Head nurses filling out diet slips, drug slips, or linen slips? The administration of medications to alert, adult patients is a very inert task 90 percent of the time. But it is a task that is often delegated to the professionally trained worker. Then we take some very active task, like admitting patients, or ambulating postop patients, and assign them to the part-task

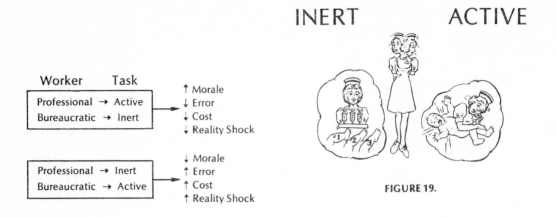

| Worker | | Task | |
|---|---|---|---|
| Professional | → | Active | ↑ Morale |
| Bureaucratic | → | Inert | ↓ Error |
| | | | ↓ Cost |
| | | | ↓ Reality Shock |
| Professional | → | Inert | ↓ Morale |
| Bureaucratic | → | Active | ↑ Error |
| | | | ↑ Cost |
| | | | ↑ Reality Shock |

**INERT          ACTIVE**

**FIGURE 19.**

**FIGURE 18.**

trained nurse aide. For example, if postoperative ambulation were done properly, i.e., if the resistance offered by the individual patient were taken into consideration then each patient's peristaltic activity would be continuously assessed and evaluated so that the nurse could determine intelligently just how much ambulation each patient needed—just enough to restore peristalsis, but not so much as to cause fatigue.

Delegating active tasks to part-task trained workers results in a greater margin of error; assigning whole-task trained workers to inert tasks results in inefficiency, lowered morale, and boredom. This then is the missing ingredient—the margin of error we are willing to tolerate in achieving the desired outcomes of quality patient care. It is only by a judicious blend of part-task and whole-task work organization and assignment that the margin of error will be kept at a minimum and quality health care will be delivered at a cost that society can afford.

There are a few other points to be made about this analysis of tasks as active and inert. First, knowledge of the amount, predictability, and variability of resistance associated with a task is exactly what is meant by *experience*. When a nurse says, "I have experience caring for neurosurgical patients," what she really means is that she has a repertoire of knowledge regarding the amount of resistance that neurosurgical patients offer to nursing tasks associated with their care. She has knowledge regarding the predictability of resistance. Does the patient's blood pressure always fall in response to a spinal tap? She also has knowledge regarding the variability of resistance of these patients in response to certain procedures. "Mr. Jones was very placid and quiet when I did the 8:00 A.M. neuro check, but he's irritable and resistive to the 9:00 A.M. neuro check. Is this variability in the amount of resistance characteristic of all neurosurgical patients or does it mean that Mr. Jones' condition is changing?" It is useful to look at experience as knowledge acquired regarding the amount, predictability, and variability of resistance.

What is often a very active task for a newcomer may be an inert task for the experienced nurse. When they first start out, new graduates perceive many of the things they do as very active tasks. They have not had enough experience to know what the amount, predictability, or variability of resistance is likely to be. Until they acquire knowledge regarding that resistance, the task will remain active for them. Another point here is the matter of expectations. New graduates expect many, if not most, of the tasks in nursing to be highly active—because their instructors describe them that way. And to the extent that many tasks done are new for the learner, they are active. But the truth of the matter is that, taken by themselves, many nursing tasks are quite inert. In truth, it is only the resistance stemming from the patient that makes nursing the highly active job that it is. (See Figure 19.) If we focus strictly on the tasks of nursing, such as taking blood pressures, we'll have to agree that nursing does consist of many inert tasks that would be best organized on the bureaucratic or part-task system. And, in fact, focusing on tasks is what happens in the work world. And it happens to newcomers as well as oldtimers. For example, how many of you, when you first started working, found yourself focusing on the task almost to the exclusion of the patient? Did you hear yourself telling your friends, "I did my first cath today," or "Boy, I really feel good. I had three IVs today and I managed all of them fine." There are lots of examples of how we nurses focus primarily on tasks. "You've got to keep all postops well sedated for the first 24 hours after surgery, or you'll really have trouble." "I always irrigate Foleys that way, and I've never had any trouble before." This is not to say that we shouldn't look for patterning or consistencies in our work. No, the point is that by focusing on task performance, rather than on the *resistance offered by patients* to task performance, we are in grave danger of treating patients like things. And when we do this, our work comes close to being just a series of inert tasks, best organized on a part-task system. But most important, when we do this, we must be willing to tolerate a large margin of error between the actual and desired outcomes of patient care.

In your school shoes, or school value system, you were taught to look at patients as individuals. Actually, this is a cliché and sort of nebulous. What is being suggested is that you look at your patient in relation to the task to be done, and ask yourself, can I predict the amount of resistance Mr. Kelley will offer to being ambulated? to being turned? to his upcoming surgery? Is this resistance likely to be more or less than that offered by Mrs. Jones, who had the same surgery last week? Why? What do I need to do to reduce this patient's resistance? (See Figure 20.) Thinking about and planning your nursing care around these kinds of questions will not only result in an individualized plan of care, but a plan of care in which the actual and desired outcome will be much closer and the margin of error reduced.

**FIGURE 20. CONSIDERING RESISTANCE TO INDIVIDUALIZED CARE**

Think about doing this same kind of thing when you are working with nurse aides or part-task trained workers. You will help them individualize and humanize patient care if you stimulate and motivate them by asking them questions such as: "Do you expect more or less resistance from Mrs. Smith when you give her a bed bath than you got from Mrs. Arthur? What can you do to reduce this resistance?"

Before this module closes, we should make explicit something that heretofore has been only implicit. In English usage, the term *resistance* often has a negative connotation. As the term is used here, it does *not* have a negative connotation. Resistance simply means the weight, inertia, or lack of motivation that must be overcome to accomplish some task. In and of itself, resistance is neither negative nor positive, but simply something to be considered. Because of its connotation, you may well have to orient others to your usage of this term before springing it on them.

This module addressed itself to the question: What makes the difference between the kind of nursing I was taught to do in school, and what I'm doing as a nurse now at work? (The world looks different when you're in work shoes than it did when you were wearing school shoes.) To answer this question, we looked at two different systems of organizing work: the bureaucratic system in which each worker does part of the task, and the professional system, in which workers perform the whole task, The question is not whether one system is good and the other bad; they are simply two different ways of looking at and organizing work. Within each system, there is logic and consistency. For the most part, nursing as it is presented and learned in school is organized on the whole-task system and promulgates such values as independent judgment, decision making, one-to-one comprehensiveness, continuity of care, family involvement, and so on. In the work

world, nursing is usually organized on a part-task system, and organization, efficiency, coordination, and cooperation are highly valued. Role deprivation or reality shock occurs when students prepared in one system must work in another system.

In response to the question, "Why are nurses educated to give care on the whole-task system approach if care can be given more economically on the part-task basis?" we introduced the idea that the organization of work depended upon the amount, predictability, and variability of resistance to task achievement. The relationship between active and inert tasks and the best systems of work organization to achieve the desired outcomes of tasks was discussed. And the module ended with this major point: to utilize school values in the work scene, to humanize and individualize patient care, one needs to focus not on the task itself, but on the resistance to task achievement offered by the patient. This will help you operationalize your goal of individualized patient care.

# Module 10

# The Work Shoes Speak

*by Patricia Benner and Marlene Kramer*

In the last module, we looked at two value systems in their more or less pure form. We saw the inherent logic and consistency of the part-task system's valuation of such characteristics as speed, efficiency, getting the task done, cooperation, coordination, etc. But in the real world, things are not as they are portrayed in books. You may find that some of your co-workers personify the value system described above, but in all likelihood most of your co-workers will be at different points along the school-work continuum of values. They will combine a focus on total patient care with a focus on part-task achievement. What is important is that you learn how to recognize the value systems of others, and be aware of similarities and differences in the value systems of different people. The purpose of this module is to help you:

1. To identify the values contained in verbal messages.
2. To discover similarities and differences between your value system and those of others.
3. To predict the consequences that are likely to occur if you over-estimate similarity in values.
4. To apply the process of value identification to your own group of co-workers.

This module will consist largely of excerpts from tape-recorded interviews with nurse aides, orderlies, practical nurses, and registered nurses. Its overall purpose is to acquaint you with some of the "practical, everyday, work values" of co-workers. No doubt, you will discover that some of their values, beliefs, and their commitment to helping people are similar to your own. It is hoped that your recognition of some of these shared values may provide you with a basis for establishing cooperative working relationships. However, in the instructions and exercises, your ability to spot differences between your work values and those expressed by others is emphasized. The reason for this stress on identifying differences is that it is the differences that are apt to produce conflict and misunderstanding. If you can identify value differences, you can interpret your health care goals to people whose value framework is different from your own. Increased empathy, or understanding another's perspective (that is, walking a mile in the other guy's shoes), increases one's potential for relating to and influencing the other. For example, Figure 1 shows a new graduate standing on her value system of individualized patient care, assessment, teaching, and so on. (Sound like really neat values, don't they?) When she looks across at the cliff of work values, they look pretty awful. But look now at Figure 2. Here the staff nurse is standing on the nursing service value system of safety, best care possible for all patients—they sound real good, right? When she looks across at the new graduate's world and her value system, it doesn't look so good—disorganiztion, lack of skills and so on.

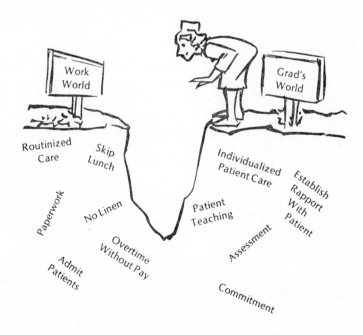

**FIGURE 1. WORK WORLD: AS SEEN BY NEW GRAD**

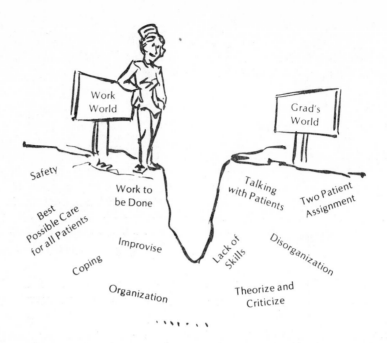

**FIGURE 2. WORLD OF NEW GRAD: AS SEEN BY NURSING SERVICE**

Each of us sees our own value system as logical and rational. It's very difficult for any of us to view the other guy's value system so favorably. This is where empathy comes in. Awareness of the differences between your value system and those of your co-workers, appreciation of the logic and internal consistency of their value systems enables you to view a situation as they would. And by doing this, you will be in a much better position to influence others, to put your school shoes to work.

Let's begin learning about others' values by reading some co-workers' responses to the open-ended statement, "A good team leader will. . . ." What do you think auxiliary workers expect from a team leader?* These interview excerpts will give you an idea of their expectations. How closely do their expectations match your expectations of yourself as a team leader? To find out, first complete the learning activity entitled, "The Most Important Duties of the Team Leader Are. . . ."

---

*Some readers may not be working on a unit organized on a team nursing basis, but will be functioning in some other kind of directive position. The same question and responses will fit their situation.

**THE MOST IMPORTANT DUTIES OF THE TEAM LEADER ARE . . .**

List what you think *your team members*—aides, orderlies, LVNs—would consider to be the most important duties of the team leader.

  1.

  2.

  3.

  4.

  5.

  6.

  7.

  8.

  9.

10.

List what *you* consider to be the most important duties of the team leader.

  1.

  2.

  3.

  4.

  5.

  6.

  7.

  8.

  9.

10.

Now that you have completed the learning activity, you are ready to read the recorded responses of some aides, orderlies, and nurses to the statement, "A good team leader will. . . ."

The team leader first has to know her co-workers and she has to be the team leader, really *be* the team leader. After you get report, she sits down with you and gives you her second report and tells you what she expects of you and what you can expect from her. You can go to her at any time with your problems and she'll be ready to sit down and talk them over with you. And that's what I really call a good team leader. (Interviewer: "After the report, what are some of your expectations of her?") After we have report with our team leader, we go around, make rounds on all the patients. We come back to the desk, and help the team leader do the paperwork, and then get everything out of the way. After we do that, if an emergency comes up, the team leader can take care of the emergency or a co-worker can take over.

A good team leader can get the floor straightened out by eleven o'clock. Everything, well, not everything, but the most important things done by eleven. That's what I call a good team leader. Everybody done up, floors run straight, everybody not happy but working. I would like my team leader to be firm but nice, you know. Keep the unit running smoothly, be firm, and *keep us busy doing what we are supposed to do*, you know, and if we're not doing it, remind us and let us know when we're slack in our duties, and be loyal. I expect her to be loyal to her team members and helpful when they need help with something—particularly new nurses, you know, they need help. Instead of standing off watching them goof and make mistakes and keeping track of what they do wrong, help them to do better.

To me a team leader is just another nurse. And I really don't like to say this, but I think I forget she's there.

In my mind I don't know what a team leader is for, so she doesn't really exist, except . . . . . . the only thing I see a team leader's role is, is passing medication, nothing else. I mean, on my floor everybody knows what they're doing and they go to it and do it.

I think her most important job is to know what's going on. If you have a team leader that don't know what's going on, it's very hard for you to think for her, and think for the patient and yourself too.

There ain't too much you can expect from your team leader in the morning time especially if you got ORs going. That is team leading right there in itself.

I don't feel bad when one of them comes up to me and says, "Well, did you get that sputum for Mr. So and So." I say, "Oh, I forgot," and just go and do it then. Now, *she's* doing a good job.

Yes, nurses that are experienced do not assist their team. But a graduate nurse who is new on the ward wants to make a big impression so she overworks herself, in fact most of them do when they first start out. And then after being there for a while they sort of get into the same routine as everybody else, and, well, sometimes you can make more work for yourself than there really is to do. (Interviewer: "So you're saying that some of the things a new graduate does in terms of helping everybody else are good but sometimes they get fouled up because they do too much.") Right. The first one or two days is hard but after she's been there a week she should become organized. (Interviewer: "By 'organized' you mean. . .?") In her work and with personnel. She usually knows who needs help with their patients. She would know who needs help by what type of patient they had because she knows which patient is sickest and which team members would need help.

A good team leader keeps you up on everything that happens with your patients and what you're expected to do and doesn't wait till late in the evening and come all of a sudden and say, "I forgot to tell you something to do." I think a team leader as soon as she gets a report should report to the person in charge of that patient. For instance, when we go in we get a report on everything that should be done to these patients. Sometimes the doctor hasn't even put the orders down. Okay, when the doctor puts the orders down, the team leader's supposed to look at those orders and come fill you in. It can become very difficult if she waits until the last minute or later and says, "I forgot, she's supposed to have a tap water enema till clear," and so who knows how long it takes her to get cleared. Our team leader is supposed to have people in order so they go to lunch at a certain time and get back at a certain time and not make the other person wait for lunch and things like that. I think the team leader is supposed to take care of the whole wing where she is team leading and all the people working under her. When a patient comes from surgery, she's supposed to get the report, she's supposed to call me, and tell what kind of care this patient is going to need.

What I don't like is when the team leader comes into the room when you're in front of four or five patients and tells you, "What's wrong with you, you're behind in your work." If you are not doing something right they should tell you, but not in front of the patients! They got to wait until a *little* later, but they should tell you then. . .and *not wait*. Because, well, for example, I didn't do something and the next day when I got my report from the team leader, she says, "Today I hope you do a better job." And it really bothered me. . .I asked her "What do you mean by that? Do you want me to do my job or a better job? What have I done wrong?" She said, "I noticed you didn't do this and that," and I said, "Well, listen, this is not the time to tell me, why didn't you tell me the moment when I was supposed to do it. Why are you telling me now?" That's really bad. They should tell you right at the moment and not wait until you can't do anything about it. If somebody tells you, "I hope you do a better job," you know, it hurts you, you cannot do anything at that time, then it's too late.

A good team leader is one who will pitch in and help. That's what I call a good team leader, not sit at her desk and ask you if you need help or something. She should come down and ask if you're having difficulties and then help.

I like a team leader to help when help is needed. Say, you want to get up a patient and the patient won't get up. Have the team leader come down and kind of talk to them a little and help them get up. I could do the talking, but it's better when someone higher up does it. Because the patient seems to approve of the nurses more than me because I'm lower than the nurses.

I would think a team leader should try to get to know the team member and what he's capable of doing and if he's new, or just came out of the hospital assistant course, he might not be up on everything. And some people are too proud to come and ask for help. Besides, if you passed the course, the hospital *expects* you should know how to do everything. A team leader is supposed to come ask you if you're up with your work and sometimes, "Is there anything I can help you with," 'cause sometimes you just get behind.

A good team leader is a team leader that is able to manage her work and not be all day passing pills and nothing else.

That ends this set of interview excerpts. Now, turn to the learning activity, "A Good Team Leader Will . . . .," where we have extracted and paraphrased some of the main expectations you have just read. Look them over and compare them to the two lists you made: first, to your list of what you think auxiliary workers consider to be the most important duties of a team leader, and then to your list of what you expect of a team leader.

### "A GOOD TEAM LEADER WILL. . . ."

Paraphrased Interview Excerpts:

1. A good team leader will know her patients and her co-workers. She gives an accurate report; is accessible, available to help her co-workers; organizes the work.

2. A good team leader gets the floor straightened out by 11:00 A.M.

3. A good team leader is firm but nice; she is loyal to co-workers. She helps new nurses do better instead of just standing off and criticizing them. She keeps the unit running smoothly, let's her co-workers know when they are slack. She monitors the workers and keeps them on the right track.

4. A team leader is just another nurse. I really don't know what a team leader is for except passing medications.

5. A good team leader will not be hyper . . . will listen to you when you come to her.

6. It is most important for the team leader to "be on top of what is going on."

7. About the only thing a team leader can do in the mornings (night shift) is prepare patients to go to the Operating Room. That takes all her time.

8. I expect a team leader to remind me of the important things I am supposed to do.

9. I expect a team leader to assist with bedside care. . . .I don't expect her to take all day passing medications.

10. I expect the team leader to be organized in her work. This is hard, the first day. The second day, the team leader should know who will need help with their assignments.

11. It's most important for the team leader to learn everyone's name and role. She should know what she can expect from her co-workers.

12. I expect a good team leader to keep you informed on what is to be done for the patient. If there are new orders, she should give you the

orders early. See that people go to lunch on time. She should fill you in on the patients returning from surgery.

13 If there is something you have not done, a good team leader will tell you right away, give you the specific details and not wait until the next day and give you a vague message that "she hopes you will do better."

14. A good team leader will not sit at the desk a lot. She will ask you if you need any help, or if you are having any difficulties.

15. A good team leader will not scold you in front of the patients.

16. When you are having difficulty getting a patient to comply with doctor's orders, a good team leader, because she is higher up, will intervene and get the patient to comply with the doctor's orders.

17. A good team leader will be approachable and not put you down for not knowing something. She will make it comfortable for you to learn.

How do the lists compare? If your list of auxiliary workers' expectations of a good team leader corresponds well or matches the expectations stated here, then chances are you interpret your patient care goals to auxiliary workers quite effectively. The greater your empathy, or the more accurately you can predict co-worker expectations, the more effective your interaction as a team leader and team member will be. If your list and the expectations stated here do not match well, then you probably need more practice at "walking a mile in the other guy's shoes," in seeing the world as he sees it. Continue on with this instructional program; it should help you develop or increase your empathy.

The next group of interview excerpts focuses on one particular area of role conflict between auxiliary personnel and registered nurses: the conflict that arises when the auxiliary person is caught in the middle, wanting to meet patient needs for relief of pain and lacking the power to meet those needs himself.

> The team leader is the person who sees that the medication that the patient is asking for gets down there to him. I mean he shouldn't have to wait and to say, "I asked you for medication, I'm in pain." And I have to go up there to the desk and ask again and she says, "Oh, I forgot." She got busy at the desk or something. (Interviewer: "Does that bug you?") Yeah, it does. 'Cause I'm getting prepared to take the LVN test. And I know some LVNs who passed it that now can pass out their own medication. And I'll be able to say, "I don't want to bug her about it, I can just go get it myself." I think lots of times they are busy. And of course the patient doesn't realize that. But I have run upon some RNs who just plain forget, and I don't know why they forget. It really bugs me. I had to walk right back up there again to tell her this over again. Or you may know this patient is really in pain, and once in a while one of them says, "Well, he isn't in that much pain." Who's to know how much pain the patient is in but himself?

> What I dislike most is when the patient wants something for pain and I'll go to the nurse team leader, whoever the team leader is, and tell her that this patient

wants something. She'll tell you, "I'll be there in a minute." Well then, maybe she forgets. Then the patient puts on the light again and you go back in and answer the light and it's the same thing. You have to go back and look for the person, and in the meantime this person can go on and give the patient the pills and you're still looking for her. This is what really frustrates me the most. Being an aide and RN are two different fields. The aide can only go so far because we didn't go to school and we don't know medicine or what not. If I could do all my own treatments and my own medications then the day wouldn't be so frustrating. But when you have to depend on somebody else to help you with some of the things you are doing and it don't get done, it's kind of hard—real frustrating.

I would go to a team leader and tell her that a patient wants medication and they'd say, "Okay," and that's the end of it. The patient puts the light on again and you go and say, "May I help you?" And the patient says again, "I want a pain pill." So you tell her again and she just says, "Okay, okay!," and gets really impatient about the whole thing!

The only thing I find rewarding about being an LVN is that I can give my own pain medication. I don't have to go find the RN. She'll be sitting down somewhere or say, "Don't bother me, I'll be there."

I've been the aide taking care of a patient and told the RN that this patient wanted medication. Sometimes a couple of hours go by. Some patients, you know, they don't want to think that they're bothering you. There are patients like that and if you come back a couple hours later he must be laying there in pain and feeling very bad towards you. Because he didn't ask *her* for it, he asked *you* for it. So he thinks it's your fault he didn't get it. So you are mad at her because you *told* her. Sometimes she'll say, "Oh, I didn't hear you."

All the time, a patient needs a pain shot or something. Trying to get it to him . . . the patient puts the light on again and then you keep having to go in and answer the light and tell him the same thing over and over. That really gets to me. So if the nurse can, when you tell her the patient needs the pain shot, she should try to give it to him. Each time we go into the room the patient is going to be asking us. Even though you tell him you can't pass the medication, they still bug you. What makes the patient yell at you, is they do not know, a lot of 'em, that you don't give medications and they call you back again and say, "I told you I wanted a pain pill," or "You know I'm in pain."

A team leader needs a little responsibility as far as passing medicine and things. If she has any little extra time, she should go around helping the team and I feel when you tell the team leader that a patient needs medication you shouldn't have to go back and tell her, you know, two or three times, because when you go back to the patient they ask you, "Did you tell the team leader?" They feel like possibly you've forgotten. But sometimes you have told the team leader and she's too busy or she doesn't take time to go down and tell the patient that the medication is not due yet. I think this is one of the things that the team leader really should do because if it's left up to anybody to go after medication they should do it. It's up to the team leader. I think if she has the extra time she should go down and talk to the patients, too. But actually on the floor, they are so busy that instead of going to the patient and saying, "It's not time for your medication," they'll just say, "Tell them I'll be down there. It's not time." It's like you have to go back to them and tell them and sometimes they doubt whether you even asked, you know.

You get to know your patients' habits. I think we all do that. We identify patients with friends, with family. You know, he reminds me of . . . she reminds me of so and so. You feel kind of hurt when he didn't get his medication. You wonder, *what* is the nurse doing?

After reading these excerpts, think a minute about the predicament of the auxiliary worker. What can you do to reduce this kind of role tension between the patient, the auxiliary worker, and yourself, the RN?

Now, place yourself in the auxiliary person's role. Imagine that you are your nurse aide. What are some ways you might cope with this problem, as an aide?

The theme of the following interview excerpts is that *experience is more valuable than education*. Let us assume that you agree that education *is* an important teacher, but that *you* believe that education *and* theory make *experience a more effective teacher*. Is this view the same as or different from what your co-workers believe? And if different, how might the differences affect your interactions with your co-workers? Let's read what the co-workers who were interviewed had to say about the relative value of education and experience.

So many of these young peoples nowadays learn what they know in books—but it's a lot different knowing it in books and having the experience of it. So to them, well, books, that's just a hangup with them.

It would be nice to make 'em feel free to ask anyone, but you find so many of them are so eager, they think they know so much. They *do* know the book work but they don't have the experience, and they won't accept it that someone else has the experience on the floor even though they don't have the education. They have a hard way of learning.

They have the book learning to start, but in the practical way they have to learn same as anybody else.

So it's a little bit difficult sometimes to get things done right away. So it takes them probably a few weeks before they learn the practical things.

I advise all of them to go in at least one summer to be a nurse aide. That would help them more than anything else. And also to have more patients around their last year. By the last year don't have just one or two patients. We've had them come on the floor here and take a patient load before they become a team leader and see how it works out. Then they get a little experience, I guess.

Student nurse come, I mean a new grad come on the floor. She assigned this patient, well, I guess it takes time, I guess, to learn how to cut corners when you're working. She does everything by the book.

Being at school, they know very little about what's going on inside a hospital. And all hospitals are different, I'm sure, but you have to get them trained, say like the UC way, if they're going to work here.

Well, it's difficult. For instance, if you haven't had any experience, it's kind of hard to come in and take care of eight patients even though they orientate you. It takes a few days, and by the end of the week they give you four and then they give you a few more patients. But still there is so much they have to learn from experience rather than—they have it in theory, but experience is what is needed to help them.

A new grad needs to forget some of her book learning, not forget it but work with the unit, find out what's needed on the unit that she's on. Not what they did in school or what they were taught but how we do it on this unit.

They teach them that. Most of them come in with this attitude, "I have so many years of schooling and I'm supposed to know it all," and they really *don't* know. They know the book; they know the theory, but they really don't know how to handle a patient or manage their work. In other words this is one thing I find. They know the book because they're taught that in school. . . . I'm not speaking as a professional but as an aide. They come in and they think that they're going to tell you how to manage your day—and you've been doing this work for years! They're going to come in and tell you things you already know. (Interviewer: "Can you give me an example?") They teach them in school, I guess. Well, a couple of girls and I were talking it over about the new grads. They teach them that they are going to be really in charge and over you when they come into the unit like you're their subordinate. Well, it's not supposed to be like that here. We work as a team, not somebody over you telling you when to breathe and when not to breathe, because you have sense enough. You've been on this job for so many years and you know just about what you're supposed to do to keep your job or to do your patient care. They come in with this little idea that they should tell you what to do. Maybe they teach them that in school.

The old workers and me and all the nurses should try to cooperate with the new nurses. I tell them, "Don't pay no attention to that," because everything is new to her, because she is facing the reality, not the books anymore. Until she gets the confidence from everybody and we help her in all the ways and all that. Probably she'll feel more free to learn and more able to do things without getting frustrated and tired or feeling disillusioned and saying, "What in the world did I attend school to spend five or more years learning nursing?" There's this because I have heard some of the new nurses talking like that. I say, "Don't pay attention."

There's a routine on the floor. Things are much different than a classroom or working with an instructor with you all the time. They get really nervous and you even forget a lot of stuff that you really know and you're trying to do well and it just takes a while to get into the swing and get organized and do things without any problems.

They think because they have more education they really know. Those are the ones that really have a hard time coping with the floor. That one new nurse, she comes in and says, "I had six years of schooling." What we need is good Nurses, not desk nurses. We have enough of those already!

That ends co-workers' comments on the value of experience over education. After reading these excerpts, list below at least three ways you might acknowledge to your co-workers your understanding of the values expressed in these excerpts.

1.

2.

3.

Now, assuming that you believe that education can make a real contribution to patient care, suggest at least three ways (verbal, behavioral, or
both) you might interpret your belief to your co-workers. Try these out on
your co-workers and see what kind of response you get.

1.

2

3

Now, complete the following learning activity.

**EXPERIENCE IS A VALUABLE TEACHER**

*Directions:*

> Interpret the values you have just heard expressed, that is, put into
> your own words *the messages and the feelings* you have just heard
> expressed. (For example: Nurses with book learning become desk
> nurses, not real nurses. Feelings heard are ones of disdain for desk
> nurses and superiority for nurses who are real nurses and who can
> cope with the floor.)
>
> You may want to re-read some of the excerpts again in order to
> do this. Feel free to do so.

**MESSAGES HEARD**

A. _____

_____

_____

B. _____

_____

_____

C. _____

_____

_____

D. _____

_____

_____

E. _____

_____

_____

F. _____

_____

_____

**FEELINGS EXPRESSED**

A. _____

_____

_____

B. _____

_____

_____

C. _____

_____

_____

D. _____

_____

_____

E. _____

_____

_____

F. _____

_____

_____

The next group of interview excerpts is entitled "If No One Listens. . . ." Here you will see that auxiliary workers view responsive listening as one of the most important attributes of a "good nurse." These excerpts should give you some insights into what the auxiliary person has to contribute if you listen, and how he feels about himself and you, if you don't listen.

She doesn't have time to listen to what you want to say, she doesn't have time. She says, "Oh, well, wait a minute," you know. Something could be very important, but because she's passing meds or doing something she doesn't have time to listen. And that kind of makes me uptight, you know, and then later on she'll come back and ask you what you wanted, you know, but whatever you wanted then, it might be too late or it's not important at that time—and most of the time it's about the patient!

Some team leaders don't listen to your reports about the patient. They have to *take* report, but they just don't listen. She can't give anybody else a report if she doesn't listen to report from me. But some of these nurses, they think they know the floor, and they go around and meet all the patients. But you know, as team leader, they don't know what I have run into while they were at the desk, so I think it's very important that any nurse who's team leading should have a full report from her team members because usually there is something. She can't be all over the floor at one time. You can do it all at one time but the point is that when you take report, you listen so you are able to give a thorough report to the next shift. . . . After running around quickly they say, "Give me your report right quick." I found a lot of times, I gave a fast report and then there's things I've missed and a lot of things that I've forgotten. But by the time I go back, she's already passed my report on to the P.M. shift and then it's too late. It's time for me to get off so a lot of times I leave and a lot of times there's things they don't know. There's no point in coming in the next morning and telling them what they should have known yesterday, you know.

Number one, I expect a good team leader to listen to me when a patient has problems like medication problems or maybe the patient needs treatment and I haven't been taught how to give this treatment. Not so much on my floor but I have to float to several floors and each floor is different. I would try to tell the team leader that I don't know how to do this and would prefer her to do this, but she don't want to listen. I get this little attitude—she don't answer me and well, you can tell when a person don't like something, you know. Taking off some time to give a little assistance would promote better care, because it doesn't take all day to pass medicines around.

After reading these interview excerpts, how do you think "not listening" is interpreted by auxiliary workers?

From your knowledge of human behavior, describe some possible consequences of nonlistening behavior on the part of team leaders.

Let's now consider "Ways of Influencing the New Graduate." As a new graduate you are likely to be very aware of testing and evaluating yourself according to your own standards. You may be unaware of your impact on co-workers and perhaps even less aware of their impact on you. The following interview excerpts may provide you with insight into some of the perceptions of auxiliary workers about new graduate nurses. As you read these excerpts you might want to note particularly the ways these workers try to get their messages, their standards, their values across to you, the new graduate. Note also the areas these workers identify as the most troublesome for them in adjusting to new graduate nurses.

It's annoying when you see something that needs to be done and the student doesn't do anything about it. I'm a very fussy person about things being in their proper place. (Interviewer: "I notice you are referring to the new graduate nurses as 'students.' Is that how you view them?") Of course. I think we all do. (Interviewer: "Is there a change? When?") Yes, there is a change. It is when they start doing things that. . . I don't know, like an IV or something like that. You get a better opinion of them. "She's not so bad after all." "She needs to do this and I don't." That's the only difference. But that's because she has been on the floor for a few weeks or whatever and she's got a little more confidence in herself. She transmits this.

We have a new graduate nurse on our floor and she was a student there. She was a student, and when she came to work there full-time as an RN, I still looked on her as a student, until recently. She has been there about four months now, I guess, four or five months. I've started looking at her as an RN. (Interviewer: "What made you change?") Because, I think, for one thing, we've worked together on one side. Say a week or two ago. Just her and myself. I would forget sometimes to go and check my IV in Mr. So and So's room and when I went in there I find she has done this. This is where her training comes in. This has been drummed into her head, whereas it hasn't been into mine. I would know to go check it, but if I forgot to check it, I'm not all that worried about it.

Some think they really know it all. I try to have an open mind to them, just assume they know it all. I'm sure most of them know, when something goes bad on the unit or with one of the patients, and I think, "It's just me. . . ." We've had a few though, it's *not* just me. We had a few that we've run into this problem with—they act like they know it all, but they don't.

I helped a new RN. She didn't know we could go down on the ninth floor and ask them for the meds. We're not supposed to, but we do, and without telling her, I ran down and got the medication. I brought the medication back to the floor and gave it to the nurse. She said, "We don't have a doctor's order," so I went and got the doctor and told him that we needed an order for the medication. He wrote the order and we gave it to the patient and he felt better in a few minutes. Those are the problems a new RN runs into. It's not that they don't want to do these things, it's just that they really don't quite understand how it all works yet.

They don't know where everything is all the time and if you tell them, "I know the patient," or you tell them, "Even if it's not in my field, I've been here so long I know things that are really not in my field," most times they cooperate, but every once in a while you find one who thinks she knows everything and she doesn't accept it. So that's what an aide has to be careful with. To find out the nurses, their ways, and their personality, and things like that.

They don't actually tell you, but you can judge them from their actions and tell from their work that they're not dedicated people. And they're just not really good nurses.

This new nurse, she just came, I mean she just fit right in with the people and said, "I'm new and haven't had too much experience on the floor. If I make a mistake or do something wrong I appreciate corrections, you know. If I come to you and ask you questions, do you mind?" I say, "Feel free to ask me anything you want to," you know. We worked together like making beds and I shared her time with her and she shared mine with me. This way we got along. There was more than one new grad that did this. However, when we get new nurses or new grads on the floor, they always have a chance to work with me. The head nurse, who is really very nice, sees that the new grads work with all level of personnel.

She's orientated to that floor, she knows my duties as an aide. I find her constantly asking me to do things that are not in my job description. And I was wondering one time if she was just testing me or was she just trying to be funny. One thing I really don't appreciate is when they put medications alongside the bed, the patient's bedside and say, "Would you see that the patient takes this medication." I don't think that's right, for various reasons, because it could be the wrong medication.

Then sometime you get sort of disgusted and just let them go at their own pace, and you just tell them if they need any help, just come and ask. You kind of fade out of it a bit. You see, you can't really show 'em or help 'em or explain anything because they have to learn the hard way, just like a little kid.

I tell them that was the way I was taught to do it and the way we do it here. (Interviewer: "And then what happens usually?") Well, they don't say too much. But I really get the impression that they go and tell the others, "This aide is trying to tell *me* how to do it!"

Well now, the thing about it, a new grad come into the place she knows she doesn't know or have the experience that this nurse has that has been here five years. She just *feel* like she's new and she really doesn't do anything about it. A new grad get her pin, her license, and she come in and she thinks she's a nurse. I don't think she's a nurse! She . . . she has to learn and she has to do real nursing for a few years before she's really a nurse. She's just a human. This is . . . that's it. That's one difference between a new grad and a nurse, one that's already a nurse, experienced. Because it's just not there until she's had practice.

But it's something about the . . . when they come in. They don't know too much in the actual nursing field. I guess they have to get the book work out of their mind first, and it's sure not out yet.

When you go to a new job, try to get to know everybody because you don't know who the important person is that may help you get more adjusted to the job than anybody. Everybody is little or big; and they are there for a purpose. I think any of them would help you as much as the other, but some help with big things and others help with the little things you want to know. You don't have to go up and beg people for it. I think that it's very important to know the people you work with and know what each one is not capable of doing.

Just take Janie, who's another nurse, and myself. We can sit down and talk to each other. You could come and ask me for help, whether you were over me or not. You can go to Cleo and ask her most anything. There's just this feeling you have with some people that you don't have with others. They don't mean to . . . they're just not receptive. There's a lot of things that make sense that I do but I don't know how to instruct, but she (the new grad) can come to me and ask me and I can make it much easier for her. Because I've been over those things and I know.

They won't take our word for it, they always kind of go and get the head nurse and someone else's information, something like that. There was one or two of them that I ran into like that . . . give the impression that they wanted to be boss. Some would say, "I'm going to go back and get my degree and teach, I don't care to work here."

I couldn't just say that it's new graduates, it's just about anybody. If they're not willing to learn. . . . those are the ones that have a very difficult time.

Did you note how these aides, orderlies, and nurses got their standards and values across to the new graduate? No doubt you noticed that one of the key ways was to ignore the new graduate's behavior so that she experienced some negative consequences. Perhaps you picked up on the fact that direct telling seemed to be only a last resort, and then the auxiliary worker expected the new grad to check the information given with the head nurse. The point is to ask yourself, as you're going through your first work experience, how you can open up communication about values and standards and make some of these messages more explicit and more direct and therefore a little less painful.

The final section of this module is entitled, "A Good Day Is. . . ." Before reading these interview excerpts, complete the "Survey of Work Values." It is very important that you do this *before* reading the interview excerpts. If you read them before filling out the survey, you may have difficulty sorting out your own work values.

## SURVEY OF WORK VALUES

Identify some of your work values *before* you read the values expressed in the interview excerpts. Doing so may point up potential value clashes between yourself and other workers. Knowing the differences between your values and other workers' values may help you interpret your patient care goals to your co-workers according to *their* frame of reference.

1. People have different things in mind when they say, "Today was a good day at work." What do *you* mean when you say, "Today was a good day"?

   Yourself:

2. Now do the same thing for your head nurse and co-workers. Your head nurse would say that a "good day is when . . . ."

   Your head nurse:

   Your Co-Workers:
   (Orderlies and Aides)

3. Would you prefer tasks and events at work to be *structured* and *predictable*? Or would you prefer that your work be less structured, less predictable? Indicate on the continuum below your inclinations for structure.

|_____/_____/_____|
Structured/predictable     Moderate amount of        Less structure
                           structure and pre-        and predictability
                           dictability

4. Do you like to be finished with baths, treatments, and other routine tasks by a certain time in your shift?

    Yes_____ No_____ Sometimes_____

    Does your head nurse like you to be finished with baths, treatments, and other routine tasks by a certain time in your shift?

    Yes_____ No_____ Sometimes_____

    Do your co-workers like to be finished with baths, treatments, and other routine tasks by a certain time in your shift?

    Yes_____ No_____ Sometimes_____

5. In one phrase state what you think your head nurse's goal for the unit is.

    _____

    _____

    _____

6. Of the following criteria used to judge good nursing care, which do you consider the most important? (Rank in order of importance: Use 1 to 4, with 1 being *most* important and 4 being *least* important):

    Rank in order of importance the criteria your head nurse uses to judge good nursing care.

|  |  | Your head |
|---|---|---|
| You | | nurse |
| ____ | All preventive nursing measures to prevent complications such as atelectasis and decubitus, etc., are done. | ____ |
| ____ | All diagnostic procedures are done. | ____ |
| ____ | Medications and treatments are accurate and on time. | ____ |
| ____ | The patient is assisted in understanding and coping with his illness. | ____ |

Read the following interview excerpts. See if you can identify values expressed by these auxiliary workers and nurses that might conflict with some of your values.

> I feel a good day is when you actually give good patient care, not the halfway job that sometimes you have to do. And everyone is pleasant, and no friction or hassles. (Interviewer: "What are some of the things you have in mind when you say 'good patient care'?") Good patient care . . . well, turning them properly, giving them chest percussion or vibration of the lungs. When you can turn them properly, and give them good care, and make sure that you are doing your portion to keep their skin in good order so that it won't break down, and, if they can take fluids, see that they get ample amounts of fluids. You feel good when you give patient care like that.

> A good day for me is when I'm on duty and I can get organized and take care of my patients and do the routine things that I'm supposed to be doing without too many interruptions.

> A good day? Time to get my linen and set up on each bed and then start the bed making. I like to get them done around 9:00 and get the patients all set up in time for breakfast. Sometimes I have to stop my whole routine and get them set up for breakfast. Then afterwards, when the patients are having their breakfast, I go off and have my coffee break. And by the time they are through I'm just returning and I can start my bed making and baths. And by the time I get through with that I've got 11:00 specimens to send some place, or your collection of clothes, or taking a patient different places. I try to be through with everything by 11:00, and that makes a good day.

> Enough work to keep you busy, but not too much. When your day passes fast you enjoy working with the patients and you don't get upset. Some days you're just upset about the things that the patients are doing, or the work's so hard, or you're short of help. Even when you're short of help you don't mind if there is just enough to keep you busy. It makes the time pass faster really.

> A good day is when I have six patients and I'm occupied, I mean pretty well occupied with them and with no extra excitements, no emergencies. No constant seizure patients. And then things just work out well, so I can take my time and kind of spread myself around my six patients without anybody lacking. If you have eight patients, that doesn't mean that you are giving them the best of your care. But if you have six you feel that you've done what you could that day and you don't feel that you sort of shrugged your responsibility.

> A good day? Okay, be able to finish my work the way it should be done and be able to communicate with the nurses and feel that they are helping you not just physically, but mentally. Sometimes, when you don't get along well with one, you can have the easiest day, but it sure seems the hardest. If the team leader doesn't get along with you that makes it very hard. I have a few times when I haven't been able to get along with my team leader, but usually I do. That's when I feel like I'm having a good day—when I have enough things to do and I can finish, and no one hassles me.

When a group of head nurses was asked what they mean when they say, "Today was a good day," they responded as follows:

When everyone shows up and on time, and everything gets done on time.

No fights, or frictions, or hassles, and the patients all get good care. My responsibility is to see that all the patients get good care, and if we have an emergency, or code, or problem patient, then a lot of the other patients are going to lose out.

A good day is when things aren't hectic when I come on, so I can get myself organized and perhaps even help some of the weaker staff members get themselves organized. If things are organized and if everyone keeps me informed of what's going on, then we all have a good day. I don't like my staff to bug me with every little thing, but I do want them to keep me informed about things that the doctor or supervisor might ask me later on.

When everyone, not just me, is organized and doing their work properly. That's a good day. And no one goes sour unexpectedly, and no one falls out of bed.

Safety and at least adequate nursing care. My unit is so busy that that's really all I can hope for and demand. We are so busy, that really, a good day is when everyone gets at least safe and adequate care, and everyone pulls together, and cooperates.

A good day is when the clock sort of stands still until we can get everything taken care of. And I'm on top of the situation and can sort of control things, or at least I have everything under control. I may not be able to control it, but at least I know what is happening when it happens and not later on. I just hate the days when the students are on, because I never find out till end of shift report what has been going on all day.

When there's enough time to get everything done and all the patients get at least safe, minimum nursing care. And everybody works together and takes care of and does what they're supposed to. That's a good day.

Now that you have read these excerpts, see if there are some work value differences between you and the aides, orderlies, or head nurses. You may want to go back and read some portions of the excerpts again.

### VALUE DIFFERENCES

1. List three areas of value difference between yourself and the head nurses interviewed.

   A.

B

C.

2. List three areas of value differences between yourself and the auxiliary workers interviewed.

   A.



   B.



   C.



3. Using your idea of what your head nurse thinks is a good day (from page 222), list three areas of potential value difference between yourself and *your head nurse*.

   A.

B

C.

4. Using your idea of what your co-workers think is a good day (from page 222), list three areas of potential value difference between yourself and *your co-workers.*

   A.

   B.

   C.

5. What value clashes might you expect between yourself and your head nurse in terms of the ranking of criteria used to judge good nursing care?

After completing this learning activity, you should be aware of some of the work value differences between yourself and others. By conscientiously examining work value differences, you can increase your ability to resolve interpersonal conflict based on value differences.

You would be wrong to conclude that *your* head nurse and co-workers have exactly the values expressed in these interviews, or that you are absolutely correct in your prediction of what your head nurse and co-workers think a good day is. The point of this presentation was to demonstrate a *process*, a way of finding out what value differences might exist between you and your co-workers.

Let's briefly review this process:

1. Listen to what people say in response to questions.

2. On the basis of their responses and other remarks, make inferences about their value candidates.

3. Watch what people do repeatedly and what preparations they make for various activities.

4. Make inferences regarding value candidates based on what people do. Do the behaviors coincide with their professed (verbal) values?

5. Look for the system or patterning of values (for example, determine where an individual seems to be along the whole-task, part-task system continuum).

6. See if you can predict other values within an individual's value system, based on (1) what you know about that system and (2) on his behavior and words.

7. Identify the differences and similarities in values between yourself and others.

8. Predict what might happen if you overestimate similarities in values.

It is now up to you to use the process to determine the similarities and differences in values between you and your co-workers. The following learning activity will help you use this process.


### CHECKING THE WORK SHOES AROUND ME

This is an active learning task to be done on your hospital unit or station.

*Directions:*

1. Arrange to conduct an informal interview with your head nurse, another staff nurse, and one or several of your auxiliary co-workers—individually, not at the same time. (Suggestion: invite them for coffee or talk to them over lunch.) Ask them the following

series of questions, which correspond to the questions asked of the aides, orderlies, and nurses in the interviews you have just read.

a.  A good team leader will . . .

b.  What's a good day for you?

c.  Is experience the best teacher?

d.  What do you think are some of the most important things for new graduates to learn?

2.  From their responses to these questions, itemize what appears to be their system of values.

**HEAD NURSE**                    **STAFF NURSE**                    **AUXILIARY STAFF**

3.  Remembering what you learned in "A Look at Shoes in General" module about values being operationalized in behavior, list (on the following page) some of the behaviors that you see your co-workers doing most often.

**BEHAVIORS**                                                    **VALUES**

_____

_____

_____

_____

_____

_____

_____

_____

_____

List the values that might be inferred from these behaviors. Are these the same values that you inferred from the verbal answers to your questions? (See question 2 above.) If not, which of the two lists do you think reflects the real values of your co-workers?

4. Predict the location of each of your co-workers on the Part-Task/Whole-Task value continuum below.

**NAME**

| _____ | Part-task values | | | | Whole-task values |
|---|---|---|---|---|---|
| | /1 | /2 | /3 | /4 | /5 |

| _____ | Part-task values | | | | Whole-task values |
|---|---|---|---|---|---|
| | /1 | /2 | /3 | /4 | /5 |

| _____ | Part-task values | | | | Whole-task values |
|---|---|---|---|---|---|
| | /1 | /2 | /3 | /4 | /5 |

| _____ | Part-task values | | | | Whole-task values |
|---|---|---|---|---|---|
| | /1 | /2 | /3 | /4 | /5 |

| _____ | Part-task values | | | | Whole-task values |
|---|---|---|---|---|---|
| | /1 | /2 | /3 | /4 | /5 |

5. You have learned how values are organized into systems. Infer some other values of each of your co-workers on the basis of that person's location on the above continuum. (For example, in the response to the question, "What's a good day for you?," your head nurse may have responded, "A good day is when I can get everything done and I can get in to see at least one patient and talk to him about something that's bothering him." From this and her re-

sponses to other questions, you might have placed her at about point 2 or 3 on the continuum. And from your review of the analysis of the part-task and whole-task value systems, you might predict that the head nurse would also value teaching one member of her staff something each day.)

6. List the major kinds of interpersonal conflict that are likely to occur between you and your head nurse if you overestimate similarities of values and perspectives.

   A.

   B.

   C

7. List the major kinds of interpersonal conflict that are likely to occur between you and your co-workers if you overestimate similarities of values and perspectives.

A.

B.

C

This module was designed to help you examine how value systems are expressed by your co-workers, to predict the consequences of overestimating similarities in values, and to suggest to you a process for determining the values of your co-workers so that you can anticipate areas of similarity and difference. Tuning in to some of these important value differences will help you understand some of the sources of irritation and communication breakdown in your work environment. You can use the areas of similarity in value systems to interpret your patient care goals to others.

# Putting Your School Shoes to Work

Just as you cannot assume that your co-workers will personify the part-task or bureaucratic value system simply because that is the dominant value system in the work environment, you cannot assume that, because you are a recent graduate, you will necessarily embody the whole-task or professional system of work. You may well have been taught the values of total, comprehensive patient care, family involvement, continuity, individualization of care, use of cognitive and decision-making skills to plan care and so on, but whether they are actually your values, i.e., *criticized* interests, you may not know as yet.

In school there was probably little or no competition from other nursing values, so that you may never have had to test out your interests to see whether they were values. In all probability, your school values now face competition from other interests, such as the mastery of manual technical skills, handling yourself well in emergency situations, cooperating with others and helping them complete their work even if it means that you don't spend much time on care planning for your own patients. This competition among interests has undoubtedly forced you to make some choices as to which interests are really values. Now, it's time to take a close look at your value system. This module will help you identify what your values *are at this time*, and will then examine strategies for putting your school values to work in the work scene. The objectives of this module are:

1. To show you how to identify your values.

2. To predict areas in which operationalizing your own values will likely produce conflict with your co-workers.

3. To point out strategies that will allow you to define your work situation so that you utilize the value systems of others to effect desired changes in behavior.

Let's begin by showing you how to identify your own values. You can do this in much the same way that you identified the values of your co-workers. First, listen to your words and then look at what you do. Listen for the "shoulds" and "oughts" and "musts" in your language. Then look at what you are doing and see if what you are doing is the same as what you say you *should* be doing. To do this, you might wish to refer to the learning activities that you did in "The Me Module."

Also, take a look at the kind of preparations you make so that you can do what you think is important. I know one nurse who valued patient teaching very highly. She was working evening charge, and to ensure that she could do her patient teaching each evening for the patients going to the OR the next morning, she made a number of preparations. First, she enlisted the cooperation of her aide by explaining to her that pre-op teaching was an essential and integral part of patient care. She then planned her work so that at a specified time, she would tell the aide that she was going to go to see various patients to do pre-op teaching, and that she was not to be disturbed unless it was a life-or-death emergency. The aide understood that she was to answer the phone and take care of anything that came up until the nurse had completed the teaching. Can you imagine the looks on the faces of the physicians when they were told that the nurse could not be disturbed because she was doing pre-op teaching? And can you imagine what this told them about this nurse's value system?

In addition to listening to what you say, looking at what you're doing, and noting what activities you make preparations for, there's another way to get some clear indications of your values. Turn to the learning activity labeled, "Questions! Questions! Questions!" It is best if you complete this learning activity before going on with the rest of this module, but if that is not possible, then proceed and complete the learning activity at your next opportunity when you are on your unit.

## QUESTIONS! QUESTIONS! QUESTIONS!

1. Select at least five co-workers who work with you fairly often and whom you think know you fairly well (more than five would be better, but try to get at least five). Approach them individually and ask (informally or formally, whichever is more comfortable for you) each of them to tell you *the three questions that you ask them most frequently during the course of the working day.* (Be sure they understand that you want an open and honest answer and that it will produce no undesirable consequence for them.)

2.  Write down the answers from all of them. If you talk with five co-workers, you should have at least fifteen questions that you ask frequently.

Coding

_____    _____

_____    _____

_____    _____

_____    _____

_____    _____

_____    _____

_____    _____

_____    _____

_____    _____

_____    _____

_____    _____

_____    _____

_____    _____

_____    _____

3.  Now, go back and code each of the questions according to the following instructions:

Insert PC in the appropriate space at the right to indicate a Patient Care type of question.

> Patient care questions concern direct patient care activities (for example, "What is Mr. Smith's attitude toward the coming surgery?" "Have you completed Mr. Jones' dressing change?")

Insert SM in the appropriate space to indicate a System Maintenance type of question.

> System Maintenance questions cover all indirect patient care and all activities necessary for the maintenance of the health care system. These include task monitoring questions (for example, "Are the orders all completed?" "Has the linen been distributed?"

"Nourishments been passed?" "How many IVs do you have on your side?" unit-centered questions, such as, "Need any help?" "Need any additional staff?" "Are the rooms clean?") and organization-centered questions ("What is the census?" "How many wheelchairs are assigned to your unit and where are they?" "Are you caught up with your work?")

Insert Per in the appropriate space to indicate a Personnel type question.

Personnel type questions cover all activities that develop or maintain personnel skills and/or appearance. Examples are: "Are you familiar with the tracheostomy care routine?" "Do you know how to do such and such?" "What are your plans for your day off?" "When are you going to coffee?" "How're you doing?"

4. Total the number of questions in each of the three categories. If most of your questions (say 50 percent or more) were in the patient care category, you probably have patient care *values*, not just interests or attitudes. If most of your questions were in the system maintenance category, then you probably have strong part-task, bureaucratic system values. If most of your questions were in the Personnel category, then your values lie in the direction of staff development and administration. In a nationwide study of nurses, it was found that system maintenance type questions ranked highest.*

Questions are very important cues to values: they tell us what the questioner believes to be important. Have you ever spent any length of time being unable to anticipate the kind of questions your supervisor or head nurse was most likely to ask you? The question might be, "Did you clean the bedside tables?" or, "Will you finish on time?" or "How did Mr. Jones respond to being told his leg had to be amputated?" Once you learned what was important to your supervisor, you, too, regarded it as important and you questioned those for whom you were responsible about the same items. What this means is that the kind of questions you habitually ask your co-workers not only reflects your value system, but also shapes and molds the behavior of your co-workers, who are repeatedly questioned on certain points.

From the learning activity, "Questions! Questions! Questions!," plus an examination of your words and actions, you should be able to make a list of your major work values. Please do this now. It is strongly suggested that you state your values in action or behavioral terms.

---

*If you would like to see how you stand in comparison with the nurses responding in the nationwide survey, see: Treat, and Kramer, The question behind the question. *J. Nurs. Admin.*, Vol. 2, No. 1, January-February, 1972, pp. 20-27.

**MY VALUES**

(Criticized Interests)

List your values (order is not important) in behavioral terms.

Examples:  I value talking to patients.

For me, it's very important to do procedures and treatments skillfully.

Going on rounds with the doctors is really worthwhile.

1.

2

3

4

5

6.

7

8.

9.

10.

11.

12.

13.

14.

15.

16.

17.

18.

Now that you have listed your values, examine them and see what the pattern is. Do your values tend to cluster around whole-task or part-task activities? Where are your values centered? On patient care, personnel, or system maintenance? Do they tend to reflect the school values of continuity, comprehensiveness, individualization of care, use of judgment, or are they closer to work values such as safety, adequacy, organization, efficiency, cooperation, and management of emergencies? The question of whether your values are what you *want* them to be was covered in "The Me

Module." Here, we are looking at what they *are*, as manifested by your behavior. If you find that your values have changed a great deal since you first started working, or that your values are not exactly what you want them to be, then you ought to return to "The Me Module" and redo some of the exercises on goals and barriers presented there.

Now that you've taken a good look at your values and studied their system and patterning, you are ready to compare your value system with that of the head nurse, staff nurses, and other co-workers on your unit. Retrieve the "Survey of Work Values" from pages 222–223, and the "Checking the Work Shoes Around Me" learning activity from pages 228–229 and compare the list of your values with those of your co-workers.

### POTENTIAL AREAS OF VALUE CONFLICT

1. List areas of potential conflict between your value system and those of co-workers.

_____

_____

_____

_____

_____

_____

_____

_____

_____

2. List the areas of greatest similarity between your values and those of your co-workers. What are all of you interested in doing?

_____

_____

_____

_____

_____

_____

_____

_____

_____

When you compared the list of your values with those of your co-workers, did you find similarities or differences? If there are differences, they will affect the rewards and sanctions you receive from those in your environment. The process goes something like this.

If *you* value the whole-task system of work more than your co-workers do and you are out to give "total, comprehensive patient care," when your work situation values quick, fragmented, part-task care, you will not feel rewarded or satisfied with your accomplishments and yet your co-workers may praise you for getting the job done . . . or criticize you for "spending too much time" with one patient. Thus you can be rewarded for what you do not value and criticized for doing what you do value. An example from one new graduate may help to illustrate this point:

> I think I set higher levels for myself than maybe the people I'm working with do. Because a couple of times I thought I was doing okay, you know, I was getting stuff done, but I don't think I was performing as well as I feel I should have been. But the RN I was working with said I was doing a really good job . . . One day, it was kind of a busy day and I didn't get out with the patients as much as I wanted to, and I didn't feel like I was helping the team members as much as a team leader should. But without knowing the patients and without being familiar with them, you know, that takes more time . . . there weren't any difficulties that came up or anything, but she (the RN) said I did a good job. But, I just felt that I should have been on the floor more.

Being rewarded for things you do not value, and not receiving rewards for things you do value causes a lot of discomfort, and causes pressure on you to change your values. You need to be aware of these discrepancies in rewards, and the pressure that they produce. Only through this awareness will you be able to resist pressure to change your value system — if you do not want to change it.

In the following interview excerpt, a new graduate tells about her sense of frustration and confusion with the value switch she encountered at work.

> My dissatisfactions, which I had been feeling, became nothing in comparison to what my evaluation brought forth. Essentially, the evaluation focused on my disorganization and my inability to cope with certain situations. Undoubtedly, much of what they said was true, or at least partially true. I was not really aware of these things. However, what was devastating to me was their lack of praise as to what I did do well. I should point out that my head nurse never really showed an interest in me or my work, except when I had done something wrong.

Remembering what you learned in the previous modules of this instructional program, you should try to get into the shoes of the head nurse. Is it any wonder that a head nurse would reward you only for behavior that fits *her* (not your) value system? You need to look at your values in conjunction with those of your co-workers, particularly those of your head nurse, since she is generally the pacesetter for the unit. In areas where your values differ, do not expect to be rewarded or positively reinforced. Learn to depend upon yourself for your own internal rewards and motivation in these areas. Remember also that you will probably receive rewards and encouragement for doing things valued by the head nurse. If these things are not part of your value system, receiving such rewards might confuse you, or you might decide to change your behavior so that you continue to receive those rewards. We are all human and we like and need stroking. That's OK if that is really what you want. But remember, the first step toward changing our values is changing our behavior. If you change your behavior to get more rewards and encouragement from your co-workers, do so deliberately and knowingly. And if it is at the sacrifice of one of your values, you will need to criticize the new interest in terms of your other interests.

Perhaps an example will clarify what is meant here. The head nurse compliments you on how well you ran the desk and got all the treatments done, specimens down to the lab, etc. This pleases you, but you know you did it at the expense of not getting out to see any patients or doing any pre-op teaching. And you also didn't get a coffee break that evening. You decide that you are going to criticize your various interests to see if you are still satisfied with what you think your values are. The three interests you are going to look at are: doing pre-op teaching; running the desk; and taking a coffee break. The common antecedents for all three are time and effort, with coffee taking the least amount of time, and running the desk the most time. At this point, running the desk also requires the most effort, because it is relatively new and you don't have a repertoire of experience built up yet. Pre-op teaching is fairly easy for you because you did a lot of it while you were in school.

What about the consequences of each interest? These have to be analyzed and compared. The consequences that you list for "taking a coffee break" are: you may have a chance of meeting some intern and getting asked to a party; resting your feet and relaxing a bit; the "pick-up" that you get from the caffeine in the coffee will help you be a little more alert when you get back. As you see it at this time, the consequences of "running the desk" are: first and foremost, praise from the head nurse when you do it well; co-workers smile and comment that it's nice working when you're in charge because things go well; you tell yourself that in the long run patients are getting better care, but you really haven't experienced this yet; and you don't get out to see patients or do pre-op teaching because you have to put so much time and effort into this interest. The consequences of "pre-op teaching" are: the feeling that you're doing a good job; the enjoyment of imparting information and interacting with patients; and you have seen how pre-op teaching can really make a difference in postop care and avoidance of complications. In comparing these interests and their consequences, you may decide that at this time, receiving praise from the head nurse is the consequence that is most worthwhile. You're new and a little unsure of yourself, and it really feels good. It's OK to make that decision; just realize that you are doing it and since your interests are somewhat competitive (because of the similarity in antecedents), what you are really saying is that you value the head nurse's opinion of you more than you do the consequences of a coffee break or of pre-op teaching. You may decide that all interests are important to you and that you are willing to chance a little less efficient running of the desk so that each evening you can talk to or teach one patient for fifteen or twenty minutes. Later, as you gain more skill, you can increase your patient contact accordingly. That way you might be able to reinstate your pre-op teaching interest to a high priority value.

Next, we will look at strategies that may be useful when your values differ from those of your co-workers. We will address the question, "How can I put my values to work?"

Before we proceed with a list of strategies, it's important that you understand the purpose of putting your values to work. Changing other people's values and behaviors is not a game. The purpose of doing it is to get others to work to improve patient care. It's not a matter of trying to manipulate others so that you get your own way, but rather of using influence knowingly and judiciously so that you can practice the kind of nursing you believe is best for patient care, or so that you can work most effectively with others to produce desirable changes in the health care system. It's a matter of safeguarding patient care and advancing the practice of nursing. Any occupation or profession must look to its youth, its newcomers, for a constant infusion of new ideas. Experienced workers must learn how to receive and make room for new ideas; *newcomers must know how to infuse their ideas into the system without shaking the system up so badly that chaos results.*

Manipulation serves personal ends or goals; the influence strategies we are presenting here serve the goal of improving the quality of health and patient care. Our goal in nursing is not to manipulate but rather to motivate ourselves and influence others to constantly improve the health care delivery system so that our clients receive not only the quantity but quality of health care which is their right.

Let's look now at some specific strategies potentially useful in helping you operationalize your values in the work setting.

*Strategy 1.* One of the first and most important things that you must do in this, your first job, is to select and establish your desired identity as a professional worker. You must change your concept of yourself from that of a learner who incidentally works to that of a professional worker who concurrently learns. Pivotal to this worker identification process is selecting, criticizing, and maintaining one's value system. Try out and test your interests. For those values that pass the ultimate test ("It's worth having, all things considered."), hold on to them in the face of situational constraints. Develop the abilities and traits you need to achieve your goals. Get into the habit of constant reappraisal of your values and goals.

*Strategy 2.* Develop empathy and use it to get into the other guy's shoes. Learn to see things the way they see them, and then use this insight to develop and foster plans of action that will satisfy their needs as well as your own. Some help in the use of this strategy will be found in the final module, entitled, "The Mating Process." For now, practice these steps:

a.  First, describe the value system of the other person as positively and favorably as you can. Describe it in such a way that it sounds as good to them as yours sounds to you. To show them that you understand it, try to state in your own words what you think the other's perception of the problem is, and then check your statement out with them for accuracy. For example, a new graduate tells a nurse aide that she has just changed a patient's bed. The nurse aide becomes angry and begins to sulk. As a new graduate, you may find this puzzling. You may conclude that the nurse aide does not appreciate your help, or that she thinks that the linen change was unnecessary. However, if you know that a common perception among the nurse aides on your unit is that "cleaning up patients" is their job, and if you can get into the nurse aide's value system, you will be able to interpret your actions in terms of that value system. For example, "Mrs. Smith, I wasn't doing that because I didn't think that you would do it, but I just happened to be out there and it seemed stupid for me to come in and call you when I was there and could do it in the time it would take me to walk to the desk and ask you to do it."

Or another example that might well happen in the situation cited earlier about the nurse who secluded herself for 10–15 minutes each evening in order to do pre-op teaching: Upon encountering one of the nurse aides who was grumbling about having to cover the unit while you did this, the nurse said: "Mrs. Adams, I suppose from your point of view, it looks as though I'm spending a lot, perhaps too much time, with one patient and neglecting the other patients and my other duties. You believe that all patients need attention and that it isn't fair, either to you or to the other patients that I spend so much time with one. Is that right?

b.  Show by your words and actions that you respect the right of others to have their value system, and realize that they will probably act to maintain the integrity of their system.

*Strategy 3.* Set mutual goals. Find some commonality in your value system and those of your co-workers, something you agree upon, and begin from there to set mutual goals. Remember, even if you agree upon a goal, the means you and they use to achieve it may differ. You might be able to point out that there is more than one way to reach the goal, and that all ways are workable. There will be more information on the setting of mutual goals in the final module ("The Mating Process").

*Strategy 4*. Remember, you are trying to effect a *change in behavior*. A change in attitudes and/or values may or may not occur—that is relatively unimportant. What is important is the behavior change. It is up to the individual to make a corresponding attitude or value change, if they wish to. If you want your nurse aide to answer lights promptly, or to call patients by name instead of diagnosis, reinforce and reward her for this behavior—never mind if she really has the "right attitude" toward patients. That's really immaterial for your purpose.

*Strategy 5*. Learn to choose judiciously between whole-task and part-task care. Neither system is all right or all wrong; they are simply different. At best, work organized on a part-task basis provides coordinated, well planned, efficient care to large numbers of people. At worst, it provides uncoordinated, fragmented care to large numbers of people. The professional whole-task system at best provides more comprehensive care to fewer patients, while at worst it provides less efficient care by providing some care that could be more efficiently provided by a series of workers.

Some needs are better cared for on a "whole-task" basis, while others are better met on a "part-task" basis. The important thing is not to choose either approach to the exclusion of the other, but to see the advantages of both systems and choose integrative approaches to work organization based upon objectives and patient care needs. For example, in school, you had a lot of time to set up and execute a teaching plan. Now, you have only short periods of time in which to do patient teaching with a larger number of patients. Thus, your teaching must be accomplished in short but well-focused talks. You may have only 15 minutes, but in 15 minutes of well-focused conversation, you can do a great deal of teaching. You may decide that a particular patient needs a concentrated 30-minute block of teaching and so you use the 30 minutes when bathing usually takes place to do the teaching. You may exclude the bath, or else bathe the patient while you talk. Generally, there are other staff members to cover for you during coffee, lunch, or supper breaks. You can usually enlist other staff to cover such things as PRN medications while you are doing pre-operative teaching, too. Thus, it is possible to integrate the part-task and whole-task approaches to meet patient care needs.

There is another way of organizing work according to patient care needs. When you find that safe or adequate care to large numbers of patients interferes with more comprehensive care for one or two patients, you may become frustrated and bemoan the difficulty. An effective solution is to decide what is the minimal, adequate, safe care that must be done for the majority. See if you can organize this care quickly on a part-task basis, keeping in mind that people can be rapidly trained on the job to do these part tasks. This should leave the whole-task trained worker free to meet the needs of patients requiring more comprehensive, whole-task care.

To help develop your ability to choose judiciously between whole-task and part-task care, complete the following learning activity.

**WHAT WOULD YOU DO?**

The setting is a 20-bed postcardiac surgical ward of a large county hospital. It's the evening shift—about 4:30 P.M.—and you are alone because the one aide who works with you has gone to dinner. The day shift report indicates that the ward is fairly quiet and that most of the patients are status quo. All the patients on this ward are pre- or postcardiac surgery, many having just recently transferred out of the cardiac ICU, which is adjacent to the ward. You are in the process of making rounds to see all the patients. Halfway down the large open ward is Mrs. Swape, a 52-year-old postpump patient who also works as a volunteer on the ward. She seems very sad and lonely, and you remember that the day nurse had remarked that Mrs. Swape had not been her usual cheerful self that day. You pause in your flurry of activity, approach Mrs. Swape, and gently cover her hand with yours. As she looks up at you, you think you detect tears welling up in her eyes. This is most unusual. During all of her past surgery, she has been very highly controlled: never crying or complaining, always saying "thank you" to the nurses, even when you had to do painful procedures like suctioning and turning her. You've been concerned about her and her super control.

Reflecting to yourself that maybe Mrs. Swape is ready to open up and talk, you gently pull the curtains around the bed and seat yourself on the edge. After a few minutes, Mrs. Swape begins to talk. She is in the middle of telling you how afraid she is—not about the surgery, but afraid the nurses on the ward won't like her anymore. It seems that a few years ago she had a postsurgical psychosis during which she really "flipped out" for a few days: pulling out IVs, NG tubes, throwing things, and screaming at the nurse. She remembered this after she came out of it, and now she's afraid she might do it again with this surgery, and then the nurses won't like her anymore or let her come back to work on the ward as a volunteer. Mrs. Swape is in the middle of telling you this. Her face is pinched and anxious and she looks as though she will "let go" any minute now.

Suddenly you hear the food cart clanging through the doors of the ward. At this hospital the trays do not come up from the kitchen prepared; there are just pots of food, and the staff has to serve it on plates, construct the special low-salt diets, etc. Furthermore, the cart has to be returned to the kitchen for use on the other floors. Most of your patients are fairly recent open-heart surgery patients. They need their food, particularly the potassium. If you stay with Mrs. Swape, there's no one there to serve them the food; if you don't serve them the food and return the cart, the supervisor will call or come to the ward, and you know from past experiences that she takes a dim view of this kind of "inefficiency." If you leave, even for a minute, your intuition and judgment tell you that the climate will be broken and Mrs. Swape will clam up again.

1. What would you do in this situation?

2. Can you think of a way in which you might effect some sort of compromise between the part-task and whole-task approach in order to meet the needs of all patients?

*Strategy 6.* A sixth strategy is to "reframe," that is, focus attention on the individual patient's resistance to specific tasks, for example, postoperative ambulation or a wound dressing change, instead of focusing on the task itself. This strategy was discussed briefly in the module, "Work Shoes and School Shoes," in terms of individualizing patient care. It is the predictability and variability of resistance, rather than the sheer amount of resistance, that makes a task active or inert. Individualize the task performed for each patient by focusing your attention and that of your co-workers on each patient's resistance This will help you achieve individualized patient care.

This strategy can also be used in respect to reframing the concept of work. What is the work of a nurse? For years, the emphasis has been on physical care: "When I'm finished with treatments and taking off orders, and if time permits, I'll go teach Mrs. Jones about her surgery." The work of the nurse includes both physical care and social-psychological care. The work day needs to be planned with both the physical and psychosocial aspects of work in mind. To operationalize your goals, you should interpret them to head nurses and co-workers and get them to reframe the work day to see that talking, listening, and teaching are as much a part of nursing as baths, treatments, and medication. The latter activities are not something to be done "After we finish our work."

This module was entitled "Putting Your School Shoes to Work," because we assumed that the value systems of most new graduates are closer to the whole-task or school subculture than to the part-task or work subculture. Perhaps, after two or three months of work, your school-bred value system is more an attitudinal cluster of preferences rather than a set of criticized interests, and you are experiencing some conflict within yourself. This module presented a process that can help you identify your values and it described several strategies that should help you to operationalize your value system for the betterment of patient care By mastery of these strategies, you will be able to mold your reality to fit your ideals and influence your work environment to improve patient care. In this way, you will be able to give a positive answer to Cervantes when he exclaims: "If only dreams and reality were not so far apart!"[1] They're not; they don't need to be.

**REFERENCE**

1.   Cervantes, S.M. *Don Quixote.* New York: Modern Library, 195

## BIBLIOGRAPHY

Allport, G. "Attitudes" in M. Fishbein (ed.), *Readings in Attitude Theory and Measurement.* New York: John Wiley and Sons, 1967.

Bennis, W. G., *et al. The Planning of Change.* New York: Holt, Rinehart and Winston, 1969.

Dewey, J. *Sources of a Science of Education.* New York: Liveright Publishing, 1929.

Dewey, J. *How We Think.* Boston: D. C. Heath, 1933.

Festinger, L. *A Theory of Cognitive Dissonance.* Evanston, Ill.: Row, Peterson, 1957.

Goss, M. Influence and authority among physicians in an outpatient clinic. *Am. Sociol. Rev.*, Vol. 26, No. 1, 1961, pp. 39-50.

Greenwald, A., *et al.* (eds.) *Psychological Foundations of Attitudes.* New York: Academic Press, 1968.

Hall, R. The concept of bureaucracy: an empirical assessment. *Am. J. Sociol.*, Vol. 69, July 1963, pp. 32-40.

Hovland, C.I. *The Order of Presentation in Persuasion.* New Haven, Conn: Yale University Press, 1957.

Hovland, C. I., and Pritzker, H. A. Extent of opinion change as a function of amount of change advocated. *J. Abnorm. Soc. Psychol.*, Vol. 54, 1957, pp. 257-261.

Hovland, C.I., and Weiss, W. The influence of source credibility on communication effectiveness. *Publ. Opin. Q.*, Vol. 15, 1951, pp. 635-650.

Interaction Associates, Inc: *Tools for Change, Strategy Notebook.* San Francisco: Interaction Associates, Inc., 1972, 2nd Edition. 63 pages.

Kluckhohn, F. Dominant and variant value orientations, in C. Kluckhohn, *et al.* (eds.) *Personality in Nature, Society, and Culture.* New York: Knopf, 1953, pp. 342-357.

Kramer, M. and Schmalenberg, C.E. The first job: a proving ground. basis for empathy development. *J. Nurs. Admin.*, Vol. 7, No. 1, 1977, pp. 12-20.

Kroeber, A. L. and Kluckhohn C. *Culture.* New York: Vintage Books, 1952.

McDonald, F.J. *Educational Psychology*, 2nd ed. Belmont, Calif: Wadsworth Publishing Co., 1965.

McDonnell, C., *et al.* What would you do? *Am. J. Nurs.*, Vol. 72, No. 2, February 1972, pp. 296-301.

Schein, E. H. *Professional Education: Some New Directions.* New York: McGraw-Hill, 1972.

Scott, W.R. Professionals in Bureaucracies — Areas of Conflict, in H. M. Vollmer and D.L. Mills (eds.), *Professionalization.* Englewood Cliffs: Prentice-Hall, 1966, pp. 265-275.

Scott, W. R., *et al.*, Organizational evaluation and authority. *Admin. Sci. Q.*, Vol. 12, June 1967, pp. 93-117.

Shostrom, E. L. *Man, the Manipulator.* New York: Bantam Books, 1968.

Simon, S. B., *et al. Values Clarification.* New York: Hart Publishing Company, 1972.

Smith, K. Discrepancies in the Value Climate of Nursing Students: A Comparison of Head Nurses and Nursing Educators." Doctoral Dissertation, Stanford University, 1964.

Treat, M., and Kramer, M. The question behind the question. *J. Nurs. Admin.*, Vol. 2, No. 1, 1972, pp. 20-27.

Watzlawick, P., *et al.*, *Pragmatics of Human Communication.* New York: W. W. Norton, 1967.

Weinstein, E., "The Development of Interpersonal Competence," in D. A. Goslin (ed.), *Handbook of Socialization Theory and Research.* Chicago: Rand McNally, 1969, pp. 753-775.

# CONFLICT RESOLUTION
## the mating of dreams and reality

**INTRODUCTION**

Yesterday, all my troubles seemed so far away
Now, it looks as though they're here to stay
Oh, I believe in yesterday.*

I'm a graduate with no feelings . . . no gut reactions. Patients are sicknesses and I'm paid to take care of them. Things are sterile, clean and white . . . Guess who had to have another enema this morning! . . . 512. And what a mess. We had two foleys, and the preops were thirty minutes late. 45 is still on the bedpan, check it out will you? This place has been a madhouse today. My feet are sore . . . you wouldn't believe it! Anyway, 14, ate well, 23, no complaints, 11, ambulated three times . . . No names, no faces, just shadowy shapes to wash and make well again. Total patient care is the biggest hoax ever perpetrated since the fountain of youth. I came out of nursing school with the idealism of a student. I knew I had a lot to learn and I was prepared for that. But after having my suggestions ridiculed for impracticality, and not getting answers to my questions, I had nightmares, and went home to vomit[1].

The difference between the yesterday of school and the today of nursing practice frequently results in the kind of turmoil and conflict expressed in the excerpt you have just read, which was written by a student nurse and presented in a sociodrama at a National Student Nurses' Association Convention. There is a feeling of helplessness and powerlessness in a system that neither wants nor respects the concepts of nursing care that you bring with you to the work world. Often, the new graduate ponders: "Is it worth it?," "If this is what nursing is all about, I don't want to be a part of it," or "I'm tired of beating my head against a brick wall." Such thoughts are expressions of inner turmoil, frustration, and dissatisfaction. As time passes, things may go from bad to worse, until the finale is reached: "I can't live with this kind of inner churning. I've got to get out of this before I go crazy!"

All of these thoughts and feelings can lead one to conclude that conflict is unhealthy and destructive. But this is not necessarily true. It is not the conflict *per se* that is the problem, but rather the inability to manage and deal with it. Were you taught in school to expect conflict between school and work values? Were you taught how to operationalize your professional values despite ridicule or indifference from other staff on your unit? You may have learned how to deal with resistance in general but it is unlikely that you had an opportunity to deal with the resistance of a head nurse or another staff nurse to one of your ideas or suggestions. As a matter of fact, when you ran into poor practices on a unit, your instructors probably commented, "Look, they've been practicing that way for years here. There isn't too much we can do about it, but when you get out. . ."

Because you've had no experience at making change, you don't know how to deal with the conflict engendered when you try to introduce new ideas or ways of handling everyday problems on the unit. Naturally, this leads you to believe that conflict is bad.

This instructional program, "Conflict Resolution: The Mating of Dreams and Reality," consists of three modules. In the first, entitled, "Conflict, The Cutting Edge of Growth," we explore the attitude that conflict is healthy and growth-producing. The second module, "Reality," will define and describe three major types of conflicts experienced by new graduates and will present a series of statements from new graduates to illustrate the various types of conflict they have encountered. The third and final module, "The Mating Process," presents six major principles that can be used to work out productive strategies of conflict resolution.

**REFERENCE**

1.  Caghan, S. *Conscious and Commitment: Strategies and Models.* New York: National Student Nurses' Assoc., Inc., 1970, p.1.

# Module 12

# Conflict: The Cutting Edge of Growth

This module will attempt to bring about an attitudinal change in you. Its objective is to help you develop a positive attitude toward conflict; to see conflict as healthy and growth-producing and as a means of effecting desired personal and environmental changes. For some of you, this will be a congruent attitudinal change, for you already perceive conflict this way. But for most, it will be an incongruent change. You may have been raised to view conflict as something bad, something to be avoided, something that nice people don't engage in. For you, the attitudinal change will be more difficult, but we hope to produce it by utilizing one of the ways suggested in the "A Look at Shoes in General" module: information input. (The fact that we are beginning by trying to produce an attitudinal change rather than a behavioral change does not nullify the principle that more effective change is produced if one starts by trying to change behavior rather than attitudes. But because we lack personal contact with each of you, we have to commence this way.)

To begin the informational input, we will clarify exactly what is meant by conflict. Conflict is the tension generated by disagreements that result whenever perceived incompatible activities occur between interdependent individuals over substantive issues. In other words, it is a clash between individuals who are attempting, in light of their own knowledge and beliefs, which they value highly, to either maintain or change some structure. It is important to note that these individuals must be interdependent in some way and the issue must be important to them, or there would be no conflict.

What is meant by the statement that conflict is healthy and growth-producing? Conflict is the tension that arises from individual differences over matters of importance. This tension generally causes inner feelings of unrest or frustration that motivate the individual to take some kind of action to reduce the tension. It is this force as a motivator that gives tension its growth-producing potential. Tension can move an individual to greater lengths and at a faster rate than if there is no tension. To demonstrate how tension increases the rate of movement, we will draw an analogy between sailing and conflict.

As some of you may know, sailing operates on the principle of tension. For a sailboat to move, there must be a certain amount of tension placed on the sail by the wind. If there is no wind or very little wind, the boat sits dead in the water. The sail stays limp and flaps in the breeze. This is tolerable for a time. It can be a real drag after a couple of hours, when the dock is still in plain view. When the wind freshens, the sail will fill with air, i.e., the tension increases, and the boat begins to move.

This same principle can operate in nursing. When you first start nursing, sufficient tension is generated by your feelings of uncertainty about your ability to function in this new setting to set you into motion. As you begin to master the technical skills and the organizational skills necessary to function on your particular unit, the tension begins to decrease. Things begin to go relatively smoothly and there is much less hassle. After a time, a feeling of stagnation may set in. There is a realization that the things you learned in school just aren't happening here in the work scene. New graduates often begin to formulate plans for putting into practice those principles of nursing care that were learned in school. Their attempts to implement change may be met with criticism from others on the unit. Tension increases. Motivation to implement change increases, despite possible conflict. Frustration also increases, but you continue to try to put into practice those principles of individualized patient care that you learned in school. Thus, conflict increases your motivation to make changes and improve the quality of patient care.

Perhaps some of you experienced an initial preoccupation with learning new skills. Others may never have had this preoccupation with skill learning and thus encountered the tension and frustration of trying to put your school ideals into practice quite early. In any event, it can be seen from both the sailing and nursing examples that tension produces an increased rate of movement and growth.

There is another possibility, however. The tension can be *too* great. If the tension on the sail of a boat is *too* great, the boat may keel over on its side. Or the wind may catch the sail and send the boat into a spin. The boat spins until the crew can take the action necessary to spill some of the wind from the sail and regain control of the boat.

Just as the wind can produce too much tension on a sailboat, so, too, frustration and conflict can produce too much tension for you. As you enter the work world, you will notice that many things need changing. As you attempt to make these changes, you will encounter many barriers: lack of interest and motivation among other staff, staffing inadequacies, and shortages of time and supplies, to mention a few. The frustration and tension builds to the point that it can overwhelm you. Some new graduates, overwhelmed by the tension, become "Rutters," or else they flee the work scene altogether. Others make use of their skills to become bicultural: to mate traditional concepts of nursing with avant-garde concepts of nursing practice.

Just as skill in sailing can be utilized to convert a spinning boat into a positive sailing venture, so too, appropriate skills can enable you to convert frustrating experiences in nursing into positive, growth-producing experiences. By mating the new ideas that you bring to the work scene with traditional concepts of patient care, you can help improve the system of patient care. The potential for growth lies in your ability to manage the tension, i.e., the conflicts, so that long anticipated improvements in patient care become a reality.

Because conflict often forces change and increases the rate of change, it is potentially healthy and growth-producing. It is the purpose of this program to help you develop your ability to manage conflict in such a way that it is growth-producing for you.

> The routine work, the endless lights, calling for some small comfort, the back breaking, leg aching work of it all. We need some imaginative stimulus, some not impossible idea, such as may shape vague hope and transform it into effective desire, to carry us year after year. . . . We've got to get it together[1].

## REFERENCE

1. Caghan, S. *Conscious and Commitment: Strategies and Models.* New York: National Student Nurses' Assoc., Inc., 1970, p.7

# Module 13

# Reality

The river's too wide now for crossing
The water's rush too loud for talking
We never build bridges for walking
The river's too wide.*

Conflict can and does happen in nursing. In December 1974, the *American Journal of Nursing* presented an account of the efforts of seven new graduates to introduce change and innovation on a pediatric ward. The author describes how the nurses developed a proposal that was presented to the Director of Nursing Service and accepted. The accepted proposal met obstacles of all sorts: "rigid policies, staff resistance, and most detrimental, administrative inaction." A little more than two years after beginning the project, all seven nurses had left the pediatric ward. The article concludes on a note of bitterness:

> Three cheers for the liberalized nursing education that teaches us to think and act independently and give individualized, comprehensive nursing care—but meanwhile *where* do all the creative, caring nurses go to practice nursing as we've been taught?**

*MUSIC CITY MUSIC, INC. (ASCAP) © 1973 International Copyright Secured. All Rights Reserved. (Lyrics by Bob Morrison on the album, "If You Love Me Let Me Know," by Olivia Newton-John.)

**From Genn, Nancy. Where can nurses practice as they're taught? *American Journal of Nursing,* Volume 74, Number 12, December, 1974. © 1974 American Journal of Nursing Compan··

One can't help but ask, "Is the river too wide?" Are the problems now faced by you, a new graduate trying to put into practice those things you learned in school, beyond resolution?

All of the problems facing new graduates probably cannot be resolved. But some can be. Before resolution can take place, however, the issues causing conflict between the new graduate and the work scene need to be examined. This module will examine the issues of conflict identified by new graduates who moved into the work world. The module has two objectives:

1. To identify the three major types of conflicts.

2. To describe and identify types of conflict you are now encountering.

Let's begin by taking a look at the *types* of conflict new graduates have described. They can be broken down into three types: intrapersonal, interpersonal, and organizational.

### INTRAPERSONAL CONFLICT

*Intrapersonal* conflict refers to the tension or stress that occurs *within* an individual as a result of unmet needs, expectations, or goals[1]. Discontentment and dissatisfaction result because personal goals and expectations are not being met. For example, the professional-bureaucratic conflict that was discussed at length in the "Work Shoes and School Shoes" module has an intrapersonal aspect. New graduates expect nursing to be practiced as they were taught to practice it in school. On the basis of their beliefs and expectations, they develop and set goals for themselves. When they reach the real scene, things just aren't what they were "cracked up" to be. They find that speed, organization, and efficiency are valued and that practice of these values interferes with talking, listening to, and teaching patients. As an individual and as a nurse, the new graduate feels a great deal of frustration and dissatisfaction.

The intrapersonal conflicts described by new graduates were classified into four major categories:

1. *Professional-Bureaucratic.* Conflict arises because of the differences and the incompatible expectations of the professional and bureaucratic work systems. Everyone must adjust to and pick up some loyalty to the bureaucratic system. It is not bad if you do. However, the process of adjustment is wrought with conflict. The standards that nurses are taught in school and those advocated in the work scene are different, and the nurse resents and resists the work standards. Statements made by new graduates that reflect this type of conflict are:

I'm not able to give patient care because of all the meds and paperwork.

The patients are treated like diseases rather than people.

I don't have time to talk with the doctors or the patients. There's barely time to do the physical care.

The other staff members don't follow through with the care plans for the patients. No one seems to care.

2. *Means-Goals.* Conflict arises when the means necessary to reach a desired goal—either a people-changing goal or a clinical practice goal—are lacking. Comments from new graduates that reflect this type of conflict are as follows:

We don't have adequate equipment or staffing and the problems just keep happening. No one is very receptive to my ideas about change.

Alcoholic patients are so hopeless. No matter what we do they keep coming back.

We have kids that come for heart surgery. Many times the surgery doesn't help. We try everything we know and still some of the kids die.

3. *Competency Gap.* The competency gap is due to a lack of skill or knowledge on the part of the nurse rather than to a lack of means to reach a desired goal.

There was a cardiac arrest and I didn't know what to do. That really upset me.

Sometimes I miss orders on the chart and don't know about new equipment that is used. I can't seem to get the team organized.

4. *Expressive-Instrumental.* Conflict arises from the dilemma of meeting either the technical (instrumental) needs of patients or their human (expressive) needs. You are torn between the technical work that must get done and the patient's human needs.

The patient had a ruptured aneurysm and we kept him alive for several days on the Bennett. There was no brain wave activity and his family kept saying to pull the plug. How do you decide what to do? It's really hard.

I had a patient who was really worried about having a breast biopsy and she had finally opened up and was talking about it. Then the supper trays came to the floor. I didn't know if I should stay with the patient or get the other fifteen patients on the unit their supper trays.

### INTERPERSONAL CONFLICT

The second type of conflict is *interpersonal*, i.e., conflict that arises out of differences of opinion, different orientations, power struggles, or other events between two or more persons[2]. Typical interpersonal conflicts in nursing are hassles with the other staff on the unit or hassles with the physicians. Frequently, these are labelled "personality clashes." Organizational values that you refuse to adopt but which are held by other staff can produce interpersonal conflict.

There are four major categories of conflict of the interpersonal type:

1. *Nurse-Nurse.* Frequently, conflict arises over differences of opinion as to how the unit or a particular patient should be managed. This conflict is often the interpersonal aspect of the professional-bureaucratic conflict. Comments made by nurses in relation to their differences with other nurses were as follows:

> The head nurse is so task-oriented. She tries to set priorities for me so I won't spend as much time with the patients. I think she picks on me.

> I had a plan of care set up for the patient. The staff didn't follow through with the plan and really mismanaged the whole situation.

2. *Doctor-Nurse.* The nature and the quality of physician-nurse interactions sometimes lead to interpersonal conflict with particular doctors. Here are some of the comments that nurses made:

> It never fails, when his patients go bad, he hollers at one of the nurses. He is so incompetent that we have a running battle going about what is the best way to treat some of his patients.

> Dr. Jones consistently reprimands me in front of the patients for things I am not even responsible for.

3. *Nurse-Auxiliary Workers.* Quite frequently nurses find themselves in conflict with auxiliary personnel over the quality of care delivered, the way care is delivered, and the way the worker responds to the nurse.

> I find the aides do it more than anybody. When a patient needs to be turned, they'll just take them and push them over, stuff some pillows under them and leave. They won't even ask the patient if they are comfortable.

> You come on; you don't have any experience; you're 20 something years old; and you're the boss. You tell this aide, who's 50 or so, what to do. Or just by making out the assignment that means you're telling her what to do. Or you have to ask her to do things because you can't do everything yourself. And she says, "No." Then what do you do? It's really frustrating.

4. *Nurse-Patient.* Occasionally, the nurses reported having disagreements with patients. Although we are classifying it as an interpersonal conflict, such a conflict often has intrapersonal aspects. The nurses found it very difficult to admit to themselves that they were having hassles with patients, and they experienced a great deal of inner turmoil.

> This patient was demanding and complaining, and very disagreeable. I tried making a special effort; you know, I'd go in to talk with him when his light wasn't on—things like that. It didn't make any difference. He continued to complain until I had all I could do just to be civil to the guy.

> Every once in a while we get these patients who could care less about getting well. This diabetic just refused to learn how to take care of herself. I tried reason, then scare tactics, then downright insult. It didn't matter. Finally I decided if she didn't care, why should I?

**ORGANIZATIONAL CONFLICT**

The third type of conflict is *organizational*, i.e., conflicts that arise due to the characteristics of the system[3]. In any organization, there are rules, procedures, communication channels, etc. Conflicts that arise when individual needs and goals cannot be met within the system are generally organizational in nature.

This type of conflict is the hardest to deal with, as it pits you, the new graduate, against the system. The system is a nebulous thing—it's something out there. This makes it difficult to know where and how to change it.

Organizational conflicts fell into three major categories:

1. *Staffing Patterns.* The most frequent kinds of conflict occurring around staffing patterns arise from a shortage of staff and inadequately prepared staff. Some comments by new graduates:

> There simply is not enough staff to give good patient care. We get the physical care done and have no time to spend with the patients.

> The staffing is inadequate. We don't have a ward clerk, so we do the paperwork and then there aren't enough RNs to go around, so the aides do all the real nursing.

> People make mistakes and won't admit to the mistakes. And the supervisors are incompetent!

> It's hectic: rush, rush, rush!!! Nurses are always making mistakes and poor judgments because there simply aren't enough of us.

> The continuity of care is a joke. People are pulled to float here and to float there. No one knows what is going on.

2. *Rules and Policies.* Conflict may arise when you have to abide by rules and regulations that seem to make it impossible to provide quality care.

> The supervisor came and wanted to know why the report hadn't been filled out and sent to her office. It seems that report is more important than feeding the patients.

> There is too much paperwork. We have a form or a requisition for everything we do from diets to dropping bedpans.

> I'm constantly rotating shifts. Do you know that in a ten-day period I worked all three shifts? I marvel that none of the patients had any serious consequences some of the times I went from evenings to days.

> They are very rigid around here with the routines on the units. The policies and procedures are petty. But you must follow the manual.

> The communication channels would confuse anyone. The team leader talks to the head nurse; the head nurse talks to the supervisor; the supervisor to the director; the director takes things to a committee; finally the hospital administrator; then the information is channeled back down. By the time anything happens it's too late.

3. *Resistance to Change.* Conflict occurs due to the seeming impossibility of making even the smallest change in the way things are done in the organization. A feeling of helplessness and powerlessness is reflected in the comments of new graduates.

> We lack the equipment we need and the supervisor and hospital don't do a thing about it.

> Routine and inefficient. People don't care. And the real problem is they don't want to change.

> Their ideas are outdated and rigid. You can't get your point across.

> The hospital administrator and Director of Nursing Service? I never see them. And the head nurse—she isn't open to suggestions or change.

Perhaps these types of conflict and the comments made by the new graduates sound familiar to you. They probably reflect quite accurately some of the conflicts you have experienced in the work world.

There is a relationship between the different types of conflict. Intrapersonal conflict can cause interpersonal or organizational conflict; organizational conflicts can cause interpersonal or intrapersonal conflict. The important point here is that you are able to identify whether a conflict is within yourself (intrapersonal), between persons (interpersonal), or with the system (organizational). Doing this allows you to deal with it more effectively because it tells you where to focus your energies to manage the conflict constructively.

This module has described some of the common conflicts identified by new graduate nurses, organized according to the three major types: interpersonal, intrapersonal, and organizational. In order to assess the types of conflict that you are experiencing as a new graduate, complete the "Situational Conflict Identification" learning activity.

### SITUATIONAL CONFLICT IDENTIFICATION

1. Describe several conflict situations that you have encountered in your work environment.

2. Identify the type of conflict (i.e., intrapersonal, interpersonal, organizational) in each situation.

**REFERENCES**

1-3. Derr, C. Conflict resolution in organizations: views from the field of educational administration. *Publ. Admin. Rev.*, September–October, 1972, p. 496.

# Module 14

# The Mating Process

The painter who's been painting all his life
   ain't a rich man
He's got children and a wife
But he keeps painting
though he knows that when he dies
   he'll still be poor,
But his paintings make his life
   mean so much more

And so he sings:
Won't somebody see what I have made
Don't be afraid, don't be afraid
Won't somebody come and see the thing
   that makes me whole
Before the children of my mind become
   the orphans of my soul.*

    This module tells you how to take the children of your mind—your ideas, hopes, and dreams—and make them work before they become the orphans of your soul, lost through ridicule, apathy, or frustration. When the ideas, hopes, and dreams you have for nursing and for yourself as a nurse are not realized or not even listened to, tremendous upheaval and conflict

*From CHILDREN OF MY MIND, lyrics and music by Gary Osborne. Reproduced by kind permission of the Sparta Florida Music Group Limited, London, England.

arises within you. In "The Mating Process," you will learn that your ideals can be realized if you use appropriate strategies of conflict resolution. This program deals with strategies of productive conflict resolution.

This module will first describe two different conflict courses—productive and destructive. Then, general strategies for dealing with the different types of conflict—intrapersonal, interpersonal, and organizational—will be presented. Following this, we will present the principles of productive conflict resolution. Upon completing this module, you will be able to:

1. Identify your own type of conflict resolution.
2. Identify underlying conflict issues.
3. Implement a plan for the resolution of conflict and/or for the creation of change in your own work environment.

### THE COURSE OF CONFLICT

Let us begin by reading an excerpt from a song by Olivia Newton-John that reflects the two courses of conflict:

> A gentle stream once flowed between us
> But love could cross it easily
> Till stormy skies brought bitter teardrops
> And made that stream, a raging river, come be-
>    tween you and me.
>
> Good lessons learned are not forgotten
> We gave up love to save our pride
> Next time I'm faced with rising waters
> I'll build a bridge of love and kindness
>    reaching to the other side.*

These words show how conflict can take either a destructive or a productive course. What are the factors that can turn gentle streams into raging rivers or else build bridges to the other side? The two courses of conflict are differentiated by four primary factors: (1) the issue, (2) power, (3) responsivity to needs, and (4) communication. Let's turn to a discussion of each of these four factors as they relate to the two courses of conflict.

1. *The Issue.* In a destructive conflict course, there is escalation and expansion of issues. The issue is defined broadly and is related tangentially to other items brought into the discussion. There is a great deal of *reaction to feelings.* Reaction refers to an automatic process—an individual hears the words of the other and a feeling state results. The response is dictated by the feelings rather than by goal-oriented deliberation.

---

*MUSIC CITY MUSIC, INC. (ASCAP) © 1973 International Copyright Secured. All Rights Reserved. (Lyrics by Bob Morrison on the album, "If You Love Me Let Me Know," by Olivia Newton-John.)

In productive conflict courses, the issue is focused and is maintained at a manageable size. Peripheral issues are discussed only in relation to the main point. *Action* rather than reaction is the process of choice. In this context, action refers to a deliberative and contemplated response. An action indicates that an individual hears the comments of the other and then deliberately chooses the most appropriate response rather than responding automatically according to his feelings. Action rather than reaction is the process for keeping the issue focused and preventing escalation.

2. *Power.* In a destructive conflict course, there is an attempt to maintain or change the existing system through the use of threats and coercion. The atmosphere is one of strong competition—there must be a winner and thus a loser. A win-lose stance develops so that one party tries to dictate the actions of the other involved in the conflict.

In a productive conflict course, there is no win-lose stance. All participants are seen as having something valuable and worthwhile to contribute. Solutions are sought on the basis of "Hey, let's work this out together," rather than "We'll do it my way."

3. *Responsivity to Needs.* In destructive conflict, each person insists that "his way" is the only way to do things. You listen only to those who support your point of view and disregard any other possible solutions. The more involved you become in the conflict, the more certain you are that your way of thinking and behaving is the "only way."

In productive conflict, you seek solutions that are responsive to the needs of all participants. There is a detachment from your own point of view and a commitment to that action which most allows the meeting of everyone's needs.

4. *Communication.* Mutual distrust and misperception are the main characteristics of a destructive conflict course. There is little, if any, real communication. What communication does exist is usually heard only in light of one's own preconceived ideas. Information from a person one dislikes or distrusts is not listened to.

Productive conflict is characterized by open and honest dialogue. There is sharing and a sincere attempt to understand the viewpoint of the other regardless of who that other is. The chief concern is to get the problem into the open so that it might be dealt with instead of skirted.

Put in a few words, the overall feeling resulting from a destructive conflict course is one of loss and dissatisfaction emanating from a poorly managed situation. If a problem should arise again, one would just as soon avoid any interaction as have another miserable experience.

The overall feeling accompanying productive conflict is one of gain and satisfaction from a well-managed situation. There is a sense of exhilaration in having used one's full capabilities to invent solutions that were satisfying to all those who participated. One has a sense of accomplishment, a feeling that when other problems arise, they can be dealt with even more productively.

At this point, you may wish to complete the learning activity entitled, "The General Stream of Things," which will help you identify your own style of conflict resolution.

### THE GENERAL STREAM OF THINGS

*Directions:* This exercise is designed to help you look at your general style of resolving conflict. Look back to the conflict situation you described in the previous exercise. Answer the following questions and provide comments that support your answers.

1. Do you generally attempt to resolve conflicts or allow them to take care of themselves?

2. In what ways do you keep the issue focused?

3. In what ways do you escalate the conflict?

4. Do you attempt to threaten or coerce others to act in accord with your wishes? If so, how?

5. In what ways do you attempt to persuade others to make what you consider to be appropriate changes?

6. When a difference of opinion arises over the way something should be done, do you verbalize the merits as well as the disadvantages of others' possible solutions?

7. Do you work with others on the unit to achieve resolution of conflict, or do you tend to work only with those individuals who support your ideas?

8. Are there others on the unit whom you ignore because of their "poor" ideas?

9. In what ways do the solutions to conflict reflect a consideration of others' needs as well as your own?

10. Do you make every effort to make a solution work regardless of whether your ideas were incorporated into the solution?

11. How do you generally feel about the resolution of conflicts that you have been involved in? (i.e., frustrated, angry, satisfied?)

Based on the answers to the questions and the information provided so far in this module, rate your style of conflict resolution on the destructive/productive continuum.

/_____/_____/_____/_____/_____/_____/_____/_____/
Destructive                                                              Productive

### GENERAL CONFLICT STRATEGIES

Let's now turn to a discussion of general strategies for dealing with the three types of conflict—intrapersonal, interpersonal, and organizational—so that we might begin to discover ways of dealing productively with the conflicts encountered in the work environment.

As a rule, there are only two possible options for dealing with any of these types of conflict: change yourself or change the environment. The choice depends to a great extent upon your goals—what are the hopes, dreams, and ideals you hope to realize? If you want to implement your school-bred ideals, you will probably have to change the environment. Even if you do decide to try to change the environment, there will be times when you must change yourself, because there will always be some things in the environment that you don't like but must live with.

The first step toward choosing your option is to identify the type of conflict—is it intrapersonal, interpersonal, or organizational? This enables you to decide at what level the conflict is occurring. The most crucial question in relation to the level or type of conflict is, "With whom am I dealing?" For example, there are times when you may really have blown up at another nurse or at one of your co-workers. Sometime later it may occur to you that your co-worker really didn't have anything to do with the conflict—it was something you were feeling because things were not happening as you expected them to, or you were unhappy about yourself. If you identify the level of the conflict—be it within yourself, with another individual, or with the system—you can deal with it directly rather than dealing with peripheral issues or creating more conflict by dealing with the original conflict at the wrong level.

The next step is to assess the vital issues in your work setting. As you work on the unit, you will find a number of problems that need correction. Some of these problems, or issues, will be more important than others. You must begin to choose which issues you will take a stand on. For example, should you make an issue of the amount of paperwork you have to do or do you take a stand on the need for pre-operative teaching? There are so many things in the work world that are annoying and frustrating that if you try to change them all, you will be in constant conflict with someone. Your co-workers will begin to react unfavorably to your constant efforts to change everything. So, decide what you consider to be the vital issues requiring change. Then you can take a stand on these issues.

The next question is, are the risks involved worth the expected gains? Of course, the answer to this question depends upon the issues you decided are important to you. For example, a conflict about wearing nursing caps may well be annoying, but it is not an issue worth great risk, whereas a conflict involving patient safety may well be worth attempting a change regardless of the risks. Ask yourself two questions to obtain a clear picture of the possible gains and possible risks involved in taking a stand on an issue. (1) What's the worst that can happen if I try to change the situation? (2) What's the best that can happen if I try to change the situation? If the gains outweigh the risks, you may choose to change the situation. If the risks outweigh the gains, you may choose to change yourself and live with the problem.

Armed with answers to the above questions, you can make your choice. Whether you choose to change yourself or the environment, the process for dealing with conflict and instituting change is the same; only the target is different. Let's look at the components of the conflict resolution process. The process involves the following steps:

1.  Identify the issue
2.  Explore alternative solutions
3.  Seek alternative solutions
4.  Select a trial solution
5.  Evaluate the success of the solution

Although the basic process is the same whether the conflict is intrapersonal, interpersonal, or organizational, there are some special requirements for interpersonal and organizational conflicts. If the conflict is intrapersonal, all of the data is supplied by you. You may seek help from someone else in applying the process, but nevertheless, you have a one-person data base.

Because an interpersonal conflict involves more than one individual, conflict resolution requires the following additional factors:

1. A mutually felt need to resolve the conflict

2. A balance of power

3. A phase of integration

If the conflict is organizational, the same additional factors apply. This is because all organizational conflicts must ultimately be dealt with on an interpersonal basis. There is no way of dealing with "the system" in the abstract. Some one person or group of persons is responsible for maintenance of the system. Conflict resolution, therefore, must take place with these individuals.

The basic process as well as the additional factors necessary for interpersonal and organizational conflict will be discussed in more depth when we present the principles of productive conflict resolution. You will note that, for the most part, the strategies of conflict resolution are expressed in interpersonal terms. Occasionally, techniques will be labelled as working most effectively for organizational conflict, but in general, the strategies are applicable to all types of conflict. Some modification will be necessary for application of these strategies on an intrapersonal level, but the reader can easily make these modifications.

**PRINCIPLES OF PRODUCTIVE CONFLICT RESOLUTION**

Let's look at the principles of productive conflict resolution and at strategies for achieving these principles.

*Principle 1: Productive conflict resolution is facilitated by a mutual desire to resolve the conflict.*

To make progress in resolving conflicts, all the persons involved must want to do something about the conflict. One of the unique problems of the new graduate is that many times she feels a need to change the way nursing care is given in an institution, but those who are in power or have been with the institution for a long time have no desire to make a change. This is a natural phenomenon. It is easiest and most comfortable for people to do things the way they have always done them. In a recent interview, one head nurse said: "We're all afraid to change. We have to be convinced that there is a good reason for a change before we do change." Also, established individuals want reasonable assurance that they can be *as* successful after the change as they were before. OK, so how do we convince others that there is a need for change? How do we produce a mutually felt need to resolve a conflict?

The first suggestion is that you, the new graduate, "hold in check" your feelings about the need for change. Nye hypothesizes that the "greatest danger involved in persuasion attempts is 'in coming on too strong' "[1]. The strong "come-on" tends to produce the reaction, "No one else seems to have the problem; you'll get used to it." When others do not feel the strong emotional involvement that you do, it is easy for them to dismiss the problem. Thus it's a good idea to follow the suggestion put forth in the "Reality Shock" module, i.e., find someone you can discharge your high enthusiasm for change with so that you can discuss it with others in a cool, unemotional way. Temper your own feelings until the others recognize the problem, so that there will be a mutual desire to do something about it.

To create or foster this desire in others, several strategies can be used. But before you attempt to use any of the strategies for productive conflict resolution, you must first have established yourself as a competent nurse both in your own eyes and in the eyes of your co-workers. It is the credibility and social power resulting from your reputation as a competent nurse that allows you to use "need-producing" techniques successfully. If the others on your unit do not see you as a competent nurse, able to handle the work load, your use of the strategies will probably lead to increased difficulty rather than change.

The first strategy for producing a mutually felt need is to increase your contact with the individual with whom you disagree so that you produce a conflict. Deutsch notes that for conflict to occur, interaction is necessary[2]. Interaction allows you to discuss your views on how patient care can best be accomplished, the differences between what you believe can happen and what you see happening, and how the differences affect you. This kind of discussion with the individual with whom you feel a difference of opinion will make the conflict visible and will increase the chances that something will be done about it. It is important that you merely bring the differences into the open, however, and not attack the other person or get him into a defensive stance. Once either person assumes a defensive posture, the stage is set for a competitive or destructive course of conflict. Thus, your approach must be a calm, matter-of-fact presentation of differences. Repeated contacts and discussions of differences in beliefs and views make it very difficult for either person to ignore the differences. For example, suppose you believe that adequate discharge planning is a must in patient care and yet it seems to be one of the lowest priorities on your unit. Your approach might be something like this:

YOU:    Did Dr. Smith say when Mr. Arnold was going home? He is going to need some diabetic teaching before he goes and it seems like I ought to get started before the day of discharge to be sure he understands and is able to care for himself.

HEAD NURSE:  When Dr. Smith is ready to discharge him I'm sure he'll let us know.

*Two days later:*

YOU:  Mr. Arnold understands his condition fairly well now. He still can't give his insulin though. Heard anything yet from Dr. Smith about discharge?

HEAD NURSE:  He's planning on discharging him tomorrow.

YOU:  There's no way we can have him ready for discharge tomorrow. I can call the Public Health nurse but she won't visit over the weekend. It really bothers me when we get down to the wire and have to send patients home who aren't well enough to take care of themselves.

*A couple of days later:*

YOU:  Dr. Jones discharged Mrs. Rey today. But the social worker says it will take a couple of days to arrange for her placement in a nursing home, so she'll have to stay. If Dr. Jones had let us know earlier we could have made the arrangements so Mrs. Rey wouldn't have had the extra expense and the bed could have been freed for someone who really needs acute care.

Such interactions would bring your concern to the attention of the head nurse. Once she is aware of the problem, you might be able to sit down with her, restate the problem, mention the examples you have previously told her about, and discuss what can be done about it. Such a discussion would fall on barren soil if you had not first created in her a concern about the problem and a mutually felt need to do something about it.

The consequences of this technique depend upon the power of the person with whom you have the conflict, and how this person generally uses her power. If the individual holds little power within the organization, chances are the consequences will be limited to some interpersonal friction until the issue is resolved. If, on the other hand, the individual holds formal organizational power, she may respond with formal sanctions, such as poor performance evaluations, unit transfers, etc. You need to decide what the consequences will be, based on your knowledge of the individual.

A second strategy for creating mutual motivation is to let the problem grow. If the problem is felt by you but not by others, let it grow until it affects others. The chief problem with this technique is that it requires you to tolerate less than optimal patient care for a time. Frequently in nursing, when conditions are not optimal, one tends to take up the slack by putting forth every possible effort on an individual level. This contributes to the optimum for the patient at the expense of the staff. What is being suggested is that *if patient safety is not involved, the staff needs to stop taking up the slack and allow the faults of the system to show up.* This requires judgment on the part of the nurse as to which problems can be left to grow and which need immediate corrective action. This is difficult, as the nurse's education emphasizes that she should do everything within her power to help the patient. The question, however, is do you continue to strive on an individual basis to overcome the problems encountered? Or do you attempt a system-wide change to solve the problem?

How can one let the problem grow? Let's look at an example. A frequent difficulty encountered by nurses on evening and night shifts is a shortage of supplies and staff. The technique for letting such problems grow would go like this.

You need to start an IV or hang another bottle of solution but there is none available on the unit. Rather than borrowing from another unit, you call the supervisor, tell her what you need and ask her to bring it to the unit. Later, you find that there is no Valium®  in the stock drug supply and you need some. Again, call the supervisor and tell her what you need. Each time you find there is something you need that is not available on the unit, call the supervisor to get it for you. It won't take long until others are made aware of the problem of inadequate supplies.

Another example: You find yourself on nights without enough staff to do all the duties described. You usually find yourself staying overtime in the mornings to finish up with the charting and other duties that you weren't able to complete during your shift. So you make a decision when you come on shift that these are the things that can be accomplished, given the time and staff available, and you leave the other activities undone. When the next shift comes on, you state the facts and the basis for your decision, and tell them what was not done. This will either draw attention to the problem of inadequate staffing, or, perhaps, it will teach everyone that a lot of what we do is unnecessary and can be left undone.

As you can see by the above examples, this technique does bring the problem to the attention of others so that a mutually felt need can be attained. It requires you to tolerate frustration, and perhaps less than optimal care.

The consequences of this technique vary greatly. If you do what was described in the first example, which really amounted to harrassment of the supervisor, the consequences are likely to be an increase in interpersonal tension. If you do what was described in the second example, you are increasing the likelihood of formal organizational sanctions. When employing this technique, you must be careful that you have previously demonstrated your ability to handle the work load of the unit under usual conditions, so that not doing the tasks is a reflection of choice rather than incompetence.

A third strategy for establishing a mutually felt need is to follow the established rules or procedures to the letter, a strategy referred to as "judo" by Postman and Weingartner[3]. New graduates frequently comment that the rules of an organization are petty and rigid. By following these rules to the letter, you use them to bog the organization down. This is particularly effective for organizational conflicts. A couple of examples of the use of this technique follow.

It is a common policy of hospitals that patients may not leave the unit to go to the cafeteria or other units without a physician's order. Nurses often believe that such matters could and should be left to the discretion of the nurse and patient, and in practice the order from the physician is just a formality because this rule often prevents patients from visiting with their families in the coffee shop or out on the lawn. Suppose you want to draw this rule to the attention of others in the organization. Orders are often written for x-ray, physical therapy, or other treatments without an accompanying order to allow the patient to leave the unit. If patients were not transported from the unit for any treatments without explicit orders that they could leave the unit, it would not be long before a good deal of attention would be focused on the rule. There are risks involved in this, of course, so you must be sure that the desired outcome is worth the risk involved.

Another example: The incident report is frequently a means of communicating errors directly to nursing service administration. Suppose you make use of this means of reporting to include errors that are not ordinarily drawn to the attention of the administration, but rather are annoyances for nurses on the unit. Such things as "patient received inappropriate diet because kitchen was closed," or "medication was an hour late because there was none available on the unit" are reported as incidents to nursing service.

The use of "judo" is a tricky business, and you must think through the possible consequences. You may only precipitate a change in rule or policy that puts an end to the "judo" and perpetuates what you consider to be petty and rigid rules.

The consequences of "following rules to the letter" depend upon the answers to two questions: (1) Will doing so interfere with patient care? (2) What is the likelihood that the organization will alter the rule just enough to render what I'm doing ineffective, and maintain the status quo? If there are patient consequences, how serious and long-range will they be? If the organization can block your efforts by minor changes in the existing rules, are the efforts worth the results? This technique, if used regularly, probably offers the greatest potential for interpersonal hassles and the slightest pay-off for these hassles. On the other hand, if used selectively and judiciously, this technique can have a great impact with small risk of serious long-range consequences.

A fourth strategy for creating mutually felt need is persuasion by the use of analogy[4]. The idea behind persuasion by analogy is to take an issue related to the one that you really feel strongly about and persuade another person that what you are saying makes sense so that they agree with you argument. This may not sound too clear; perhaps an example will help.

Not infrequently new graduates comment, "Patients are treated like diseases instead of people. No one really seems to care." If persuasion by analogy were used to create a mutually felt need, to give more personal care, the dialogue might proceed as follows:

YOU:    Have you ever made rounds with Dr. Craig?

HEAD NURSE:  Yes.

YOU:    His interpersonal relationships with the patients aren't too good, are they? I mean, like this morning, we saw five different patients. Each time he went in, checked the dressings, made a few comments about how well the incision was healing, and left the room without even asking the patient how he was, or if there was anything he wanted to know. I know Dr. Craig cares about his patients, but his actions sure don't convey that to the patients. What do you think?

HEAD NURSE:  Well, Dr. Craig is a busy man. He has patients on the other floors, too, and has to get back to his office to see others. It's hard to spend much time when he has so many other things to do.

YOU:    Yes. I can see that he is busy. Can you imagine though how much better his patients would feel if he came into the room and asked if they had any concerns so he could talk to them while he checked their dressings? If there were any long and involved concerns, he could always tell the patient to talk it over with the nursing staff. I just don't like the patients to get the idea that people don't care when they really do.

HEAD NURSE:  I agree, but I'm not sure that there is anything we can do about Dr. Craig.

YOU:    I don't suppose there is too much we can do directly with Dr. Craig. It seems to me though that since we, the nurses, spend the most time with the patients, there are things that we could do. As I was thinking about it, it occurred to me that some days I perhaps convey the same messages to patients that Dr. Craig does. You know, when I have a lot of surgicals or treatments and it is a busy day, I know I sort of whisk in and out of the rooms. Others have said the same thing. I remember that you once said that on busy days sometimes you hardly get a chance to make rounds. On days like those the patients must begin to wonder if anyone cares about them. We are going to have busy days and we have to get the work done. I just thought maybe we could all talk about it and that you might have some suggestions about what we might do.

As you can see, the argument moves from the way a physician treats patients to the related issue of how nurses treat patients. You could add even more supportive data by relating what the patients have said to you when the doctor is very brief and rushed, as well as patient comments about the nurses on days when they seem very rushed. Note that there is a smooth transition and direct connection between the issues. There is an easy movement from the way doctors treat patients to the way nurses treat patients. This is a key element in this technique. The issues must be closely related or the movement is too choppy and the analogy is lost. The individual you are talking to must commit himself on the related issue, or you must abandon this line. There is no way you can move to the issue of how nurses treat patients if the head nurse (or whoever you are talking to) says, "Well, the patients just have to get used to it." You must have agreement that it is not desirable to have patients feel that no one cares about them before you can move into the real issue.

This technique probably has the fewest interpersonal consequences and the greatest pay-off. The chief difficulty lies in the fact that issues related to the real conflict issue aren't always available. Also, it may be difficult to get the other to commit himself.

A fifth strategy is selective application of the rules. This technique suggests that you judge the appropriateness of rules or regulations on an individual basis. For example, you may decide to enforce the rule that patients may not leave the unit without a doctor's order for some patients but not for others. For example, it doesn't really apply for Mr. Benson, whose daughter just graduated from high school and who came with her friends to visit him, so you allow him to leave the unit to visit with them. Such selective application of rules can bring the rules to the attention of several different groups of people.

This strategy has great effectiveness for organizational conflict. Of course, it may also get you into a great deal of trouble. This technique probably carries the highest potential risk. You can expect interpersonal difficulty as well as formal organizational disapproval. You need to be aware of the consequences for the others involved in the situation. Be sure that there are no severe risks involved for either patients or other staff members.

It is well to remember that all five of the strategies described here are designed to create a mutually felt need to resolve conflict; therefore, all must be applied judiciously. Any or all of the strategies may be used, depending upon the issue at conflict. We present the following guidelines to help you decide which strategy to use.

1. Select the technique most appropriate to the issue at conflict. To do this, you need to identify what is the issue at conflict. Decide how many strategies you may select from and then work the issue through mentally, using each technique. Whichever strategy works best and is most comfortable for you is the technique of choice.

2. Start with the strategy with the least serious consequences. Once you work the conflict through, using the techniques available to you and consider the consequences, you are ready to select the strategy you wish to use. It makes sense to begin with that strategy that involves the least risk and the greatest possible pay-off. If this strategy fails, then you can always adopt a strategy having more severe consequences or more risks. The important point is that you consider the consequences so that you may make a knowledgeable decision.

*Principle 2: Productive conflict resolution is facilitated by a balance of power.*

Within our institutions there are head nurses, supervisors, and Directors of Nursing Service who occupy positions of formal power. Staff nurses generally have positional power over nurse aides, orderlies, and so on. Furthermore, there is much informal power operative in work situations. Most new graduates have probably encountered a nurse aide's power of age and experience, even though by her position, the new graduate staff nurse has greater organizational power than the aide. A balance of power does not mean a flat control structure where everyone has the same power or is equal in organizational status. What is meant by balance of power is a recognition of the legitimacy of each individual to contribute, in a positive way, to the furtherance of the quality of patient care. Balance of power is recognition by both parties of each person's right and ability to contribute to the resolution of conflict, irrespective of his formal positional power. This recognition requires an interaction style of mutual respect, as well as open communication and freedom from threat. We present some suggestions on how to establish such a balance of power.

First, get to know your co-workers. Establish a relationship that is conducive to open and honest dialogue so that when conflict occurs, it can be dealt with. Such a relationship increases the chances of productive conflict resolution. If your relationship with your co-workers is one of respect, cooperation, and open communication, keep it going in that direction. If, on the other hand, your relationship with co-workers is one of mutual distrust, limited communication, and lack of cooperation, you need to improve it if you hope to establish a balance of power. There are two ways to improve the relationship: (1) change your behavior: begin to cooperate and help your co-workers, or (2) explore with them your current relationship and indicate that you desire to improve it. If you elect to explore your relationship with others, your behavior will almost have to change, or trust will not develop. It will take some time to change your relationship with co-workers, but you can do it. Do what was suggested in the "Reality Shock" program. Find out what your co-workers think about nursing. What do they hope to accomplish and how can you help them achieve their goals? Also, make use of opportunities to help your co-workers.

A second strategy that is particularly effective in achieving a balance of power for organizational conflicts is to learn the system. Knowing the rules, policies, and procedures of the institution, the strengths and weaknesses of the system, will enable you to know who to approach and in what manner. Knowing who to approach and how will give you a better chance of balancing out the power in any situation.

A third way of balancing power is to establish your competency as a nurse and team member. One of the more painful experiences upon leaving the school and entering the work world is that although you may have been a highly successful *student*, you are not automatically seen as a competent

*nurse* by your co-workers. At work, you must deal with large numbers of patients and handle a variety of personnel. For the most part, these kinds of
things are not done while you are in school. In all likelihood, the staff will
be watching to see how well you can handle the demands of the work
world, and they may even construct some tests or initiation rites for you.
You may or may not elect to pass these tests.

You must expend a certain amount of energy mastering routines and
skills, team management, and even paperwork. Until you master these
tasks, co-workers are not apt to view you as a "good nurse." When they
recognize that you have a legitimate claim to the title "nurse," they will be
more willing to accept your contributions and suggestions. You need their
recognition before you can successfully operationalize your ideals, implement change, and resolve conflict productively.

A fourth way of establishing a balance of power is to find an ally. When
you first enter the work world, one of your major tasks is to hang onto your
idealism and dreams for nursing while you master the new system. New
graduates often feel powerless in the new work setting. "Why should I
elaborate on my views, no one cares," or "What's the use?" Comments of
this kind indicate a lack of balanced power. There is a sense of "my ideas
are not valued." It is not that the ideas *per se* do not have value for nursing,
but that in this particular setting, when contributed by me, there is no hope
for their realization.

To maintain your idealism while you are mastering the new system,
find an ally. Find support for those things you were taught in school and
believe in. Your ally may be another new graduate or another staff nurse on
your own or some other unit. You need someone to help you find ways to
make your ideas work in the work setting. You need support to help you feel
that you have something worthwhile to contribute to nursing and to patient
care. Then, you can approach others with confidence. Confidence, not feelings of powerlessness, helps maintain a balance of power.

In essence, to establish a balance of power is to establish an atmosphere of cooperation that includes mutual respect, open communication,
and freedom from threat. Actions that will help create and maintain a balance of power are (1) getting to know your co-workers, (2) getting to know
the system, (3) establishing yourself as a competent nurse and team member, and (4) finding an ally.

*Principle 3: Productive conflict resolution requires movement to a phase of*
*integration.*

In all conflict processes, there are two readily identifiable phases: a
differentiation phase and an integration phase. During the differentiation
phase, people describe divisive issues and vent negative feelings about each
other. During the integration phase, they recognize similarities, acknowledge common goals, and commit themselves to positive action to resolve
the conflict[5]. It is probable that there will be more than one differentiation
phase and more than one integration phase in the course of a conflict. It is

reasonable to expect that differences will arise as issues are explored and as alternative solutions for resolving the conflict are generated. Each time the differences occur, you will need to seek integration or a common ground.

To move from the differentiation phase to the integration phase, each party in the conflict must feel that his views are being heard and understood by the others. Unless this happens, the conflict will not reach the integration phase. The following are some strategies for moving conflict to the integration phase.

First, accept and encourage open dialogue. A cooperative relationship between parties will facilitate movement into a discussion of differences. If such a relationship does not exist, you must try to establish it. It seems most reasonable to expect that you will open up the communication, since the only behavior you can control is your own. If you approach the person with whom you are having conflict and indicate an interest in opening a dialogue, the person may respond positively. However, it does not always follow that a dialogue will happen, since the other person may not be ready to pursue the conflict issue. This may increase your frustration, but hang tight, it doesn't mean that there's no chance for resolution. The likelihood of a dialogue will be increased if you make it very clear *what* you wish to discuss and accomplish by the discussion. For open communication, the discussion must pursue not only your points of difference with the other, but also the other's points of difference with you. Set the stage for exploration and listening rather than defense of your own position.

Second, choose the appropriate time and place for a meeting. When you ask an individual to open communication channels, make sure that your timing is right. A short preliminary meeting where you and the other party decide on the best time and place for a meeting is in order. The best approach may be just to indicate to the other person at the start of the day that when he has five or ten minutes you would like to talk with him briefly. Explain what it is you would like to talk about, and mutually decide upon a convenient time for the meeting. Another option is to know when to expect quiet moments on the unit and approach the person at this time. See if he has a little time now. This may seem obvious but at times when there is tension, there tends to be forgetting of obvious things like this.

In setting aside time for a meeting to explore conflict issues and feelings about a relationship, you should consider the appropriateness of selecting time during the work day. There tends to be concern for what is happening on the unit. You may want to consider a meeting on off-duty time. Or perhaps you can find others on the unit to cover for you, so that you can set up a series of meetings lasting, say, 20 minutes to a half hour. There is some danger here that issues may not be dealt with sufficiently because of inadequate time, and both of you may leave the meeting feeling upset and not wish to continue. An initial time of 20 to 30 minutes may allow only differences to be discussed. If time runs out before common ground can be found, it may seem that the differences are so great that there is no point in continuing. You might want to plan the first meeting to last at least 45 minutes, so that no one is left feeling that this is useless and give up the effort.

In choosing a place for the meeting, you should locate a place free from commotion and interruptions. If you attempt to carry on a discussion at the nurse's station or in the charting room, you are apt to encounter frequent interruptions. If you are meeting while on duty, try to go to the coffee shop or a conference room. There are nooks and crannies in most units where you can be undisturbed. One of the most used conference rooms on a particular unit was the tub room, in the afternoon. It was large enough to take in a couple of chairs and the door could be locked. Many an undisturbed conference was held there. So find that quiet place on your unit.

If you have arranged for a meeting on off-duty time, meet outside your work environment. You might even consider going to the local pub and relaxing over a drink. This promotes a more relaxed and informal discussion.

Third, make a commitment. The first commitment you need to make is to do something about the conflict and about your relationship with the individual you're in conflict with. Encouraging an open dialogue and attempting to set up a meeting are indications of such a commitment. If there is to be a realization of goals and a feeling of satisfaction, both of you must also be committed to a productive course of conflict resolution. Choosing a productive course of conflict resolution does not mean that you and the other individual must become warm and friendly. It merely means that you must establish a working relationship that allows both of you to reach your goals without constant friction. An example may help to illustrate the point.

Two staff nurses worked together on an evening shift. One staff nurse was what might be called the "Organization Woman." She was highly efficient primarily concerned with the technical tasks that needed to be done. This staff nurse believed that patients deserved the best care possible and should be comfortable. She primarily sought to attain this goal by meeting the patient's physical needs. The other staff nurse also believed that patients deserved the best possible care, but she saw this in a different light. She was not as efficient and organized as the other staff nurse and was much less concerned about the technical aspects of care. The physical care was done but not always to the satisfaction of the other nurse. Although the two staff nurses were in charge of different teams, a rub developed because they had to depend upon each other to cover when they would go to supper. It was also a common practice to answer lights no matter what team you were on. Because of the crossing of team boundaries, the differences in their philosophies of patient care soon brought the two staff nurses into some arguments over how patients were being treated. One nurse would say, "Mr. James' light was on and he wanted some pain medication. I talked with him for a while. He was concerned about his family and when we finished, he really didn't need the med." The other nurse would then remark, "If he needs pain medication, give it to him." Then she would go immediately with the medication. Another frequent comment would be, "While you were gone to suppe., I gave two of your post-ops pain medication." The other nurse would respond, "Oh, were they having a lot of pain?" "No, they didn't even request the medication but their charts indicated that it was time. You have to keep these post-ops comfortable." Soon the nurses were crossing team barriers less frequently and then they began to carry their lunches to work so that they would not have to leave the floor during shift. Finally, they even refused to take telephone orders from the physicians if the patient was not on their team. At this point, it was decided that something had to be done about the situation. The two staff nurses came to a satisfactory resolution by setting up guidelines as to how to handle physicians' orders and such things as pain medications when each crossed team lines. There was no agreement reached as to what was the best way to accomplish the optimal care for the patients. The agreement was that the patients deserved the best care and that each would reach that goal in different ways. The resolution allowed each to reach her goal in her own way and controlled their interactions with each other and also with the others' team.

The resolution of the conflict was satisfactory to both parties and, as a matter of fact, it much improved feelings on the whole unit. No friendship, nor even warm relationship, was established. The tension was gone, however, as each knew what her role vis-a-vis the other was. Thus, the commitment to do something about the relationship only requires that the conflicting parties establish a mutually agreeable working relationship.

To accomplish integration, both (or all) parties must also make a commitment to flexibility. Each party may have a concrete goal or objective, but each must be flexible about the means of reaching the goal. In the above example, both staff nurses had objectives that they believed in and wanted to meet. They were not willing to compromise their objectives, but they were flexible about the way their objectives could be met. In other words, they recognized the validity of each other's goals, and they developed a plan to cooperate with each other when team lines were crossed, so that each could meet her goals.

When seeking flexibility, keep the areas requiring it specific and limited. In the case of the two staff nurses, flexibility was achieved more easily because the amount required was limited. The staff nurses expected each other to enact different behavior only when they crossed team lines. This made it easier to obtain positive results. Just as *you* would not like to completely change your way of doing things, so too, others feel the same way.

Fourth, try to understand the perspective of the other. The key to movement from the differentiation phase to the integration phase is that both parties feel they are understood. For this to happen, each must understand how the conflict looks from the other side. This is what is meant by empathy. Empathy requires that you view the conflict from the other's perspective and understand how the conflict affects him. To gain some notion of the other's perspective, you must explore the situation by explaining, listening, and clarifying.

*Explaining* means giving factual statements about how you see the situation and about how the situation affects you emotionally. Explaining is not an attempt to sell the other on your idea; it means only giving an account of your point of view. Each party needs to explain his point of view, or perspective.

*Listening* means understanding the other's explanation and appreciating the emotional tone of the words. You take in, without judging or diagnosing what is said. You withhold evaluation until you have heard the other's full explanation. The essence of listening is to hear the sounds communicated and to sense the shape of the other's world[6].

*Clarifying* is the process whereby you check how well you understand the other's perspective. Each individual should relate what he has heard the other say: what he understands the other's perspective to be and how the problem affects the other. This may take considerable time, as there may be a need for extensive explaining and listening. For each individual, the major task is to comprehend the other's view of the problem and conflict.

Understanding of the other's perspective, encouraging and accepting open dialogue, choosing the appropriate place and time for an exchange, and making the appropriate commitments enhance the possibility of moving from the differentiation phase to the integration phase of conflict. Remember, there may be more than one differentiation or integration phase. Continual striving toward the integration phase is necessary if conflict resolution is to be productive.

The following learning activity, "Conflict Turnabout," is designed to help you see a conflict from the perspective of the other individual involved. You may wish to complete this learning activity before proceeding.

### CONFLICT TURNABOUT

1.  Describe a conflict situation you are now experiencing.

2. Identify the type of conflict (with whom does the conflict exist?).

3. Describe the same conflict from the perspective of the other person involved.

4. Approach the other. Explore the conflict situation with the other by explaining, listening, and clarifying. After you complete the discussion, return to this learning activity.

5. Describe how effectively you were able to explore the conflict situation with the other.

6. How accurately were you able to predict the perspective of the other?

Now go on to Principle 4 of productive conflict resolution.

*Principle 4: Adequate exploration of the conflict issue is necessary if the conflict is to remain solved.*

Productive conflict resolution is often aborted by premature agreement. Ideas and values are agreed upon before underlying differences are exposed. Premature agreement leads to a recurrence of conflict—in another area. To prevent this, you must explore differences of opinion as well as areas of agreement regarding the issue at conflict[7]. Exploration will permit isolation of the real issue and will assist in the formulation of possible solutions. Exploring the issues at conflict requires the following actions:

1. *The underlying issue must be identified.* It is sometimes difficult to express the issue at conflict in its pure form. Thus, camouflage and smoke screens are used to disguise it. There are a variety of reasons for this camouflaging and the whys are not to be considered here. The important point is that you must learn to recognize when the issue being discussed is not the real one, and you must take steps to uncover the real issue.

The first step is to listen to the words, the content of the discussion. Is the discussion about staffing arrangements, nursing care plans, treatment of patients, or treatment of personnel? Does the content of the discussion focus on the rules of the institution, the principles of nursing espoused, or the way the principles of nursing care are applied? Listening to the words allows you to identify the area of the issue at conflict. While listening to the words, you must also listen to the emotional tone of the discussion. You must try to assess the congruency of the emotional reaction to the issue. Is the individual annoyed, angry, pleased, disgusted? Is this reaction proportionate to the apparent issue? If the reaction is either much less or much more than would be expected, you will feel uneasy. You will feel that something isn't quite right. This may be your only indication that the issue expressed is not the entire problem. If you can express your uneasiness to the other person you may be able to clarify the issue.

The duration of the discussion can help you differentiate between the real issue and a smoke screen issue. If the discussion continues despite efforts at resolution, chances are that the real issue has not yet been identified. The conversation goes round and round, and the participants seem unwilling or unable to move. In many cases, you may note that a seemingly reasonable solution is reached and still the dialogue continues. In these instances, one must look for a more basic issue.

At this point, taking a conflict situation and identifying the issue by looking at the three factors just discussed *may serve to clarify.*

> In a recent conversation with a group of new graduates, the issue of nurses wearing or not wearing caps came up. The general theme of the discussion was that nurses do not need caps to be nurses. "All that caps do is get in the way. This is particularly true in intensive care units." One ICU nurse noted that a decision had finally been made that nurses need not wear caps in the unit, but any time they left the unit they had to wear caps. The head nurse of the unit absolutely insisted that caps be worn outside the unit. "But, if we don't wear caps when they really count, i.e., when we are with the patients, then why wear them at all?"
>
> "Besides the fact that the caps were always in the way, the cap doesn't make the nurse. One should be able to tell a nurse by how and what she does and not by the cap on her head. It just doesn't make any sense—cap or no cap—the kind of care you give is the same."
>
> The discussion went on and on. Finally, it was put to the new graduates that if the cap didn't make any difference in the way they gave care and it didn't make the nurse, why were they discussing it at such length?
>
> "It just doesn't seem fair that we have to wear them," they replied. "As nurses, we should have some say in what the policy will be."
>
> "So, the cap *per se* isn't really the issue, but rather what the cap symbolizes?"
>
> "Right! We want some say over the policies of the institution. We have a right to have some control of the rules and regulations of the institution."

Listening to the content of the nurses' complaint first identified the issue as that of wearing nursing caps. The immediate reaction was, "There are some things that one just has to live with." However, this reaction was not verbalized because the emotional tone of the discussion was strong and incongruent with the issue. The nurses were visibly upset. By their own admission, caps didn't make the nurse and whether you wore one or not didn't matter. If caps really didn't make a difference, there was no reason for their strong emotional reaction. Not only was the emotional tone strong, but the discussion was very lengthy. The new graduates had talked for 30 minutes before they were asked why there was such a long discussion over an issue that they had labeled as irrelevant to nursing care. The length of the discussion, coupled with its emotional tone, was a clue that the content discussed was not really the issue. Asking for the reason for the long discussion was a way of expressing the feeling that something wasn't right here, and their question led to a clarification of the real issue—control.

Identification of the underlying issue is essential to the formulation of possible solutions. There may be times, however, when it is not possible to deal with the underlying issue, and thus a solution of *treating the symptoms* may be selected. This is not contradictory to the basic principle of productive conflict resolution: if you wish a conflict to be permanently resolved, you must deal with the underlying issue. If you treat symptoms only, conflict will recur, but with different presenting symptoms. If this be so, why would you want to treat the symptom?

There are a couple of reasons. First, you may realize that the issue being described doesn't seem to be the real issue, but you may be unable to uncover the underlying issue. This is not uncommon. To prevent escalation, you must deal with the presenting symptom. Later, when the real issue can be identified, appropriate solutions may be generated.

Another reason for symptom treatment is that you may be unable, for any number of reasons, to deal with the underlying issue right now. However, you know what the underlying issue is and you also know that for now only symptomatic treatment is available. For example, the issue at conflict between the two staff nurses working on evenings was their basic beliefs about nursing and the way nursing care should be given. Despite earnest attempts, they could not agree on the basic issue. Therefore, they dealt with the symptoms of the conflict—how do we handle pain meds when we cross team lines? How do we handle physician's orders? This was symptomatic treatment and the best possible conflict resolution at the time. However, the two staff nurses will have to set up new guidelines each time another symptom arises; thus, a lot of energy and time will be expended—energy and time that could be saved had they been able to deal with the underlying issue. As time passes, it is possible that they may find a means of dealing with the underlying issue. Thus, even as the symptomatic treatment continues, a way to resolve the basic issue should be sought.

A third reason for treating symptoms is that you may *believe* that you *are* dealing with the underlying issue only to find that the conflict reoccurs later. What appears at one time to be the underlying issue may only be a symptom. When this happens and the conflict reoccurs, the opportunity to explore the issue again presents itself. Hopefully, now the underlying issue can be made explicit and appropriate resolution reached.

There are really two options open to you in dealing with conflict—you can deal with the underlying issue or with the symptoms. If you choose to deal with the symptoms, it is likely that the conflict will surface again. If you deal with the underlying issue, it is likely that the conflict will remain solved.

2. *The points of agreement and disagreement must be identified.* Once you identify the real issue at conflict, you must sort out the points of agreement and disagreement over the issue. The only way to identify the specific

points of agreement and disagreement is to carry on a dialogue, which should take the form of a point-by-point discussion of each party's point of view. In the conflict over wearing nursing caps, the dialogue might go something like this:

DNS: I can agree that the cap does not make the nurse. I'm not sure that at this point I can agree that caps serve no function other than getting in the way. I see that caps serve an important function in helping patients to identify which of the numerous people they are in contact with are nurses and which have other functions. Now, this is the function which I see for caps and, indeed, the most important time to wear the cap is when you're on the unit. It does seem that putting on the cap to go to lunch or when you leave the unit doesn't serve that function. I'd be willing to agree that caps need not be worn in the nonpatient care areas. However, I firmly believe that the cap does serve a function in the patient care units. Those of you in specialized units have a different situation than most of the other staff nurses. You have stopped wearing your caps due to the machinery of your units. I don't think the majority of you have a problem getting tangled up in specialized equipment. Perhaps you would like to express your opinion on what I have said as well as the things you said earlier.

SALLY: Well, what you said is true. The cap does make me readily identifiable as a nurse. However, my name tag serves the same purpose. Also, as a general rule, I interact with the patients frequently enough so that they know I'm a nurse.

DNS: Even from here, Sally, I have difficulty reading your name and your title. I would suspect it would be impossible if we were ten feet apart. Now suppose I'm just being admitted and I don't know who you are? Or suppose I'm on the other team on your unit and I rarely see you? How would you suggest that you make yourself readily visible as a nurse?

SALLY: I hadn't really given that too much thought before. I guess we could all wear different colored uniforms.

DNS: That is a possibility. Do you think that it's possible to get the nurses in the hospital to agree to buy new uniforms?

SALLY: I was thinking more in terms of maybe the aides changing color.

DNS: I think the basic question remains the same, whether it's RNs or aides who change. Is it more practical to expect people to buy new uniforms or to have you wear your cap—which you already have?

SALLY: I hadn't given the expense any thought at all. That does seem a bit unreasonable.

DNS: Perhaps, before we explore any other alternative, we should see if we all agree that patients ought to be able to tell who is a nurse?

(*General agreement*)

DNS: OK, are there any more suggestions as to how we might make ourselves visible without our caps?

SALLY: I don't have any suggestions now. I'd like to have the opportunity to open the discussion again after I give it some more thought. It just doesn't sit right that the cap is the way we are identified as nurses.

DNS: OK, until we can think of a way to make ourselves readily identifiable, I think it best to continue to wear our caps in the patient care areas. When you aren't on your unit giving care, the choice about wearing your cap is yours. I'll see that the change in policy is announced at head nurses' meeting next week. Until then, I expect you to follow the policy we now have. Is this agreeable to you?

(General agreement)

DNS: Now, let's talk about the issue of who makes policy here. It seems from what you have said that you feel that you have no voice in the policies of this institution. Is that right?

(General agreement)

Clearly, the dialogue is not finished. However, enough content has been presented to demonstrate how areas of agreement and disagreement are identified.

## AREAS OF AGREEMENT AND DISAGREEMENT

| AREAS OF AGREEMENT | AREAS OF DISAGREEMENT | IDENTIFICATION PROCESS |
|---|---|---|
| The cap doesn't make the nurse. | | Very direct statement: "I agree." |
| Nurses should be identifiable to patients. | | Statements such as "my name tag serves same purpose" and "different colored uniforms" suggest that RNs should be set apart by some means. Direct question to make explicit the tone of the statements made. |
| | The method or means of making the nurse identifiable. | Alternatives to cap were suggested. Statement indicating a desire to explore and re-open discussion. |
| Abiding by the new policy until alternative found. | | Agreement was stated. |

The process of identifying areas of agreement and disagreement consists of examining the content for direct statements of agreement or disagreement and making *implicit* meanings *explicit*. You can facilitate the process by (1) stating whether you agree or disagree with issues; (2) encouraging others to state whether they agree or disagree; (3) asking for opinions or summarizing what you believe to be the implicit message; and (4) asking for verification.

When the areas of agreement and disagreement are identified, the focus of the conflict becomes apparent. As the identification process proceeds, it becomes evident where the disagreement lies. Since it is only the areas of disagreement which reflect conflict, limiting the number of issues and pinpointing the exact nature of the issues reduces the complexity and scope of the conflict, thus providing greater direction for seeking solutions. For example, one point of disagreement identified in the cap conflict was the means of making nurses readily visible, so a solution was sought in relation to this area of disagreement.

3. *The issue at conflict must be kept to a manageable size.* Fractionating issues seems to be the best tactic for bringing about change[8]. Fractionating issues means to break them down into their component parts. Smaller issues tend to require fewer increments of change, and therefore the possibility of success is increased. A word of caution: *never* fractionate issues until a mutually felt need for resolving the conflict has been created. Otherwise, attempts at change or conflict resolution will fall on barren soil.

There are several ways to fractionate the issue at conflict:

1. *Identify the areas of agreement and disagreement.*

2. *Define the issue.* Make a clear and concise statement of the conflict. In defining the issue, the technique of reframing is useful. Reframing means to view the issue from various perspectives and then define or redefine it with these perspectives in mind[9]. Two examples may help explain the concept of reframing.

In the first example, we present three different perspectives on an issue originally defined as, "We need histories and care plans for continuity of care."

NEW STAFF
NURSE:           Nursing histories and care plans would help us get to know the patient, and would contribute to individualized care and to continuity of care. Unless we begin to do histories and write care plans, the care of the patients will suffer.

EXPERIENCED
STAFF NURSE:  I know all I need to know to take care of the patient. Besides, it sounds to me like the information you think should go on this history and care plan is a combination of the admission notes, doctor's

orders, and the history and physical. Why should I bother with a new form which would only repeat the efforts of other people?

HEAD
NURSE:    More paperwork for a staff already overburdened with paperwork. And how will this affect the time that the staff has for completing all of the other required duties on the unit? There's already a shortage of time to do all the things necessary for the patients.

As reframed, the issue would be: "How do we best communicate the information gathered by a variety of professionals dealing with the patient?" Reframing encompasses the perspectives of all three individuals, so that the issue takes on meaning slightly different from the original statement, which was, "We need histories and care plans for continuity of care."

In the nursing cap conflict, the issue was also reframed. The issue, "Do we wear or not wear caps?" was reframed to, "What is the best way to make nurses readily identifiable to patients?" Again this gives a new meaning to the issue, and encompasses the perspectives of all parties.

An important function of reframing is to remove from the statement of the issue a built-in solution. Care plans, histories, and caps are solutions, not issues. If the solution is removed from the issue statement, a broader range of solutions is made possible.

When defining the issue, be sure to avoid defining it too narrowly. One tends to define issues in terms of one's own knowledge, beliefs, and values. Take continuity of care, for example. As a new graduate, you tend to define the problem as "a need for better nursing care plans." This definition limits the solution to nursing care plans and decreases the chance of exploring other ways to increase the continuity of care. It is better to define the issue as, "How do we best provide for continuity of care to patients?" This definition of the problem does not limit the answer to initiation of nursing care plans, but allows you to look for other solutions as well.

However, you must also guard against defining issues too broadly. Frequently, new graduates comment, "People don't follow through with care plans; no one cares." How does one find a solution to the problem, "No one cares?" What does "no one cares" mean? This kind of a broad definition of the problem not only makes it very difficult to deal with the issue but also challenges the values and beliefs of the others, thus increasing the likelihood of defensiveness. The conflict will escalate, because such a broad statement makes it likely that other issues will be raised, such as, "nurses sit at the desk all day instead of talking with the patients," or "nurses don't do any preoperative teaching." As more issues arise, it becomes more difficult to resolve the conflict.

3. *Focus on questions of application rather than principles.* Almost any conflict involves issues of principle[10]. It is difficult to resolve conflicts focused on principles, because principles are built upon values and beliefs.

Values and beliefs are acquired over time and do not change quickly. If one can see that the way one meets or reaches a principle (i.e., the application) is different from the current way and yet consistent with the values behind the principle, the chances of achieving change of resolving conflict are higher.

To focus attention on the *application of principles* rather than on the principles themselves, you must do two things. First, you must recognize and accept the other's values and stop fighting those values. This doesn't mean that you stop trying to implement change, but only that you emphasize a change in behaviors rather than in values or attitudes. Just as you would not like to give up your values, so the other does not want to abandon his. Acceptance means that you recognize the right of the other to his values; it doesn't mean that you have to like those values. Second, consider the other's values when attempting change. Ask yourself two questions when planning for a change. "How will this change influence the other?" "How can I structure the change so as to best incorporate the values of the other?" For example, you think of Marge, an RN on your unit who despises paperwork. You can be sure that if the care plans increase the amount of paperwork, Marge will not go along with the idea. So how do you incorporate Marge's values into the change? Well, it is possible to initially develop standardized care plans so that the only extra paperwork would involve noting modifications for each patient on individual Kardexes. Or the form for the care plan might be a partial checklist, so that minimal writing would be required. Or perhaps the care plans could be tape recorded and the ward clerk could put them on the Kardex. There are any number of ways that the values of the other can be incorporated into the change.

4. *Identify the level of the conflict.* As noted earlier, identifying the level of conflict (i.e., interpersonal, intrapersonal, or organizational) helps one choose the appropriate strategy for dealing with it. Dealing with the conflict on the wrong level tends to expand the size of the conflict. The suggestions given earlier in this module will help you identify the level of the conflict and thereby focus the issue.

To summarize, fractionating conflict helps you explore conflict issues. The exploration of conflict also involves identifying the underlying issues, identifying points of agreement and disagreement, and keeping the issue to a manageable size.

*Principle 5: Solutions to conflicts need to be responsive to the needs of all parties involved.*

You have now reached the point where a decision must be made about how to handle the conflict that has been identified. So far, you have been concerned primarily with creating the appropriate atmosphere, getting to know the other person or group involved, and analyzing the conflict. Now, all the work you have done will be brought to bear on your decision of just what change or solution should be made, and how that change will be implemented.

In any conflict situation, it is possible to classify the "solution seeking" behavior of the parties involved according to the degree to which each attempts to satisfy his own needs or concerns, and the degree to which each attempts to respond to the needs of the other. The attempt to satisfy the other's concerns is the cooperative dimension; the drive to meet one's own needs is the assertive dimension. These two dimensions suggest five different conflict-handling modes or behaviors (Figure 1). The first is *competition*. If I compete, I try to satisfy my own concerns at the expense of the other. I go after what I want. In a discussion with you, I don't listen to you; I argue and try to convince you that you're wrong and I'm right.

The opposite of competition is *accommodation*. In this mode, I sacrifice my concerns for those of the other. I accept whatever the other wants, no matter how strongly I feel about the issue. I hold my feelings in check at all times, and accommodate to both the feeling tone and to the solutions desired by others.

.Midway between competition and accommodation, there is *compromise*. I don't go after everything I want, but I go after some things. I don't give the other person everything he wants, but I give him some of it. Both of

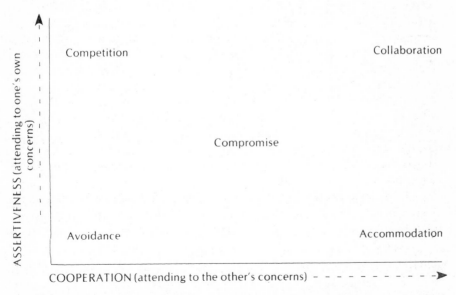

FIGURE 1.   CONFLICT-HANDLING MODES GRAPHED ACCORDING TO THE DIMENSIONS OF COOPERATION AND ASSERTIVENESS*

*From Thomas, Kenneth W., "Issues in Management of Conflict." In *Proceedings of the Fifteenth Annual Research Conference in Industrial Relations*, Los Angeles: Institute of Industrial Relations, UCLA, March 13, 1973.

us are sort of unhappy with a solution that meets only part of our needs, but we can live with it.

There are two other conflict-handling modes. It is possible to be both unassertive and uncooperative—through *avoidance* behavior. I sidestep the issue completely, I don't get involved, I withdraw. This is not to say that I don't have or don't recognize my own needs or the needs of the other. I do, but I repress or ignore both; I don't try to work toward a solution.

The opposite of avoidance is *collaboration,* i.e., to be assertive and cooperative at the same time. I try to find some alternative that satisfies both my own needs completely and the other person's needs complete-ly—not something that satisfies both of us a little and leaves both of us a little dissatisfied. For collaboration to work, both parties must recognize that a conflict or problem exists. Then they must share information about their needs and concerns. And finally, they must strive for some solution that satisfies both sets of concerns.

Which of the above modes of behavior would you select when trying to resolve a conflict? Principle 5 makes it obvious that the collaborative mode has the highest pay-off, and consequently is the mode of choice. Let's look at the pay-off, or interpersonal returns, for each of the conflict-handling modes. Which will have constructive effects and which will have destruc-tive effects? If you are cooperative, as in accommodation, the other person is going to *like* you, but not *respect* you. But if you are cooperative to the point of collaboration, the other person will not only *like* you but will also *respect* you. So you see, you will obtain more beneficial interpersonal results if you are collaborative.

In terms of getting his goals met, the other is also ahead by being collaborative. If the other continually avoids or accommodates, he will not achieve his own goals, and will be walked upon and stepped over. Num-erous research studies have shown that collaborative people receive more recognition and are far more promotable than the avoiders or accommo-dators. You might think that competitive people would achieve their goals quickly, too. Such is not the case. Competitive people appear to make trouble for themselves. If the other competes with you, you will respond by competing and mobilizing your energy against him. You will stop being very cooperative with him. Most work situations foster enough interdependence that the other's performance depends upon you. In terms of the other's interpersonal reward and goal attainment, then, collaboration appears to yield the highest returns.

It would seem, then, that in the best of all possible worlds, you would want to resolve conflict by handling it collaboratively. Unfortunately, this isn't the best of all possible worlds. Although collaboration is generally the best conflict-handling mode, sometimes it is just not wise to collaborate. First, there are *stakes* involved in each specific conflict. If the stakes are high—if something you value greatly is being challenged—you will probably be more assertive than cooperative in dealing with the conflict. The same, of course, is true for the other. Second, there is *conflict of interest*. If your needs and the needs of the other are *clearly* incompatible and no integrative solution can be found, compromise will probably be the conflict—handling mode of choice.

Third, there is *social pressure*. Each individual is surrounded by a web of social forces in his environment. We feel pressure not only from our own constituency but also from others'. If the other has more allies and supporters for his solution than you do, you will feel a strong pressure toward accommodation and cooperation.

Fourth, our *history of interaction* with the other person will condition our choice of conflict-handling mode. Each person will have expectations about the other's behavior. However, history can be changed at any point in time; it is never too late to begin to adopt the collaborative mode.

Fifth, *time pressure* can prevent collaboration. Sometimes there really isn't time to collaborate and problem-solve on a complex conflict issue. A hasty compromise may be the best solution. However, be wary of the trap of using time pressure as an excuse to avoid use of the collaborative mode. Working together toward a solution that meets both your own needs and those of the other may take a little more time, but the pay-off is well worth it.

The above, then, are some conditions that will mitigate against the use of the collaborative mode of resolving conflict. The real challenge is to change the conditions that prevent collaboration. Rather than respond to and accept these short-term realities, think about the kind of relationship you would like to have and act to bring about the conditions that would foster that kind of relationship. If social pressures prevent the nurses on your unit from collaborating, then maybe you can change some of those social pressures by creating new norms. If the nurses on your unit have an interaction history that makes it difficult to collaborate, then maybe you can set out to *build* a relationship that will support collaborative behavior. If you haven't got enough time to sit down and problem-solve a conflict with someone, perhaps you can make more time available or set aside a time for this important work. Think of the value and benefits of change and conflict management for both yourself and the other involved. If your suggestions for change are responsive to the needs of others, you are apt to find that your ideas for change will be more acceptable to them.

The learning activity, "Guidelines for Developing Change Alternatives," is included here. The use of this tool will allow you to examine possible solutions to conflicts in terms of your own values and the values of others, so that you may formulate plans for change that will maximize benefits for yourself and others, thus enhancing the acceptability of your suggestions. This is only a tool to help you prepare suggestions for change; it does not guarantee that your suggestions will be adopted.

## GUIDELINES FOR DEVELOPING CHANGE ALTERNATIVES

Statement of specific change to be achieved:    Develop means to make nurses readily identifiable to patients.

| Possible ways of reaching goal | (1) name tags | (2) different colored uni-forms | (3) use of colored ribbon badges |
|---|---|---|---|
| a. Value and bene-fit of solution for me | get rid of cap | get rid of cap | get rid of cap; readily identifiable |
| b. Value and bene-fit of solution for other (in terms of his value system) | none | nurse readily identifiable | nurse readily identi-fiable; different colors for HN and staff nurse so charge person is also identifiable; economical |
| c. Major difficulties and consequences anticipated from other (in terms of his value system) | not readable; not a real iden-tifier as every-one wears name tags | expense | some RNs like wearing caps; will patients know what ribbons mean |
| d. What changes in possible solution will maximize benefits and mini-mize consequences for both parties. | | possibly just sweater or jacket of some type over uni-forms | use of ribbons and wear-ing of caps can be op-tional; local news cover-age and explanation to patients |
| e. Revised possible solution | | colored jackets | use of colored ribbons and wearing of caps optional |

The process of mutual decision making begins when a common goal is identified by the participants, the issue at conflict is defined, a time limit is set for finding solutions, and suggestions to resolve the conflict are request-ed. We have already explained how to identify a common goal and define an issue at conflict. The next steps are (1) to set a time limit and (2) to obtain suggestions for resolving the conflict.

Experience has shown that solutions can be arrived at within a set time period. If no time period is set, conflict resolution can drag on and on[11]. Therefore, setting a time period will prevent the individuals involved from becoming frustrated and abandoning their search for a solution altogether.

When you get to the stage making suggestions, brainstorming tech-niques are useful. This means that ideas should be tossed out and written down with no value judgment placed on them. Once all the suggestions for resolving the conflict have been made, the pros and cons of each should be examined. Each suggestion must be judged for its ability to resolve the conflict and achieve the goal, while allowing each party to maintain his values.

Finding the best solution requires that all suggestions be considered with an open mind. This is difficult, since each person has a vested interest in his own suggestion. Open-mindedness is facilitated if you don't come to the defense of your own suggestion. Point out the pitfalls as well as the value of your idea and then allow the idea to stand on its own merit. When evaluating the ideas of others, point out the positive aspects of each idea before you make any comment on its disadvantages. To be sure that each idea is judged on its merits, apply the following three questions: (1) Does this idea move us toward our goal? (2) Does this idea perpetuate the conflict situation? (3) What action does the idea require? It is at this point that the work you have done will show. If you have considered the common goal and incorporated into your solution factors that will maximize benefit while minimizing consequences for all parties, the full merit of your suggestion will be obvious.

When offering your suggestions, you can state them in terms of the other's values, thus demonstrating your consideration. For example, take the suggestion that different colored ribbon badges be worn by nurses. To offer this suggestion in terms of the other's values, you would say something like this:

> I suggest that the RNs wear different colored ribbon badges on the shoulder of their uniforms. The badge could be a simple pin-on badge so that RNs would just pin the badge on as they came on duty. This would save both time and money by allowing the common use of the badges and not having to sew badges on the uniforms. The head nurse could wear a different color than the staff nurses. Sometimes patients ask who is in charge and this would make the nurse in charge readily identifiable. The ribbons don't cost too much—I checked into the figures. And you know, the Auxiliary is always asking if there are things that we need and I bet we could persuade them to finance this venture. I'd be willing to check with Mrs. Jones about it. The advantage of the ribbons would also be that those who wished to continue to wear their caps could. I realize that at first we would have to spend some time and effort explaining to patients what the badges were all about, but that could be easily incorporated into the admission checklist and patient brochure. I think maybe we could also get some publicity for this in the local newspaper. That would sure bring us into the public eye, and show our concern for patients. What do you think?

As you can see, this kind of a presentation appeals to the values of the other. The use of badges not only makes nurses identifiable but also makes each nurse's status identifiable. This is important to many head nurses and supervisors. Economic factors are considered, as well as the factor of patient and public education. Most administrators want to keep the hospital in a favorable public light—which gives the idea an extra plus for higher-up consideration. Moreover, the idea gives freedom to those who are attached to wearing caps.

Once you have presented your idea in terms of the values of the other and have heard the suggestions of others, it is time to select the solution that most adequately meets the needs of all involved. When the selection is made, a plan for implementing the solution must be worked out. This plan needs to include the responsibilities of all individuals involved. Implementation must be based on the premise that the plan will be tried out, and then evaluated for its effectiveness.

*Principle 6:   Productive conflict resolution requires that ongoing evaluation and rewards be built into the process.*

It is essential that there be some means for assuring that everyone will work toward the desired solution. Building rewards into the process keeps everyone working toward the selected solution. In this context, rewards are what "makes it count," so that it makes a difference whether an individual works to facilitate or hinder the attempted solution.

While a solution is being tried, someone must have responsibility for letting the individuals involved know how they are doing. For example, if care plans are being tried as a means of assuring continuity of patient care, then someone has to pay attention to those care plans. Is everyone doing care plans? If not, why not? Are the care plans being done as was planned? If there is no monitoring, then it doesn't make any difference whether any given individual does care plans or not. Thus, it is necessary that some type of ongoing evaluation and rewards be built into the trial period.

Long-term rewards are also needed. It is difficult to achieve any kind of change without commitment from the individuals involved. This commitment can usually be gained if everyone understands that if the solution works it will be adopted. And secondly, the commitment must count in terms of a negative find to the solution—if it doesn't work, you or the other will not be saddled with the solution for "time immemoriam."

The best way to evaluate the solution is to set up criteria when the plan to implement the solution is written up. Such criteria should measure (1) whether there is movement toward the goal and (2) whether the conflict issue is resolved. Means for measuring progress toward the goal and toward resolution of the conflict must be devised. Measurement landmarks will vary with different issues and should be decided upon by the individuals involved. For example, in implementing the use of ribbon badges in place of caps, a means for determining whether the badges made the nurses easily identifiable is needed. One way to do this might be to send a questionnaire to the patients after discharge asking if they were able to identify the nurse, and if so, "How did *you* identify the nurse on your floor?" If the badges are the identifying factor, it should show up on the questionnaire.

Once the criteria are set up, a time schedule for implementing the plan is established. This should include the amount of time needed to make preparations for implementing the solution, and the amount of time necessary for a fair test of the solution. Specific dates should be noted so that evaluation may begin at a given date.

On the given date, the solution is evaluated on the basis of the pre-established criteria. As a result of the evaluation, the solution may be adopted, modified, or discarded. If the solution is modified, another evaluation period is set up; if the solution is discarded, another solution must be sought.

The final learning activity, "The Mating Process," is designed to help you utilize the information just presented to resolve a conflict or make a change. The activity will take some time, so first read the Summary and then return to "The Mating Process" activity.

In this module, two courses of conflict, productive and destructive, and general strategies for dealing with different types of conflict were described. Following this, six principles for productive conflict resolution and techniques for achieving these principles were presented. The six principles of productive conflict resolution were the following:

*Principle 1:*  Productive conflict resolution is facilitated by a mutual positive desire to resolve the conflict.

*Principle 2:*  Productive conflict resolution is facilitated by a balance of power.

*Principle 3:*  Productive conflict resolution requires movement to a phase of integration.

*Principle 4:*  Adequate exploration of the conflict issue is necessary if the conflict is to remain solved.

*Principle 5:*  Solutions to conflicts need to be responsive to the needs of all parties involved.

*Principle 6:*  Productive conflict resolution requires that ongoing evaluation and rewards be built into the process.

It is hoped that "The Mating Process" will enable you to operationalize the children of your mind—your ideas, hopes, and dreams—so that they need not become the orphans of your soul.

> Won't somebody listen to my song
> It won't take long, it won't take long
> Won't somebody listen to the thing
>     that makes me whole
> Before the children of my mind, become
>     the orphans of my soul.*

---

*From CHILDREN OF MY MIND, lyrics and music by Gary Osborne. Reproduced by kind permission of the Sparta Florida Music Group Limited, London, England.

## THE MATING PROCESS

1. Describe a conflict situation or change attempt. (This may be any previously described conflict or any aborted change attempts.)

2. Identify the type of conflict

3. Describe the conflict from the other's frame of reference

4. Identify the conflict issue.

5. Complete the chart below. (You may wish to refer to the "Guidelines for Developing Change Alternatives" to assist you with this chart.) See page 294.

**ALTERNATIVES FOR CONFLICT RESOLUTION OR CHANGE**

Statement of specific change to be achieved:

| Possible ways of reaching goal | | | |
|---|---|---|---|
| a  Value and bene-fit of solution for me | | | |
| b. Value and bene-fit of solution for other (in terms of his value system) | | | |
| c. Major difficulties and consequences anticipated from other (in terms of his value system) | | | |
| d. What changes in possible solution will maximize benefits and mini-mize consequences for both parties | | | |
| e. Revised possible solution | | | |

6. Considering the perspective and values of the other involved, which of the possible alternatives is most apt to achieve the desired results?

7. How can you present the alternative identified in item 6 in a way that considers the values of the other?

8. Develop a plan, using the strategies presented (or your own) to resolve the described conflict or achieve the aborted change. (This plan should include strategies for achieving the six principles of productive conflict resolution.)

Implement your plan. Then return to this activity to evaluate the plan.

9. How effective was your plan?

   A. Were you able to create a need to resolve the conflict?

   B. Did exploration of issues lead to identification of a common goal?

   C. Were the solutions adopted responsive to the needs of those involved?

D.  How did the solution advance health or patient care?

E.  What were the most effective strategies utilized?

F.  What were the least effective strategies utilized?

## REFERENCES

1. Nye, R. D. *Conflict Among Humans.* New York: Springer Publishing Co., 1973, p. 148.
2. Deutsch, M. *The Resolution of Conflict.* New Haven: Yale University Press, 1973, p. 67.
3. Postman, N. and Weingartner, C. *The Soft Revolution.* New York: Dell Publishing Co., 1971.
4. Varela, J. *Psychological Solutions to Social Problems.* New York: Academic Press, 1971, pp. 97–99.
5. Walton, R. E. *Interpersonal Peacemaking: Confrontation and Third-Party Consultation.* Reading, Mass.: Addison-Wesley, 1969, p. 105.
6. Rogers, C. "Some elements of Effective Interpersonal Communication." Speech given at California Institute of Technology, 1964, p. 2.
7. Yates, H.W. A strategy for responding to social conflicts. *Pastoral Psychology.* Vol. 22, No. 16, 1971, p. 40.
8. Fischer, R. "Fractionating Conflict," in J. Bondurant, *Conflict: Violence and Nonviolence.* New York: Aldine-Atherton, 1971, p. 144.
9. Watzlawick, Y., *et al. Change: Principles of Problem Formulation and Problem Resolution.* New York: W.W. Norton, 1974.
10. Fischer, 1971, p. 139.
11. Varela, 1971, pp. 158–159

## BIBLIOGRAPHY

Beckhard, R. *Organization Development: Strategies and Models.* Reading, Mass.: Addison-Wesley, 1969.

Caghan, S. *Conscious and Commitment or: Who Murdered Florence Nightingale.* New York: National Student Nurses' Association, Inc., 1970, pp. 1–7.

Derr, C. B. Conflict resolution in organizations: views from the field of educational administration. *Publ. Admin. Rev.* September–October 1972, pp. 495–501.

Deutsch, M. *The Resolution of Conflict.* New Haven: Yale University Press, 1973.

Druckman, D. The influence of the situation in interparty conflict. *J. Conflict Resolution,* Vol. 15, No. 4, 1971, pp. 523–554.

Ewing, D.W. Tension can be an asset. *Harv. Bus. Rev.,* Vol. 42, September–October 1964, pp. 71–78.

Fischer, R. "Fractionating Conflict," in J. Bondurant, *Conflict: Violence and Nonviolence.* New York: Aldine-Atherton, Inc., 1971, pp. 135–145.

Genn, N. Where can nurses practice as they're taught?, *Am. J. Nurs.,* Vol. 74, No. 12, December 1974, pp. 2212–2215.

Goffman, E. "On Cooling The Mark Out: Some Aspects of Adaptation to Failure," in W. Bennis, *et al.* (eds.), *Interpersonal Dynamics: Essays and Readings on Human Interaction.* Homewood, Ill.: The Dorsey Press, 1968, pp. 377–391.

Kelly, J. Make conflict work for you. *Harv. Bus. Rev.,* Vol. 48, July–August 1970, pp. 103–113.

Kiresuk, T.J. Goal attainment scaling at a county mental health service, *Evaluation.* Vol. 1, No. 1, 1973, pp. 12–18.

Kriesberg, L. *The Sociology of Social Conflicts.* New Jersey: Prentice-Hall, Inc., 1973.

Mager, R.F. and Pipe, P. *Analyzing Performance Problems.* Calif.: Fearon Publishers, 1970.

Mudd, E.H. "Conflict and Conflict Resolution in Families," In S. Mudd (ed.), *Conflict Resolution and World Education.* The Hague: Dr. W. Junck Publishers, World Academy of Art and Sciences 3, 1966, pp. 58–69.

Nye, R.D. *Conflict Among Humans.* New York: Springer Publishing Co., 1973.

Patchen, M. Models of cooperation and conflict: a critical review. *J. Conflict Resolution,* Vol. XIV, No. 3, 1970, pp. 389–407.

Postman, N. and Weingartner, C. *The Soft Revolution.* New York: Dell Publishing Co., 1971.

Rogers, C. "Some Elements of Effective Interpersonal Communication," Speech at California Institute of Technology, 1964.

Schein, E. *Process Consultation: Its Role In Organization Development.* Reading, Mass.: Addison-Wesley, 1969.

Smith, C. (ed.) *Conflict Resolution: Contributions of the Behavioral Sciences.* London: University of Notre Dame Press, 1971.

Spiegel, J. The resolution of role conflict within the family. *Psychiatry,* Vol. 22, 1957, pp. 1–16.

Swingle, P. *The Structure of Conflict.* New York: Academic Press, 1970.

Tanter, R. (ed.) Why fight? Conflict models for strategists and managers, *Am. Behav. Scient.,* Vol. 15, No. 5, May–June 1972. 128 pages.

Thomas, J. M. and Bennis, W. G. *Management of Change and Conflict.* Baltimore, Md.: Penguin Books, 1972.

Thomas, K. W. "Issues in Management of Conflict" in *Proceedings of the Fifteenth Annual Research Conference in Industrial Relations.* Los Angeles: Institute of Industrial Relations, UCLA, March 13, 1973, pp. 5–13.

Varela, J. *Psychological Solutions to Social Problems.* New York: Academic Press, 1971.

Walton, R. E., *Interpersonal Peacemaking: Confrontations And Third-Party Consultation.* Reading, Mass.: Addison-Wesley, 1969.

Watzlawick, P. *et al. Change: Principles of Problem Formulation and Problem Resolution.* New York: W.W. Norton, 1974.

Weinstein, E. A., "The Development of Interpersonal Competence," in Goslin, D. (ed.), *Handbook of Socialization Theory and Research,* Chicago: Rand McNally, 1969, pp. 753–775.

Yates, H. W. A strategy for responding to social conflicts. *Pastoral Psychology,* Vol. 22, No. 16, 1971, pp. 31–51.

## SUMMARY

Although the *Path to Biculturalism* ends with the conflict resolution program, the journey toward biculturalism has just begun. Biculturalism is not something that is achieved once and then abandoned or forgotten. Acquisition of the skills and strategies of providing and eliciting effective feedback, empathy toward co-workers, and skill in productive conflict resolution are the essential ingredients for developing interpersonal competence in new subcultures. Such interpersonal competence is absolutely necessary if an individual is to establish his identity in a new subculture, and to influence the productivity and quality of performance of colleagues.

> The problem of community,
> Which is the form of personal life,
> Is the one of deciding on whose terms it shall be lived.
> Simply to impose my terms on the other person
>    is to deny his freedom and responsibility;
> Simply to accept his terms without demur
>    is to abandon my own.
> In either case, there is no community
>    but a kind of fusion or absorption instead.
> For community implies a mutuality of distinct
>    initiatives as an on-going project.*

If the community of nursing is ever to provide society with the quality health care that people need and have a right to, then the wisdom of experience found in the work subculture must be blended with the innovative avant garde ideas of the school subculture by bicultural nurses who care enough to dare to work within the system to change it.

The techniques and principles discussed in this book are universally applicable and are useful to individuals in a wide variety of disciplines and settings. Role strain and role conflict are likely to occur anytime an individual moves out of one subculture and into another subculture where, for a time at least, he will find himself to be deviant. If fusion and absorption are to be avoided, then biculturalism is the necessary mode of conflict resolution.

It is important to remember that the development of biculturalism is reciprocal. While one individual struggles to become bicultural, he must remember that, in all likelihood, he himself is simultaneously serving as a cultural stimulation model for others who want to develop their biculturalism.

---

*From Johann, R.O. *Love Is Not Enough.* New York: America Press. © 1965. All rights reserved. Reprinted with permission.

# Index